FOR DUMMIES
BESTSELLING
BOOK SERIES

Tour de France For Dummies®

Cheat Sheet

The Yellow Jersey (Maillot Jaune)

Henri Desgrange, co-creator of the Tour and the first Tour de France race director, introduced the yellow jersey in 1919, while he was experimenting with several gimmicks in the Tour's early years. The yellow jersey allows riders, race officials, and spectators to easily identify the race leader. It remains Desgrange's most well-known innovation and the Tour's most renowned icon.

- ✔ The first yellow jersey of each Tour de France is awarded to the winner of the Prologue (pre-race) or Stage 1, depending on the race's stage itinerary.

- ✔ After each stage, the yellow jersey is awarded to the cyclist who has the lowest cumulative time (after calculating his finishing times and all time bonuses and penalty time assessments).

- ✔ Although it has occurred, it's rare for a rider to maintain the yellow jersey from race start to finish. But for each successive day a cyclist remains race leader, he receives a new yellow jersey on the finish podium shortly after each stage.

Ironically, the first cyclist to wear the yellow jersey, colored to match the yellow newsprint of the newspaper Desgrange published, didn't need to wear the brightly colored top for recognition. Desgrange introduced the new jersey during Stage 10 of that year's race, but by that time, only 11 of the original field of 69 remained racing during the final two stages, and Eugene Christophe, the leader, was easily visible on the race course — with or without his yellow jersey.

The Polka-Dot Jersey (Maillot aux Pois Rouges)

The Tour's best climber award is the second most-coveted jersey. It's a white jersey featuring bright red dots, and is known as the *polka-dot jersey*. Often called the King of the Mountains competition, the polka-dot jersey began in 1975 and reminds some Tour observers of horse racing jockeys' outfits. Like other specialty race jerseys, it began as a marketing campaign.

A chocolate manufacturer was of the race's sponsors in the mid-1970s, and one of the company's popular offerings was a chocolate bar with a white wrapper featuring red dots. Seeking more exposure for the chocolate brand, the idea for a jersey to designate the race's best climber was born.

The polka-dot jersey is awarded after each stage to the rider with the most climbing points. Points are awarded in decreasing amounts for top finishes in climbs of various difficulties throughout the race.

Tour de France
For Dummies®

Green Jersey (Maillot Vert)

As part of the Tour's 50th anniversary, the green jersey was introduced in 1953 during a stage in Strasbourg. It's awarded daily to the Tour cyclist with the most points accumulated during intermittent sprints at the end of stages.

Points for the green jersey are earned in road races, time trials, and designated sprint locations during stages called *hot spots*. Sprints for points at the end of road races are considered the Tour's most exciting and revered stage segments.

The White Jersey (Maillot Blanc)

Honoring the race's best young riders, the white jersey was initiated in 1975 to designate the highest-ranked cyclist age 25 and under in the overall standings.

Like other colored Tour jerseys, the white jersey is awarded after every stage. The highest-placed young rider in the final overall standings claims the race's final white jersey. This jersey is also known as the *young rider's yellow jersey*.

Some young riders who've claimed the white jersey have also earned the final yellow jersey. French rider Laurent Fignon (1983) and Jan Ullrich of Germany (1997) were both age 23 when they respectively claimed the final white and yellow jerseys the same year.

The Rainbow Jersey

The winner of the world road race title each year is awarded the rainbow jersey. He wears the jersey (with sponsors' logos) in races for one year until the next year's World Championships.

The world road race winner wears a white jersey with five horizontal, colored stripes — blue, red, black, yellow, and green — in his other races throughout the year. The rainbow jersey is the most coveted cycling jersey after the yellow jersey. After you've become a World Champion, it is customary to bear the rainbow stripes on an article of clothing for the remainder of your career. Most former World Champions will don the stripes either on their collars or on the sleeve openings of their jerseys.

For Dummies: Bestselling Book Series for Beginners

Tour de France
FOR
DUMMIES®

**by Phil Liggett, James Raia,
Sammarye Lewis**

Foreword by Lance Armstrong

WILEY

Wiley Publishing, Inc.

Tour de France For Dummies®

Published by
Wiley Publishing, Inc.
111 River St.
Hoboken, NJ 07030-5774
www.wiley.com

For general information on our other products and services, please contact our Customer Care Department within the U.S. at 800-762-2974, outside the U.S. at 317-572-3993, or fax 317-572-4002.

For technical support, please visit www.wiley.com/techsupport.

Wiley also publishes its books in a variety of electronic formats. Some content that appears in print may not be available in electronic books.

Library of Congress Control Number: 2005923417

ISBN-13: 978-0-7645-8449-7

ISBN-10: 0-7645-8449-9

Manufactured in the United States of America

10 9 8 7 6 5 4 3 2 1

1B/RT/QV/QV/IN

WILEY

About the Authors

Phil Liggett, a former competitive amateur cyclist, has attended every Tour de France since 1973 and is universally known as "the Voice of Cycling." A television commentator since 1978, Liggett has also covered six Summer Olympics and four Winter Olympics. He has been recognized throughout his career with several international broadcasting awards and was nominated for an Emmy in 2003 as Outstanding Sports Personality.

Trained as a journalist in his native Great Britain, Phil worked for *Cycling* magazine for four years. He has held freelance positions with *The Guardian* and *The Observer* and currently writes for the *Daily Telegraph* in London. He has reported for BBC World Service radio, and in recent years has covered the Tour de France for the Outdoor Life Network. Phil is author and coauthor of several other books, including *The Tour de France 1988 and 1989, The Complete Book of Performance Cycling,* and *The Fastest Man on Two Wheels: In Pursuit of Chris Boardman.*

Phil has been married since 1971 to Pat Tipper, a 1968 Olympic speedskater. A masseuse, Pat has worked on five Tours de France for women and managed British teams at World championships and other major races. She currently works as a university lecturer in dance science. The Liggetts live outside of London.

James Raia has been a journalist since 1978. He has worked as a staff writer and columnist for three daily newspapers and has been a fulltime freelance writer since 1987. While traveling to more than a dozen countries on assignment, James has contributed sports, business, travel, and lifestyle articles to numerous newspapers, magazines, news services, and Web sites, including *The New York Times, Associated Press, USA Today, Golf Magazine,* and *The Miami Herald.*

James first reported on cycling in 1980 and has covered many domestic and international races, including four World Championships and every Tour de France since 1997. He also publishes two electronic newsletters, *Endurance Sports News* and *Tour de France Times,* and a car review column *The Weekly Driver,* all available on his Web site: www.ByJamesRaia.com. He has provided Tour de France radio commentary for several networks, including National Public Radio. A long-distance runner who lives in Sacramento, California, James has completed more than 75 marathons and ultramarathons.

Sammarye Lewis has many roles in the cycling world, including photojournalist, cycling fan, and event management consultant. Reporting from the Tour for four years as Velogal, she writes a daily online Tour de France journal for Paceline.com, the Web site for Lance Armstrong and his team. She has contributed to Active.com, Athletic Insight.com, CyclingNews.com, and the Daily Peloton.com as well as several print publications. Sammarye is author of the book *The Podium Girl Gone Bad — Twisted Tales from the Tour de France*. She also created and markets Podium Girl Gone Bad apparel and works in race management and coordinator capacity for the U.S. Pro Cycling Tour.

Sammarye is Web master for the Unofficial Lance Armstrong Fan Club and Discovery Pro Cycling Team Fans Web sites as well as www.velogal.smugmug.com and www.velogal.blogspot.com.

Authors' Dedications and Acknowledgments

To Trish, my long-suffering wife, who has never seen me in July since 1972, and to David Saunders, a television commentator and journalist who invited me to be his driver on the Tour de France in 1973 and who died in a car crash in 1978.

— Phil Liggett

To Gretchen Gaither, Marilyn Raia, and Elinore Raia, my wife, sister, and mother, for their encouragement and support, and to my deceased father, Anthony Vincent Raia, who taught me about the sportsmanship of life.

My sincere appreciation to coauthors Phil Liggett and Sammarye Lewis for their enthusiastic collaboration, and to editors Mikal Belicove and Tere Stouffer for their patience and professionalism. Also, many thanks to Jim Mohan, this book's technical reviewer, for his insights and corrections.

— James Raia

I would like to thank Mikal Belicove, Acquisitions Editor, for his unwavering support and belief in this book and in me. Thanks also to Tere Stouffer, Project Editor, and the staff at Wiley Publishing, Inc., who worked so hard on this first-of-a-kind book. And special thanks to coauthors Phil Liggett and James Raia, who love the Tour as much as I do.

I would also like to thank the people of France and Belgium for their gracious hospitality and generosity every year. Thanks, too, for their unhesitating assistance during the times when I was hopelessly lost along the Tour route. *Merci beaucomp por tout. Vive Le Tour!*

— Sammarye Lewis

Publisher's Acknowledgments

We're proud of this book; please send us your comments through our Dummies online registration form located at www.dummies.com/register/.

Some of the people who helped bring this book to market include the following:

Acquisitions, Editorial, and Media Development

Project Editor: Tere Stouffer

Acquisitions Editor: Mikal Belicove

Technical Editor: Jim Mohan

Editorial Supervisor: Carmen Krikorian

Editorial Manager: Michelle Hacker

Editorial Assistant: Melissa Bennett

Cover Photos: © Graham Watson Photography Limited

Cartoons: Rich Tennant (www.the5thwave.com)

Composition Services

Project Coordinator: Adrienne Martinez

Layout and Graphics: Joyce Haughey, Stephanie D. Jumper, Clint Lahnen, Melanee Prendergast, Heather Ryan, Julie Trippetti

Special Art: Sammarye Lewis (all photos except front cover)

Proofreaders: Laura Albert, Leeann Harney, TECHBOOKS Production Services

Indexer: TECHBOOKS Production Services

Publishing and Editorial for Consumer Dummies

    Diane Graves Steele, Vice President and Publisher, Consumer Dummies

    Joyce Pepple, Acquisitions Director, Consumer Dummies

    Kristin A. Cocks, Product Development Director, Consumer Dummies

    Michael Spring, Vice President and Publisher, Travel

    Kelly Regan, Editorial Director, Travel

Publishing for Technology Dummies

    Andy Cummings, Vice President and Publisher, Dummies Technology/General User

Composition Services

    Gerry Fahey, Vice President of Production Services

    Debbie Stailey, Director of Composition Services

Contents at a Glance

Table of Contents

Chapter 9: Having the Best Equipment in the Bunch 119

Foreword

Since 1993, when I rode and for 12 days in my first attempt at the Tour de France, the annual July event has become my sporting life. Until 1996, I had finished the three-week race to Paris only once, and when I was diagnosed with cancer, the Tour de France became a memory. A much harder battle — that for life itself — began. Life since that black period has taken on a new meaning to me, and the Tour de France has been my target every year since. I returned to racing in 1998, and by 1999, as a fitter and mentally different rider, I returned to the Tour, racing for almost a month in any kind of weather, over any type of terrain. I had around me the best team of riders any Tour leader could wish for (you'll understand what I mean by that as you read this book).

I am often asked why, as the overall winner, I do not win the last stage into Paris. But as you find out in *Tour de France For Dummies*, it doesn't always work that way. Instead, those who feel they can win the Tour go in search of gaining time on the specialist stages, like the time trials or the grueling legs through the mountains. These are the stages where the race is won and lost. Winning the final stage would just be the icing on the cake.

When you look at your television screen and see these stages, where a pack of riders all appear to be pedaling along together, you may wonder where the excitement is. But the truth is, the Tour de France is a happening bigger than any other annual sporting event. Millions of roadside spectators derive pleasure from watching us sweat it out in the heat of a French summer. In fact, for more than 100 years, the race has stopped France in its tracks each July. Elections have even been moved to another date, because the public has wanted to hear only about the race's progress. During the Tour, France is inundated by a media army numbering more than a 1,000 and an entourage of more than 5,000, all of whom follow the daily events as we journey around France and its neighboring countries. Meanwhile, the 198 starters in the race are gradually reduced to perhaps 100 by the finish in Paris.

In this book, you come to understand an event that appears complex, but is, in the end, pretty simple: The rider who gets back to Paris in the fastest overall time is the winner. British cycling expert Phil Liggett and Americans James Raia and Sammarye Lewis have covered 44 Tours as writers, and Phil has not missed a wheel turning since 1973. Together, they take you through every detail of this great event; after you read it, your next step is to turn up in France and catch that most infectious enthusiam known as Tour Fever.

— Lance Armstrong

Introduction

Maybe Lance Armstrong's recovery from cancer and his subsequent Tour de France titles piqued your curiosity. Perhaps a television video clip of a massive group of cyclists sprinting furiously on the cobblestone streets of Paris caught your attention.

That's the way the Tour de France works. A fleeting glimpse of the race triggers an interest. All of a sudden, you want to know more. You're a fan. Then you're hooked on everything about the race. You can't get enough and want to find out all you can. *Tour de France For Dummies* can help. It provides race strategies, details riders' skills, examines rules and regulations, and explains nuances of the three-week race and its more than 100-year history.

About This Book

Many available Tour de France books highlight its history and champions. From early years, when the race almost ended two years into its tenure, to the legacies of great riders, volumes detail the Tour's more than 100 years. This book covers that same information, but it's not only about specific race information. In this book, you also find out about the people and places around the event. Here, you find all the information you need to watch the race in person, view it on television, or surf the Internet for results and rider profiles.

In this book, we also examine the intricacies of bikes and how race equipment has evolved through the years. There's a century of personalities, technology, history, and legend sprinkled throughout this book — the Tour's famous icons, infamous characters, and fleeting moments that stand as epic testaments to the great race.

Conventions Used in This Book

The Tour de France resonates with the lexicon of France. As such, French words and phrases used throughout this book are printed in italics. We also help you pronounce them, in case you want to sound like a cycling guru to your friends.

The most critical term to know is *peloton* (*pell*-oh-tawn), a French term that means the main pack of riders. This term appears many times throughout this book.

In gray boxes throughout the book, you also find sidebars — short clips of information about interesting cyclists or other Tour information. Skip these if you're short on time, or head right for them if you want a colorful lowdown on the Tour.

As a global sport, the Tour is followed by millions of fans via the Internet. So, all Web sites listed in *Tour de France For Dummies* are printed in a special font, `like this`. In some instances, Internet addresses listed may have needed to break across two lines of text. If that happened, rest assured we haven't put in any extra characters (such as hyphens) to indicate the break. So, when using one of these Web addresses, just type it exactly the way you see it in this book, pretending as though the line break doesn't exist.

What You're Not to Read

Technically speaking, the Tour de France is not easy to follow. So, throughout this book, text preceded by a Technical Stuff icon designates specific areas of technical overload. You don't have to examine technical sections to understand the subject it represents, so feel free to skip these, if you want.

Foolish Assumptions

We make only one assumption about you, dear reader: You have an interest in one of the world's most enduring and popular sporting events: the Tour de France. You may have watched the race on the Outdoor Life Network or on one of the Tour's many international television network outlets. Or, you may have seen riders swiftly cruise past an avenue of a French city you were visiting. However you caught the Tour de France bug, this book explains event basics to you (if you're a newcomer) and also provides additional details about the people, places, and equipment associated with this race (if you already have some familiarity with the event).

How This Book Is Organized

Like all *For Dummies* books, information in *Tour de France For Dummies* is divided into five parts. Each part of the book contains several chapters, as follows.

Part I: A Bicycle Race Unlike Any Other

The Tour de France is the world's most popular and prestigious bicycle race. In this part, you find out the event's history, traditions, and basic elements as a team sport.

In Chapter 1, we discuss how the Tour began and how the race is conducted as a team event — that is, individual riders competing within teams. All details necessary to follow the event, whether you're watching from the sidelines in France or sitting comfortably on your living room couch, are also featured in Chapter 1. In Chapter 2, specifics are highlighted: from how the race route is chosen each year to the varied unique subcategories of competitions within the overall race.

The Tour is replete with tradition, and in Chapter 3, you get the scoop on race jerseys and find out why certain riders wear jerseys like no one else in the race. You also discover the meaning and nuances of the podium and its awards and honors. Finally, you get a look at other race specialties, like the honor of being in last place and how racers manage to please their sponsors.

Part II: How the Race Is Run and Won

It's not always apparent on a day-to-day basis, but the Tour is won by an individual who's part of a team. In this part, all individual riders' responsibilities are detailed, as are the race's varied rules and protocol. You're also introduced to teams' non-riding personnel — from managers to massage therapists. They orchestrate teams' daily operations.

Interpersonal relationships are integral to a team's success in the Tour. In Chapter 4, riders' individual roles are described as well as the characteristics that make cyclists successful as climbers, sprinters, and team riders. How the race progresses each day — its rules, time limits, drug tests, and race fines — are explained in Chapter 5.

Astute racing strategy helps teams get their star riders to the podium. How it all works is explained in Chapter 6.

Part III: Loving the Ride: A Man and His Bike

It has changed throughout the years, but now nearly 200 riders begin each Tour on the first weekend in July. This part introduces riders and tells you how they do what they do. You find out how the sport's best athletes prepare and maintain their bodies. You find out how riders train for months — even years — and then persevere while pedaling for more than 2,000 miles around France and other nearby countries.

Chapter 7 explains how riders take care of their bodies before, during, and after every Tour stage. From proper hydration to withstanding sickness and mechanical failures, it's all part of a Tour rider's typical day. So, a special chapter (Chapter 8) takes you through a day in the life of a Tour cyclist, including eating teams meals, finding a little relaxation time, getting daily massages, and dealing with fans.

Technology is critical to success at the Tour, so Chapter 9 provides all sorts of information about cyclists' different bikes and the mechanics who make sure the riders pedal their machines in top mechanical condition. What the riders wear in all kinds of weather conditions is also detailed in Chapter 9.

Part IV: Watching the Race

When you're a Tour fan, more is better. The race is followed passionately around the globe, and millions of fans attend the race each year and follow it in newspapers, on television, on the radio and TV, and on the Internet.

Whether you're watching race action from a French roadside or a reclining chair in the family room, Chapter 10 gives you a multitude of information resources. You find out where to watch Tour action at home and where to cybersurf to get instant race updates. If you're planning to watch the Tour in person, Chapter 11 gives options and suggestions for planning a perfect Tour de France experience.

Part V: The Part of Tens

Every *For Dummies* book concludes with signature lists of ten items called The Part of Tens. In this book, the Part of Tens includes honorees as best riders in Tour history, ten important editions of the Tour de France, unique Tour statistics, dramatic tour moments, famous race climbs, and a list of other cycling races around the world.

Icons Used in This Book

Small pictures placed in the margins of this book are used to alert you to specific kinds of information. Icons point to cycling terminology, racing nuances, information suited for memorizing, and complicated regulations. Here's what they mean.

 This icon gives you snippets of information, various tricks, and special shortcuts. It also designates cycling jargon. The sport has a vast selection of terms used by those involved with the sport. Use these terms, and your "guru status" appreciably improves.

 Facts and figures are integral parts of the Tour de France. This icon identifies information you want to know just as well as you know your phone number or ATM pin number.

 Controversial or bizarre sections of the book are designated by this icon. When you see this icon, what follows may be alarming, graphic, or at least out of the ordinary.

 From radio communications along the race course to lists of prohibited over-the-counter and prescription drugs, the Tour is replete with technical details. The icon designates percentages, various mileage totals, and other Tour statistics and highlights.

Where to Go from Here

If you want to know how and why cities host Tour de France stages, turn to Chapter 2. Ever wonder how much money Tour cyclists win for claiming a stage or winning a jersey competition? Check out Chapter 4. And if you're thinking about attending the Tour or want to watch it on television, details to both possibilities are in Chapter 10.

You can turn to any chapter in *Tour de France For Dummies* and get specific Tour information. If you're watching a stage and there's a quick, significant development, look for the topic in the Table of Contents or index, find your subject and flip to the appropriate chapter. That's the format trademark of *For Dummies* books. You can read chapters as self-contained minibooks. Of course, you can also start with Chapter 1, if you wish, and read straight through to the end.

Part I

A Bicycle Race Unlike Any Other

The 5ᵗʰ Wave   By Rich Tennant

"Cambrai is that way, I think."

In this part . . .

In this part, you discover Tour de France basics — its history, race rules, strategy, and how the three-week event operates. From watching the race at home to traveling to witness it in person, this part provides specifics on how to spectate and understand the different kinds of cycling that make up the Tour.

This part also details cyclists' different jerseys and why some cyclists wear identical outfits, while a handful of other riders wear vastly different jerseys. You're also introduced to finish-line customs and to various nuances and race traditions.

Chapter 1

Answering All Your Tour Questions

*E*very July, daily life changes in France, and has for the past 100 years or so. That's when the Tour de France — a fast-moving circus of cyclists — makes its way around the country. The Tour consists of nearly 200 riders from a couple dozen countries pedaling through fields of sunflowers and vineyards and climbing into thin mountain air.

Why do cyclists want to do this? This chapter tells you why. You discover how and why the Tour began and how to understand race operations and strategies. You get all Tour basics: what equipment riders are using, what apparel they're wearing, and what they're eating and drinking. You also find out how they do what they do, every day, for three weeks. You find out how, as a Tour de France fan, you can follow the Tour in person, watch it on television, or follow every kilometer of the race on your laptop computer.

Understanding the Race and the Strategies

Condensed to its basic premise, the Tour de France is a simple athletic contest: The cyclist who completes a strenuous and often perilous course of more than 2,000 miles in the lowest total time wins.

Yet, the event is so much more. Steeped in history, tradition, and racing lore, the Tour defines endurance and global sportsmanship. Unlike professional sports played in stadiums and arenas filled with fans who've paid for tickets, the Tour stands alone in the sports world. Its arena extends past countries' borders, and for fans, it's the best bargain in sports, because it's free.

For riders, it's a job with an equally simple equation. While progressing along the course like chess pieces on wheels, riders face the limits of endurance. They battle inclement weather and attempt to outwit and outrace each other while using the same strategy — conserve energy as much as possible for the times when it's needed most.

Working together

Riders participating in the Tour compete at the top of the sport. The Tour is the Super Bowl, Stanley Cup, World Series, Winston Cup, and NBA Championship of bicycle racing. Functioning as a team sport (see Chapters 4 and 6 for details), the race features teams of nine cyclists selected from a larger group of teammates. Reaping the benefits of synergy, teams work as units, and each rider has varying responsibilities. As riders make their way around France and into neighboring countries, teams that use sound racing strategies tend to have the most success — for the group and for the team captain.

Winning individually

Individuals win stages and one rider claims the overall title. Winning a Tour de France stage is the career highlight for many cyclists. Every day, one rider is victorious, and he climbs onto the finish podium after a stage win and hears fans' cheers and receives various accolades. But a rider's individual triumph, at least to some degree, is the result of selfless teammates. It's rare for a cyclist to win a stage without acknowledging teammates who've put him in a position to ride to a triumph.

Understanding Those Colored Jerseys

Riders on each team are required to wear the same color jersey (as discussed Chapter 3). Each team's jersey features logos of sponsors who pay the riders' salaries. The result is a kaleidoscope of moving billboards on wheels. Some teams' uniforms feature subtle colors; other teams opt for brighter colors. Some teams' uniforms look surprisingly similar, further adding to the blur of the often fast-moving *peloton* (the main pack of riders).

A few riders wear special jerseys. Throughout the race, the reigning World Champion wears his team colors, but on a special jersey with horizontal stripes. National current road champions wear team jerseys featuring their country's colors.

Four other cyclists also wear different colored jerseys each day (see Figure 1-1).

 ✔ The yellow jersey represents the race leader.

 ✔ The green jersey represents the race's best sprinter.

 ✔ The polka dot jersey designates the race's finest climber.

 ✔ The white jersey designates the highest-ranked rider in the overall competition age 25 or younger.

Figure 1-1: Winners wearing their jerseys on the podium at the 2004 Tour de France. From left, Robbie McEwen, Lance Armstrong, Richard Virenque, and Vladimir Karpets.

In most instances, cyclists wearing specialty jerseys like to wear them as long as they can during the race. But the colored jerseys of the Tour change often, and the anticipation of those costume changes each day helps make the Tour a race of many races. See Chapter 3 for additional details on special jerseys.

Choosing the Right Stuff: From Bikes to Snacks

Since the Tour began, the equipment that riders use and the methods they employ for keeping themselves nutritionally prepared to ride have changed a lot and not very much at the same time. Bikes still have two wheels, two brakes, two pedals, a frame, handlebar, gears, and a saddle. Riders still wear cycling shoes. But technology (see more in Chapter 9) has catapulted current Tour bikes into the forefront of aerodynamic efficiency. Tour cyclists' machines were once steel. Aluminum, titanium, and carbon fiber materials are now in the mix. Gearing options have also dramatically improved since front and rear derailleurs became common in the 1950s.

Cyclists ate bread and pasta in the Tour's early days, just as they do today. But riders' nutrition (discussed in Chapters 7 and 8) is now a science. Tour cyclists drank alcohol like water during the race's infancy, and it was many a rider's delight to smoke cigarettes. And while a celebratory sip or two of champagne is still traditional during the Tour's final stage, there's no smoking. The infamous tales of riders lighting each other's cigarettes are now only billows of smoke in Tour lore.

Pedaling through decades of technology

Imagine Tour riders in 1903 riding a saddle that included synthetic gels for comfort. What would those pioneering Tour riders think of today's clipless pedals and aerodynamic handlebars that allow cyclists to ride in tucked positions like downhill racers?

Tour riders now use equipment built by computer-generated formulas. It's tested in wind tunnels and perfected by a battery of engineers and mechanics. Just like the riders of yesteryear, competing in the Tour today includes a man-versus-machine dynamic. Riders are hard on their bikes; bikes are hard on riders. Throughout the Tour's history — from ancient bikes to state-of-the art machines — one constant has remained: Something will go wrong with riders' bikes during the race. Whether riders use steel or titanium frames, mechanical problems occur every day at the Tour de France, and always when riders least expect them.

Tour de France teams employ riders, managers, physicians, masseurs, trainers — and cooks. While riding an average of more than 100 miles per day, Tour cyclists eat nearly constantly. It's rare when they can adequately keep up with their bodies' nutritional requirements. Team cooks do their best to keep riders properly nourished. Cooks prepare riders' meals for breakfast, dinner, and a prerace meal, when the Tour's starting time allows. But it's not just quantity that counts, rather the quality of the quantity. As endurance athletes, riders need specific amounts of carbohydrates, protein, and fat. If the equation isn't right, it can mean the difference between riders' successes and failures.

Spectating During the Tour

Unlike stadium and arena sporting events, there are no official attendance figures for the Tour de France. Many kilometers of the course are nearly spectator free. But at each stage's starting and finishing lines, on mountain climbs, and along the final-day cobblestones of Paris, watching the Tour (see more on this in Chapter 10) is a way of life. Millions of spectators attend the race every year (see Figure 1-2), some of whom camp for days to reserve key viewing perches. Millions more enthusiasts around the world watch the event live and on a tape-delayed basis. Radio listenership is global and massive. Cycling-specific Web site traffic grows exponentially during the Tour.

Figure 1-2: Spectators waiting in the rain for the finish of Stage 5 in Chartres, Tour de France 2004.

Watching the Tour from home

Tour fans in France who don't attend the race in person are still fortunate. The event is broadcast live on the French national network every day (see Chapter 10). Most stages are organized to finish around 5 p.m. in France, the prime viewing hour.

Dozens of countries have similar broadcasts, including, since 2001, daily live coverage on the Outdoor Life Network (OLN), the first North American network to offer live daily coverage.

Searching for Tour information

Daily European newspapers provide vast Tour information. It's front-page news and often dominates sports section coverage. *L'Equipe,* the French daily sports newspaper, is a Tour sponsor, so it publishes specialty magazines on the Tour and provides the public with an overwhelming amount or race information — from race reports to rider profiles, from road closures to columnists' strong opinions. The *International Herald Tribune* and *USA Today*'s international edition provide major English newspaper coverage.

The Tour's online presence (see Chapter 10) has reached its saturation point. The official Tour Web site, www.LeTour.fr features near-immediate details of every stage. Commercial sites — from newspapers' online editions to specialty magazines' sites — battle for fast and more comprehensive Tour news coverage. Many sites feature riders' daily diaries from inside the *peloton,* while blogs, cycling forums, and chat rooms burst with activity.

Making the trip to the Tour

By plane, train, automobile, or bicycle, attending the Tour has become an increasingly popular way for cycling fans seeking a vacation to get their fill. Most major international airlines fly into Orly International Airport and Charles de Gaulle International Airport, the two major Paris airports. With rare exception, the start of the Tour is within a few hours' drive or train ride from either of these airports. July is the busiest time of year for travel to France, so make airline, hotel, and car rental reservations by early spring — at the latest.

Traveling with a tour group is another increasingly popular option. Numerous retired Tour riders have lent their names to tour outfits that provide on-course training rides, varying accommodation options, and catered meals. Regardless of the travel method, Tour visitors should firmly adhere to one well-known Tour spectators' creed: Get there early and prepare to stay late.

Chapter 2

Understanding the Tour de France Race Routes

Coordinating the Tour de France each year takes years of planning. Law enforcement agencies, government officials, tourism departments, and many businesses all cooperate. And when it all comes together, this huge traveling sporting event — and the carnival surrounding it — envelopes France for three weeks.

This chapter details how the Tour is methodically planned and how the event advances on a day-to-day basis. Where does the route go — and why? Why is the race divided into stages? How do teams know about each day's route?

What's a Stage, How Many Are There, and How Long Are They?

Although there's no theatrical stage, each day's race at the Tour de France is called a *stage,* and each one offers plenty of theatrics. Riders encounter and endure miles of country and mountain roads throughout France and other countries, including Germany, Italy, Belgium, and Luxembourg. The accumulation of its stages makes the Tour de France what is called a *stage race.*

No set number of stages is required in the Tour each year. But in recent years, at least 20 stages and a total of approximately 3,300 kilometers (2,047 miles) have comprised the race. The cyclist with the lowest cumulative time after the 20 stages wins.

The Tour's owner: Amaury Sport Organization

How the race progresses each year is the responsibility of its owner, Amaury Sport Organization (ASO), a French athletic sports promotion and marketing company. In addition to the Tour de France, the Paris-based ASO oversees more than 100 days of sports competition per year. The company has more than 200 employees and manages events from golf tournaments to marathons, equestrian events to car racing.

As part of the French press group Philippe Amaury Publications (E.P.A.), owner of several publications, ASO has a close relationship and has worked for many years with two prominent Tour newspapers, *l'Euipe* and *Le Parisien,* daily papers that report extensively on the Tour de France.

Created in 1992, ASO has expanded its cycling responsibilities in recent years and also overseas other races, including Paris-Nice, Tour of Qatar, and Tour du Faso.

Individual stage mileage and total race mileage are secondary in importance to the route cyclists take each day to get from start to finish. For example, a shorter mountainous stage is generally more difficult than a flat stage that's twice the length. How race organizers choose to design each year's race course keeps the more than 100-year-old race fresh and appealing to long-time fans and to event newcomers.

Choosing the Route and Stage Each Year

Teams, riders, and cycling fans eagerly await the announcement of each year's Tour route. Race dates, the cities in which stages start and finish, the rest days, and details of every stage are announced at a lavish Tour presentation luncheon in Paris in late October. Tour organizers do their best to keep the majority of the route locations undisclosed until the fall extravaganza. But media leaks occur every year, and the race provides it owns teasers to the media. In fact, the starting city, known as *Le Grand Depart,* and a few early race stages are sometimes revealed more than a year in advance.

A huge media contingent, many past and present Tour stars, sponsors, and race management attend the Tour presentation, where every detail of every day of the following summer's race is revealed. Attendees then debate for hours whether the new course is more difficult or easier than the previous year's journey.

One major consideration each year is whether the Tour follows a clockwise or counterclockwise route. Here are some examples from six Tours:

- **2000:** The 2000 route began in Futuroscope, France, advanced north toward the west coast, and then circled back toward the start on a north to south, counterclockwise route. The course reached the southern tip of France after about a week. It then progressed east and then north along the coast for more than a week before abruptly heading northwest into the heartland for two days toward the Paris conclusion.

- **2001:** Starting near the northern tip of France in Dunkirk, the 2001 Tour immediately moved into Belgium for three days before returning to France. The route followed a north to south, clockwise route along the country's eastern border. The course reached the southern tip of France at mid-race, moved west along the coast for three days, and then moved inland for the final week toward the Paris finish.

- **2002:** Beginning in Luxembourg, the 2002 Tour entered France after three days and followed a nontraditional counterclock-wise path east to west across northern France. The race progressed to the west coast, and then moved south and followed the border before advancing into the mountains and into the heart of France to the Paris conclusion.

- **2003:** The 2003 route began in St. Denis, France, and progressed on a traditional clockwise route north, and then moved directly south toward Lyon and into the Alps. The route then advanced to the southern border and followed a coastal route north for more than a week before heading inland for the Paris finale.

- **2004:** The 2004 route began in Liege, Belgium, and followed a nontraditional, counterclockwise direction toward the north-western coast of France, before heading inland, and then south. The route meandered around the country's southern coastline before heading north into the Alps, and then headed toward the center of France and onward to the traditional conclusion in Paris.

- **2005:** The 2005 route advanced clockwise around France fol-lowing an opening stage from Fromentine to the Noirmoutier-en-lile off the coast of the Vendee region of western France. The race concluded with a 160-kilometer (100-mile) stage from Corbeil-Essones to Paris. When the Tour followed a counter-clockwise route, it advanced first into the Pyrenees, the more rolling of the two most famous French mountain ranges, and then into the Alps. In a clockwise route, the more jagged-peaked Alps were scheduled in the second week, followed by the Pyrenees.

Paris has been the host city of the final day of the Tour de France every year since 1975. The wide cobblestone streets and renowned architecture, history, and cultural icons make the capital of France the ideal concluding city. Paris has hosted the beginning or ending of a Tour de France stage 131 times, well more than any other French city.

Figuring Out Where to Start

Each year's starting city is the Tour's primary concern. Cities place bids years in advance, particularly if a city outside of France seeks to host *Le Grande Depart.* Ample hotel accommodations, historic significance to the race, and famous past Tour riders are all considerations, as are available railway and airport routes.

Why would a city want to host a Tour de France stage? Just like the World Series or Super Bowl, being part of the event adds prominence to a city or a region. When a Tour stage begins or ends in a city, it guarantees several situations — some good, some not so good.

Economically, a departure or arrival hosting city will have its hotels, motels, and bed and breakfasts packed for days. Restaurants and pubs will likely have one of their best financial days of the year.

At the same time, each departure and arrival city, particularly those in the mountains, can expect horrendous traffic jams prior to and after stages are held. For many hosting cities, a visit from the Tour alters much of the city's normal way of life.

The process for choosing cities for the next Tour begins shortly after the final day of the current year's race. Tour organizers visit interested areas, and interested cities' representatives present proposals to the Tour organizers.

Interested cities can choose to host a start, finish, or both. Some cities have held only one departure or one finish, while others have been involved regularly since the race began in 1903.

Here's a list of cities with long tenures of hosting Tour stage starts and finishes (see Figure 2-1 for a map of France to help you get your bearings):

- Bayonne (32)
- Bordeaux (78)
- Briancon (31)

- Caen (34)
- Marseille (32)
- Metz (40)
- Nice (35)
- Paris (131)
- Pau (57)
- Perpignan (35)
- Toulouse (25)

A special stage for a special year

One year after the Tour's hundred-year anniversary, Tour organizers needed to do something powerful. The 2003 edition received even more vast global attention than regular Tour years, and after that, potential interest could have waned, so what did organizers do? They came up with perhaps the most unique and widely publicized stage in race history.

Traditionally, the finishing climb to L'Alpe d'Huez, a mountain ski resort in south-eastern France, is the most famous section of road in the race. The narrow route is a 13.8-kilometer (9½-mile) ascent that features 21 switchbacks (steep, zigzagging roads) or what the French call *bends.* The average grade of the road is 7.9 percent, with some sections increasing to 14 percent. The course ends at an elevation of 1,850 meters or 6,102 feet.

The climb to L'Alpe d'Huez has been included in the Tour 23 times dating to 1952. Italy's Fausto Coppi won the inaugural stage, en route to capturing the second of his two overall race titles. In every race prior to 2004, however, the famous climb occurred after cyclists had already pedaled for hours; they then had to finish the day's weary effort with the arduous climb to the ski resort.

The exception was 2004. Tour organizers decided to contest *only* the climb, as an individual race called an *individual time trial,* as the 16th of the race's 20 stages. Riders competed in reverse order of their position in the overall standings. As every cyclist rode alone up the mountain with only a team car and police motorcycle as escorts, an estimated 750,000 spectators, camped on the mountain road, cheered and jeered throughout day, and then celebrated late into the night.

Lance Armstrong won the stage in 39 minutes and 41 seconds, defeating Jan Ullrich of Germany (Telekom) by 1 minute and 1 second. Armstrong rode at an average speed of 14½ mph (just over 23 kph), an extraordinarily fast pace considering the severity of the terrain.

ROYAUME UNI

BELGIQUE

MANCHE

Lille

LUXEMBOURG

Amiens Châlons-en- Metz ALLEMAGNE
Rouen Champagne

Caen Strasbourg

PARIS

Rennes

Nantes Orléans Dijon Besançon

FRANCE SUISSE

Poitiers

Limoges

OCÉAN Clermont- Lyon
ATLANTIQUE Ferrand

ITALIE

Bordeaux

Toulouse Montpellier

Marseille

MER
MÉDITERRANÉE

ESPAGNE

ANDORRE

Ajaccio

Figure 2-1: Map of France.

Time Trials, Mountains Stages, Prologues, and More

Despite its century steeped in tradition, one great appeal of the Tour de France is its flexibility. Organizers arrange the course as they choose, but always with a plan to include a balance of most of the different types of races or all of them. And each year, organizers spice up the course with something new, like successive mountaintop finishes or unique starting cities, like the 1998 start in Dublin, Ireland.

Tour organizers mix and match different types of races into the Tour:

- ✔ **A Prologue (time trial):** In most recent years, the Tour has started with a short individual race called a *Prologue*. Winners of the brief event (it's always shorter than eight kilometers) claim race leadership for the first official opening stage the following day.

- ✔ **Flat and rolling stages:** Flat and rolling stages across the French countryside often comprise the first week.

- ✔ **Mountain stages:** Strenuous mountain stages high into the sometimes snow-capped peaks of the Alps and Pyrenees are held in the second week and into the third week.

- ✔ **Individual time trials:** *Individual time trials,* in which cyclists pedal solo and are timed against the clock, are interspersed strategically throughout the race.

- ✔ **Team time trials:** *Team time trials* — that is, each team riding together individually against the clock — aren't held every year (see Figure 2-2, which shows the start of a time trial course), but are added some years for variety.

Each is explained in more detail in the following sections.

Figure 2-2: The host town of Cambria gives a giant welcome to Stage 4 of the 2004 Tour de France.

Prologues and high speeds

As a ceremonial prerace, Prologues provide a quick, exciting Tour start. Individual time trials less than 8 kilometers (5 miles) in length, Prologues comprise a few minutes of individual, high-speed pedaling for every cyclist in the field. The race's winner wears the leader's yellow jersey for the first official stage held the following day.

Prologues aren't held every year, but when contested, the short distance gives fans immediate knowledge of just how fast cyclists can pedal. Prologues also provide the first look at the condition or lack of condition of overall title favorites, and showcase the most technological advances in bikes, wheels, helmets, clothing, and so on.

In the 2004 Tour, young Swiss rider Fabian Cancellara surprised the favorites, including Lance Armstrong. Riding for the Italian team Fassa Bortolo, Cancellara claimed the Prologue in 6 minutes and 51 seconds — an average speed of 53.560 kilometers per hour (33.22 mph). As an omen for what was pending in the rest of the race, Cancellara's effort was the third-fastest Prologue in race history and 2 seconds faster than the effort of runner-up Armstrong.

Flat and rolling stages

For the first week of the race, the course usually offers long, flat stretched that are gobbled up by the *peloton*. Stages may include some brief, low-graded climbs, but in general, teams try to get their sprinters in position for furiously quick dashes to finish lines.

Despite the less technical nature of the Tour's early stages, the week can be dangerous. Riders are nervous when the Tour begins, and it's not uncommon for the entire *peloton* (pack of riders) to ride en masse into finishing towns. Race organizers utilize as much of the finishing cities' geography as possible to appeal to crowds and to capitalize on sponsorship opportunities. As such, narrow, tight turns are common in the waning miles of flat stages, and one false move in the group when it's moving at high speed can result in disastrous crashes.

The first week of racing in the Tour can also provide some of the most scenic and panoramic views of the race. Because early stages encompass long stretches of flat terrain, France's vast vineyards and miles of sunflowers are often omnipresent. It's these scenarios — large groups of cyclists moving across the country together with postcard perfect backdrops — that provide travel brochure images for Tour organizers.

Making the grade: Mountain stages

Mountains, with their snow-capped peaks, thin air, winding and steep climbs, and harrowing and narrow descents, define the Tour de France. Some Tour routes in mountains are as famous as the race itself. And it's the strength and talent of some cyclists to get to the top of mountains swiftly that separates them from the rest of the field.

Like all the stages, mountain stages included in the Tour change each year, depending upon how race organizers coordinate the route. The course logically encompasses departure and arrival cities and at least a few of the numerous famous peaks of the French Alps and Pyrenees.

Mountain stages include climbs categorized by number, ranging from 4 (easiest) to 1 (hardest). The most difficult climbs are so steep, they're beyond categorizing, or *hors categorie*.

Categorizing climbs is objective and subjective. The length of the climb, the difference in altitude from the bottom to the top, its average grade and steepest grade, and where the climb is positioned in the stage are all important factors. The elevation of the climb's summit and the width and condition of the road are also contributing factors. Figure 2-3 shows a mountainous stage.

Certain general guidelines dictate how climbs are categorized, but race directors in different races rate climbs differently. Even year to year in the Tour de France, discrepancies occur.

In general terms, Category 4 climbs are short and easy. Category 3 climbs last approximately 5 kilometers (3.1 miles), have an average grade of 5 percent, and ascend 150 meters (500 feet). Category 2 climbs are the same length or longer at an 8 percent grade and ascend 500 meters (1,600 feet). Category 1 climbs last 20 kilometers (12.4 miles) with an average 6 percent grade and ascend 1,500 meters. Beyond category climbs include an altitude difference of at least 1,000 meters (3,280 feet) from start to finish and have an average grade of at least 7 percent.

A 1 percent grade means a road ascends 1 meter (3.28 feet) for every 100 meters (328 feet) it advances.

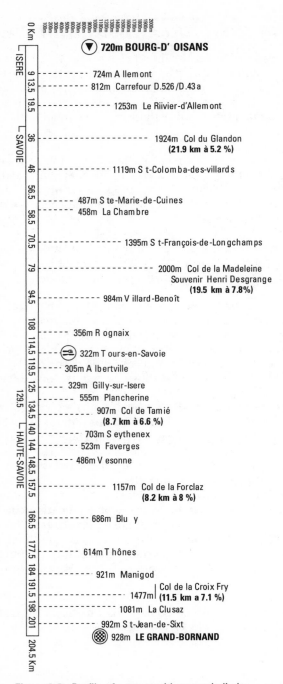

Figure 2-3: Profile of a stage with several climbs.

Mountain men on wheels

Two types of cyclists excel in mountain stages — riders in contention for the overall title and mountain climbing specialists who seek single stage wins, which are prestigious in their own right. A rider who doesn't climb well can't win the Tour, but some cyclists who climb well are not in contention for the overall title. They don't have strong time trial skills or aren't part of strong teams. Instead, mountain specialists pick specific stages and attempt to grab the glory — just for the day or for a few stages scattered throughout the race.

Every year at the race announcement there's plenty of discussion of whether race organizers have devised a course with hopes to dethrone the defending champion. Race tradition dictates that organizers plan a course that doesn't favor the reigning champion's strengths, but they never admit such practices.

As Lance Armstrong added to his six (as of this writing) consecutive race victories, Tour race director Jean-Marie Leblanc has dramatically altered the route. Some years during Armstrong's reign, new routes have featured fewer strenuous climbs and less taxing individual time trials. Armstrong's career success has been built with a simple formula: The harder a race, the better.

Leblanc's course alterations have made little difference. Like other champions, Armstrong doesn't react strongly to varying course routes. Leblanc doesn't react strongly, either. With a staff of colleagues and other experts' opinions, each year's course is chosen via logistical and financial considerations — and with the defending champion's mastery in mind. The route is also selected with an additional subjective consideration — just how severely the race director wishes to torture or not torture cyclists in any given year.

Individual time trials

More than any other Tour de France race, time trials allow the most riders to showcase their strengths. Cyclists compete individually and against only one competitor — the timing clock. Unlike road racing's team strategy, *drafting* (riding close behind another rider so as to cut down on the effects of wind) and the flow of the *peloton,* success in an individual time trial is entirely a solo accomplishment. Every split seconds counts. Riders' aerodynamics matched with their physical skills add up to a simple equation. The fastest man on a bike on any given day wins.

Course distances and routes vary greatly, but time trial routes are generally around 50 kilometers (31.2 miles) and encompass hilly, flat, undulating, and curved road sections. Riders negotiate the course as fast as possible while keeping an appropriate pace and utilizing superior bike-handling skills.

A successful time trialist is not unlike an endurance runner or an ultradistance swimmer. In some ways, time trials are cyclists' marathons. Start a time trial too fast and there's little hope for maintaining a proper steady pace for the duration of the stage. Start too slow in a time trial and a rider may never find the proper rhythm. Unlike endurance sports where certain athletes' body types are conducive to success, great individual time trial riders come in all shapes and sizes.

Race organizers can adjust starting time gaps between riders, but most time trials begin with riders leaving a starting ramp 2 minutes apart. Cyclists compete in the reverse order of their position in the *General Classification* (the current standings). If a faster rider is about to overtake a slower rider, he must pass while leaving at least a 2-meter distance to prevent drafting, which is illegal only at this point in the race. A passed slower rider then must ride at least 25 meters behind to prevent him from getting the drafting benefits of a slipstream from the leading rider.

A team vehicle carrying spare bikes and wheels must follow every rider in an individual time trial. The vehicle must remain about 10 meters behind the rider, and it can't pull even with its riders at anytime during the stage. Any information exchange between a cyclist and his team vehicle must occur from behind and at least from a 10-meter distance. A vehicle can be positioned between two riders if there's at least 50 meters between riders.

Team time trials

Team time trials seem like oxymorons. Individual time trials test riders' solo strengths; Team time trials bring team strategy back into the race equation. Often cited as the most photogenic cycling discipline, each team's riders ride together, beginning 5 minutes apart. They pedal in a tightly packed, single- or double-file procession.

Cyclists rotate in and out of the front of the group to take advantage of opportunities to draft. Each rider alternately blocks the wind for teammates and then returns into the team formation to conserve energy. A rider may take a turn at the front of his group for 20 seconds and then fall back into the mix of his teammates. Like fast-moving, human-powered, aerodynamic trains, teams advance around corners, over railroad tracks and undulations, and through roadside villages. Visually, the swift packs moving in unison provide excitement for spectators and delightful opportunities for race photographers' keen eyes.

Despite their intriguing nature, team time trials present unique difficulties. If a rider just slightly falls out of rotation, he can initiate a sudden and disastrous crash involving his entire team. If a rider can't keep the same pace as his teammates, he quickly falls off the back of the team and diminishes his team's collective strength.

While important, team time trials are not often held during the long racing season. Teams rarely have opportunities to practice, but done properly, a team time trial takes precise cooperation and coordination among team members. Teams must find an ideal pace despite riders' varying skills. When a team in a team time trial accomplishes its goal, synergy is defined.

 Teams must start a team time trial with all their riders. Teams use different strategies. Some squads hope to finish with all riders together and rotate positions until every rider is close to the finish. Other teams have designated strong riders stay at the front for longer durations, only to purposely fall off pace near the conclusion. All teams must finish with at least five riders to get an official time. The time of the fifth rider crossing the line determines the team's finishing time.

Scouting the New Route: Practice Makes Perfect

Marathon runners sometimes opt for training runs on their hometown marathon course weeks and even months before marathon day. The same isn't often possible for Tour de France cyclists. Many French riders live in France, and their extended backyards comprise at least part of the Tour de France course.

But what do other Tour de France cyclists do to familiarize themselves with the race and its varied stages? With a global race schedule that includes more than 100 races from January through October, teams have difficulty during the season viewing announced Tour venues or potential race routes.

With increasing regularity in recent years, many teams have discovered a new way to test mountain stages or specific road routes. In preseason training camps or when there's a break between racing schedules, teams find accommodations in the Alps, Pyrenees, or other centralized locations and set up temporary training bases.

Most top international pro teams have rosters with more than two-dozen riders, so at any given time of the year, part of a team may be competing in one race while another part of the team competes in another race. The same scenario occurs in some training camps. A core group of a team attends the camp, while other teammates are competing elsewhere.

Climbing L'Alpe d'Huez

Climbing L'Alpe d'Huez is a coveted experience for Tour de France cyclists and amateur riders seeking a riding memory of the event to relate to friends. The ascent to the ski resort has been done hundreds of times during the Tour, but never just as a time trial.

As such, by the time the new stage was held during the 2004 Tour, rumors of riders pedaling up the hill repeatedly in training sessions began to circulate. And when Lance Armstrong pedaled to his dominating win over Jan Ullrich, one sure reason was that practice makes perfect. Armstrong reportedly rode the course more than a half-dozen times in practice.

During the Tour, riders preview courses, particularly time trial routes. If riders' starting times are later in the day, they may ride the course early on the morning of the race and then watch a teammate ride the course while in the comfort of a team vehicle. Riders who contest a time trial course early in a stage can help their teammates riding later in day. After completing the course, an early day rider relates any problem areas on the route to his teammates and team director. And all riders receive a daily map that fits into their jerseys' pockets.

Riders aren't necessarily familiar with the route of every stage of the Tour before race day. After the overall route is announced, teams analyze the course and decide what stages are likely key days. During minicamps, cyclists may ride a designated Tour stage route repeatedly, noting the ascents, descents, bends, and potential hazards.

Chapter 3

The Races within the Race

*O*nly a few riders compete for overall victory each year at the Tour de France. But every day, there's plenty else going on in the *peloton* (the main group of riders). Beyond racing for overall victory, the best sprinter, best climber, and best young rider competitions progress daily, sometimes with battles more intense than the quest for the overall title.

Stage winners are honored each day on the finishing podium, as are leaders of other competitions. Every rider in the field has a good opportunity to claim something — a stage win, a midrace sprint, a kiss from a pretty girl at the postrace awards ceremony, a bouquet of flowers, a stuffed lion, or even the unofficial but respected honor of finishing last. The overall race leader is, of course, also acknowledged, and he gets his share of awards and recognition.

The Tour de France also has a team competition and daily and overall rewards for the most competitive riders. These competitions aren't represented by jerseys, but are important parts of the race.

This chapter describes races within the race that add excitement and keep each day's racing animated. Why do some riders wear different colored jerseys? What is the podium and what happens there? What's the red lantern or *lanterne rouge?* What do the awards mean, and who are those pretty girls on the podium, anyway?

Timing: Every Second Counts

Every Tour de France stage is timed, and there are no timeouts for trains, planes, or automobiles. There's no stopping the clock for railroad crossings, for animals in the road, or for slow-moving farm equipment. And there are no television timeouts.

Every rider is given a time as he crosses the finish line, and all riders' finishing times are visible on a large digital clock positioned above the finish line. The race's overall time is the accumulated time of all stages, but there are exceptions. In designated places during stages and for top placings at the finish, riders get bonus seconds subtracted from their overall times. Riders are also given points in predetermined sprints during and at the end of stages. Riders can also be penalized for various rule infractions, from holding onto team cars to public urination.

Getting sprints, points, and bonus seconds

Depending on the type of road stage — flat, medium mountain, and high mountain — the top-25 finishers in each stage are awarded points.

- ✔ Stage winners in flat stages receive 35 points, and the total decreases to 1 point for the 25th-place finisher.

- ✔ In medium mountain stages, winners receive 25 points, and the 20th-place rider receives 1 point.

- ✔ In high mountain stages, winners receive 20 points, and the 15th-place finisher receives 1 point.

In the Prologue and in individual time trials, winners receive 15 points and the 10th-place finisher receives 1 point. During intermediate sprints, the first three riders to pass designated lines receive 6, 4, and 2 points.

The best climber competition has similar point totals. Points are doubled for the final climb in each mountain stage.

Winning stages doesn't equal winning the Tour

A rider can win a dozen stages and not win the Tour de France. How is that possible? Suppose a cyclist wins all these stages by 1 minute each. He'd accumulate at least a 12-minute margin and various bonus times. But there's still a good chance he wouldn't win the race. The reason: With one bad day, a rider can easily lose 30 minutes in a mountain stage. It's unlikely a rider who wins 12 stages would lose a half-hour in one day, but it can easily happen if a rider gets sick, crashes, or misses a key break at the front of the race. In rare instances, overall Tour winners haven't won any stages. Yet, their strategic stage finishes give them the lowest cumulative time in the field.

Getting to Know Jerseys

Cyclists are minimalists — at least when it comes to attire. They have bicycles, of course, but riders' apparel is simple and streamlined. A pair of shoes and socks are required, and also a well-fitting pair of shorts and a jersey.

Like a well-tailored suit, proper jerseys mean a lot to cyclists in the Tour de France, as in any other race. Nearly all riders wear identically designed jerseys that differ by the sponsors' names on them. In addition, the race leader and the other race competition leaders wear different colored jerseys, but their primary sponsors' logos still appear on their jerseys.

What's a jersey and why not just wear a T-shirt?

Woolen jerseys were once all the rage at the Tour de France, but tight-fitting Lycra/Spandex and other high-tech polyester materials have been the standard for many years. Jerseys are made with a lightweight synthetic fabric that has great elasticity and contours to varying body shapes; it's often referred to as a cyclist's second skin.

Because of their tight fit, jerseys are very aerodynamic. During road stages, cyclists wear separate jerseys and shorts, but in time trials, races in which every second counts, cyclists wear one-piece *skinsuits*. Some newly developed skinsuits actually have different thicknesses in different areas to further enhance aerodynamics.

How did this jersey thing start anyway?

Pictures from early Tour de France years show riders dressed like businessmen pedaling to their offices. Like early professional golfers, cyclists at the turn of the 20th century wore knickers, dress shirts, bow ties, and suit coats. But riders soon figured out more appropriate attire. A Tour race picture from 1905 shows French race pioneers Lucien Petit Breton and Jean-Baptiste Dortignacq side-by-side on their bikes at the race start. Both riders are wearing short, above-the-knee, tight-fitting woolen pants and form-fitting long-sleeve woolen jerseys.

Brightly single-colored or striped jerseys remained standard until 1919, when race director Henri Desgrange instituted the first significant apparel change. As a marketing tool, Desgrange introduced a yellow jersey. It designated the race leader and it also matched the color of *L'Auto,* the newspaper Desgrange published, which was printed on yellow paper.

How many jerseys are used during the race?

In early Tour years, cyclists' uniforms were limited, and riders sometimes looked like they slept in their riding clothes. Compare that to today, when Tour riders wear clean outfits every day. Who wants a corporate logo looking all dirty?

Cyclists usually wear the same jersey for a complete stage, even when shorts or jerseys tear or become muddy, salt-stained, or bloodied during races. Exceptions occur after crashes. It's common to see riders complete stages with holes in their shorts and jerseys, but if tears are too large or prevent a rider from continuing, riders change jerseys. A rider can fall back from the *peloton* and change his jersey while on his bike, or he can momentarily stop at a team car for a replacement pair of shorts.

Cyclists who compete in the Tour are on top teams, and these teams can provide a single rider with up to 275 pieces of clothing per year — approximately 20 to 30 short-sleeve jerseys alone. Teams provide extra clothing during the three-week race, but riders are so sentimental that they wear the same clothing every day (washed, of course).

Showing sponsors' logos

One of the Tour's most anticipated scenes is a stage winner's protocol as he approaches a finish line. In a sprint finish, there's not much time to react. But a cyclist with a substantial lead near a finish doesn't have to worry about being caught. As such, there's plenty of time to prepare for the throng of photographers, television camera operators, and spectators waiting at the finish line.

Tour de France cyclists know the importance of winning a stage and how much it pleases sponsors and team officials and advances their respective careers. Some stage winners develop finishing celebrations that are as elaborate as cheerleaders' routines. Other cyclists prefer more subtle approaches. But all pending Tour stage winners know that, as they cross the line, it's best to have their apparel and equipment in good view to show the sponsors' logos.

During hot days, Tour riders pedal for hours with their jerseys partially or completely unzipped. But a cyclist about to win or claim a top-three finish does himself and his team a disservice if he forgets one final important finish-line tradition. That's right: It may be 100 degrees, and a pending stage winner may be exhausted, dehydrated, or sick, but he's not likely to forget to zip up his jersey in the final meters of a winning stage. The reason? Stage winners and other top finishers not only have their images in thousands of publications, but sponsors also use the same shots to promote their products and services.

If a stage winner forgets to zip up his jersey as he nears the finish line, the names of his various sponsors aren't likely to be readily visible. It's a mistake that could help sway a company from not renewing its contract because of lack of media exposure.

Explaining the Overall General Classification

Every day during the Tour, riders' finishing times as well as any bonus or penalty seconds are calculated and recorded as overall or General Classification times. *Overall standings* and *General Classification* are synonymous terms, but race organizers and cycling enthusiasts most often use the preferred General Classification, or shorten it to just *GC*. Finishing times of all stages and the Prologue are cumulative, so that the rider with the lowest accumulated total time (factoring in bonus times and penalties) wins the race.

Race site computers record riders' finishing times. Within minutes, results are posted on the race's official Web site, distributed to teams, given to on-site media members, and sent electronically to thousands of worldwide media outlets. Results that are available immediately after stages are partial, unofficial results and include stage and General Classification times of only the leading finishers. Particularly in mountains stages, when an hour may separate the first and final finisher, official results aren't available until all riders' times, as well as bonus points or penalty times, are calculated.

Official times are distributed at the race and around the world within a larger packet of results that includes individual stage placings and best climber, best sprinter, best young rider, and team results. Additional race information — from medical reports to the next day's team departure protocol — is also included.

The yellow jersey

As a man of marketing savvy and gimmicks, race director Henri Desgrange introduced the yellow jersey to the Tour de France in 1919. The tradition has remained since Eugene Christophe wore it in its debut while assuming the overall race lead after the 10th stage to Grenoble.

The *yellow jersey,* or *maillot jaune,* allows the rest of the field, spectators, and media to easily identify the race leader (see Figure 3-1, although, admittedly, it's hard to see the color in a black-and-white photo; see the color section near the center of this book for a better sense of the brightness of the yellow jersey). But in its first year, the yellow jersey was hardly necessary to make the leader stand out. Christophe assumed the race lead after the fourth stage, but when he donned the jersey the first time, only 11 of 69 race starters remained for the final two stages. With the Tour's current larger fields, spotting the race leader is more difficult, particularly for network television camera operators, so the yellow jersey is more appreciated.

Figure 3-1: Lance Armstrong in the yellow jersey in Villard-de-Lans.

Respect for the yellow

There's a lot of respect for the yellow jersey. Although Team ONCE from Spain usually has the same color yellow in its jerseys, for several years of the Tour, they have donned entirely new uniforms in pink, just to show respect for yellow and not to confuse spectators.

A new yellow jersey is awarded on the finish podium after every stage to the leader of the overall race standings. If the overall leader remains the same for two or more stages, the race leader doesn't just keep the same jersey; he gets a new one for every day he holds the race lead.

If two or more riders have the same general classification time, the tenths and hundreds of seconds recorded in individual time trial stages are added to riders' overall times. Two additional tiebreaker calculations are used, if necessary:

- ✔ **First tiebreaker:** The rider with the lowest total number after adding his Prologue and stage finishing places together wins.

- ✔ **Second tiebreaker:** The rider with the lowest finish place among the tied riders in the final stage wins.

Only three riders have won the Tour de France while leading from start to finish. Maurice Garin won all six stages of the inaugural event in 1903. The *maillot jaune* didn't debut for another 16 years, so Garin never wore the yellow jersey. Instead, as race leader, he wore a green armband. Ottavio Bottechia of Italy held or was tied for the lead in every stage of the 1924 Tour, and accordingly had the yellow jersey for all 15 stages. German riders Nicolas Frantz (1928) and Romain Maes (1935) also won the Tour while leading start to finish. The Tour had 22 stages in 1928 and 21 stages in 1935.

The polka-dot jersey for climbing

Introduced in 1975, the *polka-dot jersey,* or *maillot aux pois rouges,* is worn each day by the rider leading the best climber — or King of the Mountains — competition. The polka-dot jersey (see Figure 3-2) is reminiscent of horse racing jockeys' attire, but like other Tour jerseys, the best climber jersey design began as a marketing concept.

Figure 3-2: Richard Virenque in the polka-dot jersey on the Champs Élysées.

The jersey was introduced when a chocolate manufacturer was a major race sponsor. One of the sponsor's best-known chocolate bars had a white wrapper with red spots. The race and sponsor quickly came up with an idea: A jersey with the same white background and red polka dots would provide additional exposure for the sponsor. The polka-dot jersey was born.

Like the other jerseys, a polka-dot jersey is awarded after each stage to the leader of the mountain climbers' standings. He wears it during the following stage.

Determining the yellow jersey competition is easy, but the King of the Mountains category has an elaborate calculation of points, each awarded in a different way on all mountain climbs. Riders in contention for the polka-dot jersey title must finish the Tour.

 ✔ On the most difficult mountains, called *Beyond Category* or *hors categorie,* points are awarded from 1st through 10th place as follows: 20, 18, 16, 14, 12, 10, 8, 7, 6, and 5 points, respectively.

 ✔ In the next most difficult climbs, called Category 1 climbs, points are distributed for the first eight places: 15, 13, 11, 9, 8, 7, 6, and 5.

 ✔ In Category 2 climbs, points are 10, 9, 8, 7, 6, and 5 for the first six riders to finish.

 ✔ In Category 3 climbs, points are 4, 3, 2, and 1.

 ✔ In Category 4 climbs, points are 3, 2, and 1.

Richard Virenque: King of climbers

Richard Virenque, a native of Morocco and a naturalized French citizen, is among the most popular and controversial cyclists in Tour history. He's also the race's most decorated climber after he claimed the polka-dot jersey for a record seventh time in 2004. French cycling fans revered Virenque, who in the fall of 2004 retired at age 34. For more than a decade, race spectators etched Virenque's name on mountaintop roads throughout the race.

But this superior mountain climber who finished as high as second overall (1997) was also involved in the sport's infamous drug scandal in 1998. Festina, a team sponsored by the watch manufacturer, was disqualified during the race for using performance-enhancing drugs. Virenque and teammate Pascal Herve were the only team members who didn't admit to the offense.

More than two years later, in the team's court trial, Virenque confessed. He was suspended from cycling for nine months. When he returned, the French public forgot the doping incident and collectively embraced Virenque.

Virenque's Tour wins were all in mountain stages, and he captured wins in his final three Tours: 2002, 2003, and 2004. En route to his record-setting King of the Mountains title, Virenque rode to a 10th-stage solo win on Bastille Day, the July 14th national French holiday.

Note that for the final Beyond Category and Categories 1 and 2 climbs of stages, points are doubled.

If there's a points tie in the final climbing classification, the cyclist with the most first-place finishes in Beyond Category climbs wins. If there's still a tie, victory is awarded to the rider with the most first-place finishes in Category 1 climbs. The same process is used, if necessary, in Categories 2, 3, and 4.

The green jersey for sprinting

To help celebrate the Tour's 50th anniversary, the *green jersey,* or *maillot vert,* was introduced in 1953 in Strasbourg. It rewards the cyclist with the most points. Points are awarded during intermittent sprint locations in the Prologue and stages as well as in finishing sprints. Each day, the points leader is awarded a green jersey (see Figure 3-3, although in a black-and-white photo, colors are, admittedly, tough to see), and like other jersey honorees, he wears the jersey in the next day's stage. Points are awarded in road races, time trials, and in intermediate stage sprints, called *hot spots.*

Figure 3-3: Robbie McEwen in the green jersey on L'Alpe d'Huez.

✔ **For flat stages,** awarded points are 35, 30, 26, 24, 22, 20, 19, 18, 17, 16, 15, 14, 13, 12, 11, 10, 9, 8, 7, 6, 5, 4, 3, 2, and 1 for the 1st through 25th-place riders.

✔ **In rolling stages,** points are 25, 22, 20, 18, 16, 15, 14, 13, 12, 11, 10, 9, 8, 7, 6, 5, 4, 3, 2, and 1 for the first 20 riders.

✔ **In mountain stages,** points are 20, 17, 15, 13, 12, 10, 9, 8, 7, 6, 5, 4, 3, 2, and 1 for the first 15 riders.

✔ **In individual time trial stages,** points are 15, 12, 10, 8, 6, 5, 4, 3, 2, and 1 for the top ten riders.

✔ **During intermediate stage sprints,** points are 6, 4, and 2 points for the first three riders.

The green jersey competition, like other jersey competitions, has detailed criteria to break ties. If riders share an equal place in a stage, they're awarded the total number of points divided by the number of riders involved in the tie. If that number is a fraction, it's rounded up.

In the General Classification points totals, ties are broken based on a rider's total stage wins, second-place finishers, and so on until one rider has a greater number of finishes. Like the yellow and polka-dot jerseys, a rider must finish the Tour to place in the overall points classification.

Germany's Erik Zabel, who rides for the T-Mobile squad, holds the Tour record for green jersey titles. He won six straight years, beginning in 1996.

Being young has its advantages: The white jersey

To recognize skilled young riders, the Tour introduced the *white jersey*, or *maillot blanc*, in 1975. Sometimes known as the *young rider's yellow jersey*, it's awarded after every stage to the highest-placed cyclist 25 years of age or younger (as of January 1 in each Tour year). The highest placed young rider in the final overall standings claims the race's final white jersey (see Figure 3-4).

Figure 3-4: Thomas Voeckler in the white jersey on L'Alpe d'Huez.

Race organizers dropped the overall white jersey competition in 1988, but still awarded a prize to the best overall young rider. The white jersey was subsequently reinstated and has since been claimed by several of the Tour's finest riders — Jan Ullrich of Germany (1996 to 1998), Marco Pantani of Italy (1994 and 1995), Oscar Sevilla of Spain (2001), and Ivan Basso of Italy (2002).

Because many Tour riders mature approaching their late 20s, it's rare for a cyclist to claim the yellow and white jerseys in the same year. But it happens. Laurent Fignon of France was the first rider to claim both jerseys in 1983, when he won the first of his two Tour titles at age 23. Jan Ullrich was also age 23 when he captured the Tour and the white jersey in 1997.

Standing on the Podium (and Kissing the Podium Girls)

After every stage, the day's winner, race leader, and leaders of all other race jersey colors are required to attend the postrace ceremony. The stage winner receives flowers and other gifts. Dozens of race photographers take images of riders, and spectators loudly cheer, particularly when a French rider is on the podium.

To present podium awards, four attractive women are hired each year by Credit Lyonnais, a French bank that sponsors the yellow jersey and has been a Tour partner since 1981. The women are officially known as *hostesses,* but everyone calls them *podium girls* (see Figure 3-5).

Figure 3-5: Thomas Voeckler receiving victory kisses from podium girls on Plateau de Beille.

Through the years, podium girls' presentations have become an increasingly popular part of post-stage proceedings. Cycling Web sites post pictures of podium girls and ask readers to pick favorites. Tour riders are well aware of podium girls, too. Tour rules forbid cyclists to date podium girls, but it happens. If a relationship develops, the podium girl is asked to resign. In fact, several Tour riders and former podium girls are married and have children.

Receiving awards and accolades

Post-race ceremonies follow tradition and protocol via the Tour's Regulations of the Race or *Reglement de l'epreuve*. The awards ceremony begins a few minutes after every stage, and the finishing city's mayor or his or her appointed representative leads the ceremony and is joined by race dignitaries.

Awards are presented in the following order:

- ✔ Stage winner
- ✔ Leader of the General Classification, who receives the yellow jersey
- ✔ Leader of the points competition, who receives the green jersey
- ✔ Leader of the best climber competition, who receives the polka-dot jersey
- ✔ Leader of the best young rider competition, who receives the white jersey

Who gets to keep all the stuff?

Tour de France race leaders have plenty to worry about without keeping track of a healthy supply of flowers and stuffed lions. But because it's common for Tour race leaders to retain the yellow jersey for several days, the Tour leader has to decide what to do with a healthy supply of flowers and stuffed lions.

In many cases, race leaders give their flowers and lions to friends or family at the race. If that's not an option, a rider can give his awards to spectators or have a team representative bring the gifts to the team hotel for safekeeping or for distribution at another time.

Riders present on the podium must follow various protocol: They can't wear glasses, other than corrective lenses, nor can they wear helmets. In addition, most teams implement their own dress code for podium appearances that's more stringent than the Tour rules.

Award winners refusing to participate in awards ceremonies (or at starting ceremonies) are penalized, unless they can give extenuating circumstances for their absences.

Giving flowers and stuffed lions

The race leader is presented with a bouquet of flowers and a toy, stuffed lion after every stage. Two of the four podium girls (they rotate daily responsibilities in pairs) distribute awards. One podium girl presents the lion, the other the flowers. The podium girl who presents the gift and its recipient then kiss on the cheeks.

The Honor of the Lanterne Rouge

Since the inaugural Tour, the last-place finisher has been bestowed with a dubious but respected honor — the *lanterne rouge* or *red lantern* (sometimes also called the *red light*). The name is derived from the red lantern on a caboose — the last car of a train. The cyclist who finishes every stage within the designated *time limit* (a set time in which a rider has to finish to remain eligible — see the "Meeting time limits" section for brief details and Chapter 5 for the official rules on time limits) and is last in the overall standings at the end of the race is not only tough, he's revered.

From glory to shame

While being the *lanterne rouge* has its glory, being disqualified does not. Tour cyclists, teams, and team personnel can be disqualified for reasons beyond competition, according to general principles of the race. Disqualification reasons include

- Infringement of French law

- Infringement of the Tour de France ethical code

- Indecent dress or unsuitable behavior

- Acts of vandalism during or outside of the race

- Failure to use transportation provided by the Tour during transfer days

- Customs violations

Arsene Millocheau had a lot of difficulty during the first Tour, but he managed to finish as the 21st and final finisher from the starting field of 60. In modern Tours, Millocheau would have been eliminated, based on various stage time restrictions. But in 1903, finishing 2 days, 16 hours, 47 minutes, and 22 seconds behind the winner was acceptable. The event was new, and who knew how long it would take to complete? Millocheau's ordeal established the standard, and his epic journey remains the largest margin between the winner and *lanterne rouge* in Tour history.

From shame to glory

Through the years, the *lanterne rouge* has become increasingly popular. Riders unlikely to gain prestige during the Tour at the front of the *peloton* or in jersey competitions figure the only remaining place to seek glory is at the back of the *peloton*. In fact, the winner of the *lanterne rouge* not only gets his share of notoriety, the Tour has offered various prize monies for the honor. Time limits have changed the approach somewhat, however.

Working hard to keep last place

The *lanterne rouge* honor has become so popular at times during the Tour that cyclists seeking the title have done nearly anything they could to claim the title. Before Tour officials instituted stage time limits, riders stopped en route to the finish line in their attempt to finish last and lose additional time to the race leader.

The *lanterne rouge* is no longer an official designation at the Tour, but many riders endure injury and illness to remain in the event in order to make *lanterne rouge* history. The last official finisher has the respect of his peers and race fans, and official or not, he's still often called the *lanterne rouge*.

Riding in the Broom Wagon

Tour cofounder Henri Desgrange had great innovations, and his visions were often simultaneously respectful and direct. In 1910, to fetch cyclists abandoning the race, Desgrange introduced the *broom wagon* or *la voiture balai*. The broom wagon (a van for many years, but now a recreational vehicle) progresses along every road race at the rear of the race. Through the years, brooms have been attached to the vehicle in various ways as symbolic yet cruel icons: Riders who need to leave the race are "swept" off the course.

The broom wagon has remained part of the Tour since its inception. It's the last vehicle in a caravan of race vehicles, with the exception of police cars or motorcycles. No rider wants to ride in the broom wagon, because it signifies the end of their Tour participation for the year. Riding in the broom wagon is also the most conspicuous way to abandon the race. Television cameras like broom wagon footage, and every Tour spectator knows exactly what's happening when a cyclist enters the vehicle. If a rider abandoning the race is fortunate, he can less conspicuously leave the race in his team car.

Abandoning the race — and why

Finishing the Tour is a career highlight for many cyclists, and abandoning the race is a rider's least favorite option. Injury, illness, finishing outside of time limits, and drug test offenses are primary reasons for riders' departures.

Since the Tour returned following WWII in 1947, the finishing percentage of riders has rarely been below 50 percent. On the day a rider retires from the race, his status appears on post-race results with either the designation *DNS* (did not start) or *DNF* (started, but did not finish).

Injuries and illness take some riders out of the Tour, and the starting field can dramatically thin out as the race moves into mountain stages. Cyclists are sometimes strung across mountain ranges, and a race that's been close for a week or more can suddenly change. Often, the reason for leaving the race is that time limits weren't met.

Meeting time limits

Unlike early years of the Tour, riders must finish stages within a certain percentage of time after stage winners, depending upon the severity of the stage. Road stages are defined as no particular difficulty (Coefficient 1), medium difficulty (Coefficient 2), and particular difficulty (Coefficient 3). Each coefficient has a detailed chart of averaging finishing speeds and a corresponding time percentage in which riders have to finish to avoid elimination. If the winner's average speed is between 31 and 32 kilometers per hour (19.23 and 19.85 miles per hour), all finishers have to finish within 12 percent of the winner's time. The faster the winner's average speed, the larger the time gap allowed.

During extremely mountainous stages (Coefficient 4), the finishing deadline varies from 9 percent to 21 percent of the stage winner's time, with increasing allowances ranging from a finishing time of no more than 28 to 40 kilometers per hour. In time trials (Coefficient 5), all riders must finish within 25 percent of the winner's finishing time to avoid elimination. In uphill time trials or time trials with "special circumstances" (Coefficient 6), all riders must finish within 33 percent of the winner's time to avoid elimination.

Coefficients and various time percentages are followed strictly, but exceptions are common for many reasons. Permitted finishing times can be changed at the discretion of race officials for various weather conditions, a road blockage, natural disaster, or a serious accident.

Race officials also have the direction to extend elimination times for the good of the race, either for a group of riders or for individuals. Examples include the following:

✔ If more than 20 percent of the field is eliminated via standard criteria, finishing time limits can be extended (the riders are savvy enough to collect themselves together to make larger groups and ride more slowly, knowing they won't be eliminated because the group is too big).

✔ A particularly unique average stage speed.

✔ The point in which an accident has occurred.

✔ The effort made by the rider(s) who failed to finish within the permitted time.

✔ The severity of the course.

Surrendering a race number

When a cyclist abandons the race, he surrenders his race numbers to a race official in the broom wagon or in another manner, if necessary. If a rider resigns from the race for a reason determined unjustified, race officials can withhold prize money previously earned in the race.

Disqualified riders or riders abandoning the race may not participate in any other part of the race or in any other cycling competition during the duration of the Tour.

Part II
How the Race Is Run and Won

The 5th Wave By Rich Tennant

In this part . . .

*N*early 200 cyclists begin the Tour de France, but not that many finish it. In this part, you discover riders' roles and how individuals' skills fit into cycling as a team sport. What makes a cyclist a climbing specialist, a sprinting specialist, a team rider, or a team leader? How do cyclists help themselves and their team when they do their jobs?

In this part, you also find out about the many and varied team personnel helping riders get through the race — on and off their bikes. Race rules are explained, as well as racing strategies: from protecting the race leader to timing bathroom breaks.

Chapter 4

It's All about the Team

*T*he Tour de France sometimes looks like a huge group of individual riders pedaling across the country, every man for himself. Cyclists operate their own bicycles with the strength of their own lungs and legs. But individuals' talents, while impressive, are misunderstood.

Multiday and multiweek cycling events, called *stage races,* are team affairs. Individuals can't enter the Tour de France; only teams representing corporate sponsors and sanctioned by *Union Cycliste Internationale,* the sport's international governing body based in Geneva, Switzerland, can compete. While dozens of professional teams race worldwide, the challenge to get selected to ride in the Tour is nearly as intense as the race competition.

Only 21 or 22 teams, each with nine riders, are chosen to participate in the three-week event. Beginning in 2005, the newly organized ProTour will automatically include 20 selected top international teams for the Grand Tours (Tour de France, Tour of Italy, and Tour of Spain) and for other key races. Tour de France organizers may also select one or two wildcard teams.

Every team is also more than just its riders. Just like in baseball, basketball, football, hockey, and NASCAR, cycling teams have owners, managers, assistant managers, trainers, mechanics, and various other support staff members.

This chapter explains the inner workings of a team. You find out how a team is organized, who's in charge, and how the cyclists and non-riding team members work together before, during, and after each day's stage. You also get the lowdown on the roles of each team's riders and what all the other people around the team are doing, day in and day out, for three weeks.

What's Team Got to Do with It?

Riders on every Tour de France team wear jerseys emblazoned with various sponsors' names and logos. Many teams have one or two *title sponsors* (major sponsors), and then they allow other companies to buy the rights for smaller advertisements on riders' shorts and jerseys. It's the cycling equivalent to NASCAR or Formula 1 racecar advertising. If space is available on a rider's jersey, it's prime promotional real estate. When careening downhill, or around corners, at high speeds, or struggling and profusely sweating while inching up difficult climbs, Tour cyclists are billboards on wheels.

Cycling team title sponsors, who give racing *squads* (another word for teams) multi-million-dollar budgets, are as varied as the terrain of France. Coffee machine manufacturers, floor covering companies, and even national lotteries of European nations all sponsor pro teams competing in the Tour. The squads are called *international trade teams.* Some squads have riders all from one country, like the Spanish Euskaltel-Euskadi team, with riders all from the Basque region of Spain. But most teams, like the 2005 sponsored U.S.-based team (The Discovery Channel Pro Cycling Team), have cyclists from many countries and who speak several different languages. The only exceptions are during the World Championships and Summer Olympics — during these prestigious events, riders represent their native countries and wear national attire.

Does the guy in yellow win every stage?

The yellow jersey, or the *maillot jaune,* is the most coveted jersey in the Tour de France (see Chapter 3). The cyclist leading the race — that is, the cyclist who has the lowest cumulative time — wears it each day.

The cyclist wearing the yellow jersey is a marked man. Every rider, every spectator, and every television camera filming the race knows the exact location of the race leader.

During his six consecutive Tour de France wins, Lance Armstrong has worn the yellow jersey for more than 60 days. That's about half of the days he has raced during his title years. It's not the goal of the yellow jersey wearer to win every stage, though; in fact, when American Greg LeMond won the Tour in 1990, he didn't win any stages. The idea is to attempt to win only on days when it's strategically prudent, and more importantly, to win the Tour overall.

Riding for dollars

Every cyclist in the Tour has a yearly salary. But the race also offers an elaborate prize money structure. In recent years, the overall race winner has earned 400,000 euros, about $480,000. The total purse of the event is three million euros, or $3,750,000, plus sponsor incentives and bonuses. Individual prize money at each stage is awarded deep into the standings. The team competition and overall standings also have prize money. Races within the race — most aggressive rider, best sprinter, best climber, and best young rider (under age 25) competitions — all have prize money, too. See Chapter 3 for more on these competitions.

Riders have additional incentives to sprint for midstage performance bonuses — the French word *primes* (pronounced preems). A cyclist on a long solo lead wins a prime when he crosses a predetermined point of stage first. Cyclists with the ability to accelerate quickly, or *sprint,* for short distances also often earn primes. They move to the front of the *peloton* within a few hundred meters of a prime location and pedal furiously to cross the line first. In the first week of the Tour — before the mountains arrive — these bonuses also allow riders not in contention for the overall title a chance to wear the yellow jersey, at least for a short while.

Armstrong spreads his wealth

Lance Armstrong's cycling career made him wealthy. But like other Tour de France winners, he doesn't ride thinking about the race prize money. Instead, triumphant cyclists in the Tour greatly benefit financially via increased sponsorship and endorsement deals, not from the money presented by the Tour itself.

Each time he has won the Tour, Armstrong has not accepted the winner's share of the purse. As per tradition, he has taken his winnings and put them back into the total amount of the team's winnings. This total is divided among his teammates and other support staff.

Many mid-stage sprints in Tour de France stages don't offer additional prize money, but do offer bonus points. These intermediate sprints are included in most stages and are designated in the course profile. Riders who cross the line in the top-three positions are respectively rewarded six, four, and two points and are likely interested in the race's best sprinter competition (the green jersey, the second most prestigious competition in the Tour — see Chapter 3). Riders seeking bonus points do so at risk, sometimes in a furious pack-filled sprint at nearly 50 mph (80 kph). Completing each day's stage is hard enough, but sprinting for short bursts at top speeds during a stage quickly zaps a rider's energy.

Selecting a Team — All Shapes, Sizes, and Skills

The nine cyclists selected to compete for each Tour de France team represent only part of each international trade team. Most international pro trade teams have at least 20 riders; some have more than 25 cyclists on their rosters. Riders selected to participate in the Tour are chosen based on their varying skills. Each team's management also chooses riders by considering their personalities and abilities to get along with teammates. The Tour is a team event, and the team's synergy and dynamics must be heavily considered — much like a business. One key to a team's success is cycling's equivalent of business world terminology. In short, are the cyclists *team players?*

The ideal Tour de France team includes a *team leader,* the squad's best overall rider. At his best, the team leader is in contention for the race overall title, called the *General Classification* (or *GC*). Some teams are so strong that they have two members who, depending on how the race develops, are capable to compete for the overall title or a very high finish.

Not every team has a superstar like Lance Armstrong or Germany's Jan Ullrich, who won the race in 1997 and has finished second five other times. Without a cyclist capable of competing for the overall crown, some teams enter the race fielding riders who seek individual stage wins. Other teams hope only for titles in sub competitions, such as the best climber, best sprinter, best young rider, and team competition, within the overall race.

In addition to team leaders and *specialist riders* (those who are capable of winning particular stages, like sprints or climbs), teams have riders who are generalists. They know the event well and are primarily responsible to ride in support of the team leader. Given the chance, these riders could also race to win individual stages. But they're primarily chosen for one overwhelming characteristic — selflessness.

Injuries, illness, fatigue, and elimination via time limits (discussed in Chapter 5) deplete many teams. By the end of the race, in Paris, some squads are grateful just to have their riders complete the final day while still being coherent and upright on their bikes. While Lance Armstrong would be disappointed to just finish the Tour de France, for many cyclists, crossing the final finish line of the sport's most difficult race on the cobblestones of the Champs Élysées is a career highlight.

The team leader

Only a handful of cyclists who enter the Tour de France each year have a legitimate chance to win. Surprises occur, but top contenders are usually well-known riders with vast experience and multiple talents. Cyclists who win the Tour de France are great climbers and have superior abilities in time trials, the races timed individually against the clock.

Team leaders don't have any standard body style or characteristics, other than possessing a low body fat percentage and extreme fitness. Miguel Indurain of Spain won the Tour de France for five consecutive years ending in 1995. During his career, Indurain carried 175 pounds on his 6-foot-2 frame. Armstrong weighs about 160 pounds and is 5-foot-10.

Team leaders advance through cycling ranks just like rookies and younger players in other pro sports. A pending team leader competes for a few years, honing his skills with the hope of advancing into a team leader's role as he matures into his mid to late 20s. Many team leaders endure failure early in their careers, however. Indurain didn't finish the Tour de France in his first two attempts in 1985 and 1986. Armstrong withdrew from the event in his first two attempts in 1993 and 1994 as well as in 1996. He has completed the race seven times in ten appearances; Indurain finished the race ten times in twelve attempts.

Tour de France team leaders improve their chances for success if they have a good relationship with their teammates throughout the rest of the season. Armstrong has won many other races, but the Tour is his top priority. During less prestigious one-day races or shorter stage races leading up to the Tour, Armstrong often rides in a supportive role for his teammates. And when cycling's grand event arrives in July, guess what? Armstrong's teammates don't forget what he's done for them. The Tour is Armstrong's time to reap the benefits. His teammates are doing their jobs only if they ride to support him.

The climbers

Cold and rainy, overcast and snowy, or hot and sun-baked — it doesn't matter. Tour de France fans flock to the mountaintops of the Alps and the Pyrenees for one reason: to witness great climbers and not-so-great climbers.

Unlike in some sports, in which the athletes' bodies and faces are hidden by gear or helmets, the emotions of riders climbing steep grades in the Alps and Pyrenees are in plain view. It's high drama, and for cycling fans it's well worth the wait — rain, snow, or shine.

Great climbers appear as if they're practicing Zen meditation. They're focused, in control of their emotions, and completely in sync with their efficient bodies. Great climbers are often smaller in stature than the rest of the field, but not always. Regardless of size, the best climbers have the ability to produce vast amounts of power for extended lengths of time.

Back-of-the-pack riders, on the other hand, struggle on steep mountain roads. They waver from side to side; their energy is depleted. The biggest time gaps between the front and back of the pack occur in the mountains. More than an hour sometimes separates leading climbers' finishing times from those struggling and hoping only to finish and avoid time elimination (discussed in Chapter 3).

Timing and patience are the integral components of how a climber in the Tour plans his moves. If a race finishes with a long, extended ascent, the riders with the best climbing skills rely on teammates to pace them as far as they can. The best climbers then forge ahead alone to battle both other riders and the rigors of the mountain.

The sprinters

The first week of the Tour de France traditionally includes several consecutive days of flat stages. It's the best time of the race for sprinters, the cyclists who have the uncanny ability to quickly accelerate their bikes to more than 40 mph (65 kph).

Sprinters are the most muscular-looking and often the most opportunistic cyclists in the race. During flat stages, riders compete strategically with the flow of the day, slow if the group is unmotivated, fast if the *peloton* is spirited. Each team's riders attempt to surround their designated sprinter as the race enters the final mile(s).

Mario Cipollini: Best sprinter ever?

Mario Cipollini of Italy is arguably the greatest sprinter in cycling history. Flamboyant, outspoken, and charismatic, Cipollini ruled the sprints in the Tour France and in the Tour of Italy for more than a decade.

Cipollini is a showman, too. With a trademark wide smile and a gregarious personality, he plays to crowds throughout the world. Cipollini won the World Championship road race in 2002, but he has primarily built his persona with furious sprint finishes. As of the writing of this book, Cipollini has won a record 42 stages of the Tour of Italy and 12 stages of the Tour de France.

Cipollini, 37, retired once and has threatened retirement on other occasions. For many years, he's had a tumultuous relationship with Tour de France race director Jean-Marie Leblanc. The reason: Cipollini has participated in the Tour de France eight times, but he never intends to finish the race. Leblanc believes Cipollini's approach is disrespectful.

As the riders, en masse, jockey for position at the front, the premier sprinters do their best to follow just behind. If they've coordinated their efforts correctly, each team positions rider after rider just in front of their sprinter. The support riders each take turns for short, quick bursts of acceleration as the race's waning stretches approach. These bursts are called the *lead-out* and accomplish two things:

- The lead-out discourages riders from breaking out to the front, because it keeps the pace high and consistent.

- The lead-out allows the designated sprinter to *draft* (reduce the wind for) the riders in front until the last possible second, and then sprint on his own for the win.

For sprinters, it's like getting a high-speed police escort by several vehicles. Imagine each officer taking a turn at the front of a single-file caravan, leading you in your vehicle to the local mall or grocery store. One by one, each police vehicle pulls to the side and another vehicle goes to the front. Within seconds of your designation, all the police cars are gone and you get to go as fast as you can — legally — to your arrival point. Sprinters' final furious assaults occur within the final few hundred meters of a stage. With their escorts gone, sprinters spread across the road in a blurry combination of bodies and bikes.

Winners of sprint finishes are often victorious by a margin of inches. Spectators may not know who has won, but the riders are so experienced, they know who's victorious — at least most of the time. The winner dramatically thrusts one or both of his hands into the air just as he crosses the line. Sometimes, though, only photographs taken as the racers cross the finish line can determine the winner of a sprint finish. And on more than one occasion, a rider has made a victory gesture while crossing the finish line, only to find out he didn't win.

A common term in sprinting is called the *throw,* which means lunging at the finish like a runner but on a bike. A bike throw can give a sprinter a few extra inches at the finish line. And if it's done correctly, a sprinter who looks as though he is beaten can win with a throw.

The rouleurs

Unheralded and largely out of the limelight, most of the Tour race field is comprised of cyclists called *rouleurs.* They're the riders who can "roll" for hours at a steady, strong pace. On windy days, rainy days, and any other kind of day, during flat or rolling stages, *rouleurs* have the most thankless jobs in the *peloton.*

Rouleurs are often each team's biggest riders. They go to the front of the race and act as windbreaks. As the cyclists in control of the *peloton, rouleurs* are invaluable, yet their individual time for glory is rare, if ever. *Rouleurs* use more energy than other cyclists in the field because they don't get the benefits of drafting; they provide the draft for the riders on their teams who have a greater shot at winning.

Frankie Andreu: Consummate *rouleur*

Frankie Andreu of Dearborn, Michigan, completed the Tour de France nine times, the current American record for finishes. He retired after the 2000 season following 12 professional years packed with hard work, little notoriety, and few victories. He now works as a cycling television analyst for the Outdoor Life Network and writes columns for cycling Web sites.

A two-time U.S. Olympian, Andreu was captain of the U.S. Postal Service team (now called the Discovery Channel Pro Cycling Team) that propelled Lance Armstrong to the first two of his Tour de France titles. Andreu had one second-place Tour de France stage finish; he placed eighth in the 1988 Olympic road race in Seoul, South Korea; and he was fourth in the Olympic road race in Atlanta, Georgia, in 1996.

But Andreu primarily spent his long career as a team rider and well-respected *rouleur.* Day after day, year after year, he raced at the front of the *peloton* on beautiful days and in inclement weather. He spent a good portion of his career helping control the pace of the Tour de France, always with his team leaders in mind.

Every team has several *rouleurs*. When they're not counted on to pedal like human battering rams, *rouleurs* work as *domestiques* or consummate team players, sometimes going back through the pack to the team car for bottles, food, clothing, and so on. *Rouleurs* often exert so much energy during a stage that they finish low in the stage standings. But standings don't tell the race story. It's *rouleurs* who have likely gotten the top finishers into a position where they can vie for the day's honors. *Rouleurs* don't get glory, but they get a lot of respect.

The time trial specialists

Individual time trials have the most direct and appropriate name of the Tour de France: They're called the *Race of Truth,* because riders advance via their own skills and without the benefit of drafting. Time trials range from short Prologue distances of 8 kilometers (5 miles) to more than 50 kilometers (31.2 miles).

In individual time trials, the field competes rider by rider, with the cyclists usually starting two minutes apart. The last rider in the standings starts first, and the cyclist wearing the yellow jersey begins last. Riders begin time trials with a hand countdown, signaled by a referee standing next to each cyclist on a starting ramp.

The best time trialists master the ability to pedal at a sustained high rate of speed without exceeding their cardiovascular limits. This is why time trial specialists, and the bikes they ride, are the epitome of cycling efficiency. Time trials require state-of-the-art equipment. Everything from the helmet to the shoes needs to be aerodynamic, so teams spend countless hours and money developing and refining their equipment. Cyclists ride time trial bicycles (these ultraquick bikes are illegal to use in road stages) that have different wheels and handlebar configurations more aerodynamically aligned than their road bikes. Depending upon individual preference, a time trialist may use solid wheels, called *discs,* that don't have spokes. Time trial cyclists also wear tight booties over their cycling shoes as another way to cut wind resistance and prompt faster times. They also wear skintight suits, called *skinsuits,* that are a one-piece, body-clinging suit with no pockets and made with Lycra/Spandex.

Time trialists also wear elongated helmets as a mandatory safety measure. The rear of the helmet extends farther down a rider's neck and back, form-fitting the contour of his upper back. This is commonly referred to as *tear-drop.* The design of the futuristic helmet helps reduce wind resistance. Time trial specialists are often contenders for the overall race title, and their skills are overtly apparent. Even though cyclists begin two minutes apart, the best time trialists overtake slower riders, and they can average more than 30 mph (48 kph) during the stage. In Figure 4-1, Lance Armstrong warms up before a time trial at Stage 19 of a Tour.

Figure 4-1: Lance Armstrong warming up for a time trial.

LeMond's great time trial win

Greg LeMond became the first American to win the Tour de France in 1986. He returned to the race in 1989 after a two-year recovery from a hunting accident that nearly took his life.

The second year he won, LeMond trailed Frenchman Laurent Fignon by 50 seconds at the start of the final stage, a 24.5-kilometer (15¹⁄₁₀-mile) individual time trial stage that ended on the cobblestone streets of the Champs Élysées in Paris. LeMond used two novel approaches en route to the closest overall finish in Tour history.

In modern-day time trials, riders are given their elapsed times (called *splits*) at designated places on the course. But LeMond told his team director he didn't want the distraction of knowing his time on the final day of the 1989 race. He preferred to ride by "feel." He went all-out from the start on a make-or-break mission.

LeMond also used now-common triathlete handlebars in the final stage, a first in the Tour de France. The new handlebars allowed LeMond to ride in an aerodynamic tuck, like an alpine ski racer. As the second-to-last rider on the course, LeMond quickly narrowed his time deficiency. LeMond crossed the line in 26 minutes and 57 seconds. Fignon, the last rider on the course, finished 58 seconds later and collapsed as he crossed the finish line. LeMond won the Tour de France by eight seconds, and his average speed for the day was a record 54.5 kph (33.8 mph).

Recognizing the Team Behind the Team

Cyclists in the Tour de France don't need help pedaling, but they do need assistance before, during, and after each day's racing to allow them to showcase their talents.

For every team's nine riders, there are seemingly an equal number of team support personnel. Team owners, team directors, physicians, chiropractors, massage therapists, trainers, cooks, mechanics, media relations and sponsor representatives, and team car drivers. They all travel with their respective teams throughout the Tour. With the riders, the contingent comprises each squad's substantial entourage.

While cyclists ride, teams' complementary staffs advance throughout the race in team cars identified with sponsors' logos. Some team support staff members progress through the course in the caravan of race vehicles that follow cyclists during the entire route. Other team personnel, media, and sponsor representatives travel ahead of the race and prepare for the cyclists' arrival in the finishing city.

The directeur sportif (team manager)

How teams prepare and execute daily strategy during the Tour is the responsibility of the *directeur sportif,* or team manager. With some exceptions, team managers are former Tour cyclists who've remained in the sport following their retirement. After years in the *peloton* and with intimate knowledge of cycling nuance, team managers are hired by team owners to hire the riders. Team managers run the day-to-day operations of the team — from preseason training camps to races throughout the season.

During the Tour, every team has a *directeur sportif,* and many teams have an assistant, too. Both managers have varied responsibilities, from race strategy to cheerleader and from disciplinarian to lobbyist, while negotiating with Tour de France management. Team managers meet with their riders daily, stay in the same hotels, and eat the same meals. Teams usually meet at breakfast prior to the stage and following the day's race at dinner.

Many *directeurs sportif* have close relationships with their team leaders. The duo collaborates on selecting key riders for races throughout the season, including the riders from the Tour de France.

Team directors are positioned in their respective team cars at the start of each stage, according to a specific starting order distributed by the race organization. As the stages progress, team cars follow the riders with the *directeur sportif* communicating with his riders via two-way radios. (Note that before two-way radios, a rider would fade back through the *peloton* to ride alongside the team car to give or collect information to relay back to his teammates in the *peloton*.) *Directeurs sportif* have varying styles, but they all share one common trait: They're not shy giving directives to their teams during a race.

Team directors maneuver through the *peloton* to assist team members and further discuss strategy. Because so many vehicles follow the riders on sometimes less-than-ideal roads, team vehicles must advance along course routes via protocol. In addition to communicating with their riders, *directeurs sportif* communicate with the race director and his colleagues, who ride in vehicles at the front of the race.

Directeurs sportif are also diplomats and opportunists. They constantly look for advantages to help their teams, sometimes by stretching the rules of race protocol. It's common, for example, for a rider to illegally hang on to a team vehicle while discussing race strategy with his director. It's also common for a rider to hang on too long while receiving a new water bottle from a team car. Team directors and riders try to take these little advantages when they think race organizers aren't looking. But after many stages, *directeurs sportif* and riders are either warned or fined nominal amounts for various course protocol infractions.

A list of the day's infractions and the penalties levied are identified and distributed with daily results to teams, race management, and the media reporting on the race shortly after each stage. Race infractions and other nonresult information are written on notices called *communiqués*. These infractions range from fines to time penalties, which are worse than fines because they affect the standings of the riders and teams.

The team mechanics (a.k.a. wrenches)

A loose spoke or a frayed cable — that's all it takes for a mechanical problem to abruptly end a cyclist's Tour participation. It's also why mechanics are so important to teams' successes. Every Tour team has several mechanics who work on riders' bikes with the precision of Swiss watchmakers.

Before each stage, mechanics fine-tune riders' racing bikes and spare bikes, too. Operating out of trucks stocked with tools of the trade, mechanics seemingly never stop working. This is one of the more rigorous jobs in the Tour, offering little sleep to those who do it. Once a stage begins, mechanics may get to rest for a while or may immediately be called to the job if there's an early race flat tire, a malfunctioning gear, or a mangled bike that needs repair or replacement.

Mechanics are on the move in every stage. When a rider has a mechanical problem, he raises his hand to notify the team. The mechanics quickly find their way to the scene and replace, for example, a flat tire and wheel in a few seconds, similar to mechanics in the pit crews at the Indianapolis 500.

Tour mechanics also make repairs at high speeds. When a cyclist needs a repair, but it's not a good time to stop, a team car approaches the rider and a mechanic leans through a window, tools in hand. He does his best to make repairs while his vehicle and the cyclist travel at speeds that can exceed 40 mph (65 kph).

Cyclists' jobs are done for the day when a stage is finished. Mechanics' responsibilities continue for hours after racing is done. Tour bikes get cleaned, repaired, and tuned up after every stage, so that they're ready for the riders again early the next day.

The soigneurs (all-around assistants)

Imagine having a valet or butler at your job. Every Tour de France team has one; they're called *soigneurs* (pronounced swan-yers). The exact job description of a *soigneur* is hard to define because it varies from team to team. But one thing is certain: *Soigneurs* can be called on anytime to do almost anything for a cyclist or his team.

From massage therapists to social workers, errand clerks to cooks, maids to confidants, *soigneurs* work as hard as anyone at the Tour de France, and they sleep as little as anyone at the race.

Throughout the Tour's three weeks, *soigneurs* buy food, deliver riders' mail, organize their team's suitcases, and negotiate for special needs with hotel owners. If a rider needs a special favor, he asks his team's *soigneur*.

Good *soigneurs* have temperaments of saints. They listen to riders' complaints. They hear all the private details of each day's events, and they're counted on to keep private team matters private. Good teams also reward good *soigneurs* with a percentage of the riders' pooled prize money.

The masseurs

Daily massages during the Tour help cyclists revitalize their muscles. Every team employs a masseur who helps in the recovery of riders' muscles. Massages are usually done in riders' hotel rooms, a few hours after every stage. Some of the best pro cyclists, including Lance Armstrong, have personal masseurs.

The drivers: Skills, stamina, and street smarts

In addition to team cars, ever Tour team has a bus. Cyclists arrive at the race each day in the team bus (see Figure 4-2), and every starting city has a special parking area for it.

Figure 4-2: The team cars and team buses arrive before the start of Stage 6 of the 2004 Tour de France.

The race also has a huge caravan of equipment trucks that, just like the team bus, advance city to city. Riders get the most attention, of course, but the caravan of buses and equipment trucks have a parade-like following. After stages begin, the team buses leave each city to crowd applause. The French public also acknowl-edges the vehicles along the route, particularly in small country villages, where the caravan has to negotiate narrow roads.

Several hours after stages, race barriers, banners, and barricades are disassembled and loaded onto equipment trucks by fast-working crews. The *equipment caravan* leaves en masse to travel overnight to the next starting city. There are no cyclists, no team directors, no music, and no race announcers. But the truck drivers toot their horns as they're leaving town, and the scene often attracts curious, festive crowds.

Chapter 5

More Tour Rules Than You Ever Want to Know

. . . .

In This Chapter

▶ Knowing Tour rules

▶ Eating, drinking, and keeping time

▶ Communicating in the *peloton*

▶ Doping tests and race fines

. . . .

A large group of cyclists, pedaling along country roads and flanked by sunflowers and vineyards, may appear tranquil. But each day, Tour de France cyclists follow a vast set of strict rules. Signing in at the beginning of every stage, taking mandatory drug tests, wearing proper attire, and ensuring the proper weight of their bikes are among the Tour's long and varied regulations for riders and their support staff.

Tour rules aren't only for riders. Team personnel, race vehicle drivers, and media also adhere to specific race rules, all compiled by Tour organizers in conjunction with French law and the International Cycling Union or *Union Cycliste Internationale (UCI)*, the sport's governing body. Rules of the race and rules of the road are listed in the official *Technical Guide* or, as it's often called, *The Race Bible*. This chapter details all those Tour rules and day-to-day operations.

Knowing Some Important Tour de France Regulations

Tour rules and regulations are detailed in race *Articles*. Listed in the Technical Guide, they range from participation to disqualification, medical care to prize money. Rules are written and detailed in French and English. Because French is the universal language in cycling (Lance Armstrong, for example, is fluent), French interpretation of rules prevails in instances in which a language barrier may cloud a definition.

Helmets: Mandatory, dude!

To reduce or eliminate deaths from crashes, every rider in the Tour must now wear a helmet during every stage of the race, including time trials (see Figure 5-1). At their own risk, cyclists may remove their helmets during the final climb to the summit if the climb is at least 5 kilometers (3.1 miles) long. A Tour course marker designates the point on the course where cyclists can remove their helmets. Removal of helmets on mountain stages is never allowed before the start of a climb.

Figure 5-1: The Giro Time Trial helmet used by the U. S. Postal Service Professional Cycling Team in the 2004 Tour de France.

Oh, no, we're wearing the same outfit

Every rider must wear his team's official outfit — shorts, jersey, socks and shoes, gloves, and helmet. Unless a rider withdraws prior to the event, each of the 21 participating teams has nine riders, attired identically, at the start of the race.

Several exceptions exist, however. Leaders in overall standings and best climber (polka dot), sprinter (green), and young rider (white) competitions wear their respective colored jersey. Each of the sub-competition jerseys includes the appropriate team advertising banners. In individual time trials, competition leaders are provided with appropriately colored skinsuits instead of jerseys and shorts.

If a rider leads more than one race competition, he wears the jersey in accordance to priority of importance: yellow jersey, green jersey, polka-dot jersey, and white jersey. The runners-up or next highest-place riders in the competitions wear leaders' jerseys in the remaining categories.

The reigning world road race titlist wears a white jersey with horizontal adjoining blue, red, black, yellow, and green bands during the Tour. The rainbow jersey also includes the rider's team sponsors' logos. Reigning national road titlists also wear their national champion jerseys with the same allowance for team names and advertising banners.

Riders can wear additional clothes over or under their jerseys, including rain gear, tights or leg warmers, or other overgarments. And they can wear additional clothing at the start or during a stage. A rider seeking additional attire during a stage drops back to receive items from a team vehicle or from motorcycle drivers designated by race organizers.

Riding by numbers

Tour riders are identified by race numbers. The defending race champion wears No. 1, and his teammates follow in order through No. 9. Every rider considered as his team's overall title contender wears the lowest number on his team. He's listed first on all official rider lists; from there, there's an alphabetical order to the numbers.

Every rider must have an official double-sided number plate on each side of his bike frame and in a designated position. Riders must also wear two numbers, one over each hip. During individual time trial stages, cyclists' two small hip numbers are replaced by a larger single number affixed on their lower back. Race organizers provide number plates and race numbers, and they must be worn without alterations.

Sign on the line, or you don't pass start

Prior to every Tour stage, riders must sign in on a pre-race staging area. The procedure is required in part as tradition, in part to appease spectators gathered near the starting line, awaiting the arrival of their favorite riders minutes before a stage start.

During road stages, riders and team managers must arrive at the *signature registration area* at least ten minutes prior to a start. Riders who don't sign in are fined 100 Swiss Francs, or about $85. If a rider is prevented from signing in because of traffic congestion or another unavoidable circumstance, a fine is not levied.

After the entire field registers, the race manager begins a stage in one of three ways;

- ✓ A *standing start* begins at the riders' sign-in or signature area.

- ✓ A *deferred standing start* occurs if a stage begins some distance from the sign-in area because of area restrictions.

- ✓ A *rolling start* or *flying start* occurs when a stage begins when the cyclists casually pedal from the sign-in area, and then begin at the stage where the course is designated as Kilometer 0 (Mile 0).

Feed zone and feeding rules

During the Tour, riders must continuously replenish foods and liquids. Before, during, and after stages, cyclists' eating and drinking habits are reminiscent of scenes of stokers shoveling coal into steam engines — they eat and drink that much.

Riders' nutritional needs are the responsibility of individual teams, with some exception. During every Tour road stage, there's a designated area on the course called the *feed zone* or *feeding station*. Team representatives carrying *musettes,* or feeding bags with sandwiches, fruit, and energy bars. They hand off supplies to riders as they advance through the feed zone. It's cycling's version of take-out food. New water bottles are also distributed to riders in the feed zone, but *musettes* and water bottles must be those supplied by Tour sponsors or otherwise Tour approved.

Outside the feed zone, riders in a breakaway can also receive supplies from their team managers' vehicles or a Tour-supplied motorcycle. *Musettes* and water bottles can be used in these feeding options, but these resupply situations and the designated feed zone must follow Tour-established regulations. Consider:

- ✔ To receive replenishment from a team car, a rider must drop back to the vehicle, and that vehicle must be situated behind race organizers' vehicles.

- ✔ Feeding is permitted at the back of a group of breakaways as long as at least 15 riders are represented in a group and as long as it has established a sustained break from the *peloton*.

- ✔ Feeding is permitted during a road stage any time after the 50-kilometer (31¼-mile) mark to a marker on the course designating the end of the feed zone at 20 kilometers (12.4 miles) from the stage finish.

- ✔ Radio communication from teams on the official Tour radio frequency is not allowed in the 12 kilometers (7.4 miles) before or in the 10 kilometers (6.2 miles) after the feed zone.

- ✔ Spraying anything from team vehicles is prohibited.

- ✔ Glass containers may not be carried or used by riders.

- ✔ Riders accepting food or beverages from spectators do so at their own risk, which includes potential prosecution.

- ✔ Riders must throw away food, feeding bags, bottles, or any other accessories with caution and must dispose of items on the roadside, not on the road below. Items discarded into the path of another cyclist can cause bodily harm or prompt a crash.

- ✔ Race organizers can alter feeding rules for inclement weather conditions or under other exceptional circumstances.

Team cars: Position and passing

The group of vehicles that travels with the riders in every Tour stage is known as the *caravan*. Television, radio, and newspaper journalists; race officials; police escorts; and publicity vehicles all follow Tour regulations. Caravan vehicles are identified with various colored stickers placed across front windshields. Priority is given to vehicles based on race responsibility, number of occupants in the vehicle, and how the vehicle is equipped.

The same rules apply for team vehicles, but team cars also have a complicated and vast additional list of rules. Each team is assigned a starting position as designated in the results packet from the previous day's stage; teams are positioned in the caravan in the overall standings order of each team's leading rider. Every team can have two team vehicles following the race, and each vehicle can have a maximum of four passengers. Passengers who have been accredited by race organizers can join the team's *directeur sportif* and his assistants in team vehicles. Non-team passengers riding in team vehicles must remain in their car during stages, and they're not permitted to aid riders or hold team equipment.

Team cars carry riders' spare bikes, wheels, water, food, and medical supplies. During the race, the primary team vehicle must be driven by the *directeur sportif* on the right-hand side of the road and in the order designated at the stage start. Each teams' additional team car is positioned in a second group of vehicles. Teams' second vehicles are positioned identically as the first group, but the second group of team vehicles must be separated from the first group by at least 200 meters (⅛ mile).

Every team vehicle must be equipped with a radio tuned to the Tour's frequency. Every team's place in the caravan is confirmed prior to every stage, and every team's radio must broadcast Tour radio throughout stages. Team vehicles must ask permission or must receive a request from race officials to overtake a race management vehicle.

Teams must attend to their riders under Tour and *Union Cycliste Internationale* rules. Fines are levied for infractions according to the sanctions list in race regulations. In addition to race penalties, vehicle infractions are subject to French legal action.

Staying within the time limit

Tour organizers have a pretty good idea how long every stage will take. They've toured the routes numerous times while planning the route during the preceding year. And after more than 90 race editions, race organizers know within a certain time frame how long individual mountain ascents and descents, long and flat sections, and wind-swept open roads will likely take. Most stages are geared toward finishing during the nationally televised broadcast in France, between 5 and 6 p.m.

Every route of every stage is detailed in a course itinerary distributed to every team and to every race vehicle — from equipment trucks to publicity cars, service technicians, and the media.

Every city of every stage is designated on the itinerary according to its kilometer distance into the stage. Stage starting times are listed, as well as the time the *peloton* is expected to arrive. National and regional French newspapers print the itinerary, so that cities' spectators know when the Tour is likely to come to their town.

Tour organizers, anticipating varying weather, list expected arrival times in each city via three average speeds. Average estimated speeds vary depending on a stage's terrain, motivation of riders, and weather conditions. But one common trio of predicted finish times is 44, 42, and 40 kilometers per hour (27.3, 26.1, and 24.8 mph).

Tour stage time estimates are surprisingly accurate, but exceptions occur. On some occasions, riders race particularly fast and arrive in cities and finish sooner than expected. Stage finish times can be underestimated by a few minutes or by more than a half-hour for several reasons — a severe crash, extreme weather, or particularly unmotivated riders.

Beyond city-by-city estimated arrival times, each stage itinerary includes a topographic stage profile. It details all categorized climbs (length and gradient), stage sprints, and feed zones. An alternative course route from the stage start to finish of every stage is also provided.

Race organizers diligently estimate stage times, but circumstances can force cancellation of a stage or stages. In special circumstances, including an accident or natural disaster, race officials may:

- ✔ Change a course route

- ✔ Temporarily halt a stage

- ✔ Consider that the stage has not been held and cancel the results

- ✔ Cancel part of the stage, nullify intermediate stage results, and restart a stage where an incident occurred

- ✔ Restart a stage but keep time gaps recorded to the point where the stage was stopped

Drug testing at every stage

Every rider in the Tour is tested for banned substances prior to the race. Various cyclists are tested after every stage, according to a selection process determined before the race. Under current rules, at least 180 urine drug tests are given, including daily drug tests for the race leader and stage winner and six to eight cyclists selected at random throughout the field.

Prohibited substances

Riders participating in the Tour compete under the anti-doping drug rules established by *Union Cycliste Internationale.* In addition, the World Anti-Doping Association (WADA) does random drug-testing all year long. The list of banned substances categorizes substances and other restrictions into two categories: prohibited substances and methods.

✔ Banned substances are divided into nine categories: anabolic steroids, hormones, beta-2 agonists, agents with oestrogenic activity, diuretics and other masking agents, stimulants, narcotics, cannabinoids, and glucocorticosteroids. Okay, most of these words won't mean much to you, so suffice it to say that these are bad for the body.

✔ Banned methods of use categories include: enhancement of oxygen transfer, chemical and physical manipulation, and gene doping. Again, the kind of Frankenstein technology that serious athletes want to stay away from.

Individually banned drugs, testing regulations, athletes' failure to cooperate, penalties, and other anti-doping stipulations and rules are available on the *Union Cycliste Internationale* Web site at www.uci.ch.

Tour drug tests are administered in accordance with the rules of the *Union Cycliste Internationale* and the French Federation of Cycling or *Federation Françoise de Cyclisme.* The Tour conducts banned substance testing under secure and strictly monitored conditions. A specially equipped caravan is established near the finish line of every stage to transport drug samples to a private location following the race. Drug test samples are then transported by private plane for analysis, and results are quickly reported to Tour officials.

Who's Keeping Score and Why?

Throughout each road race, you can often see a motorcycle with two passengers zipping through the *peloton.* The driver positions himself in various breaks in the race and reports time gaps between two or more riders or groups of riders.

The passenger on the back of the motorcycle gets time gaps via his radio earplug from race officials, and he notes those time gaps on a chalkboard or time board. Gaps likely include the time between the race leader, a chasing rider or group of riders, and a secondary chasing group or individual rider. If time gaps between riders are smaller, the time gaps aren't as difficult to estimate without radio report and chalkboard postings. But particularly on mountain climbs, it's often difficult for riders and the public to know time gaps between riders that can be strung out across a mountain range.

Cheating and other dastardly deeds

Since the early years of the Tour, cheating has been an unfortunate part of the race. Just like the infamous incident in the 1980 Boston Marathon when apparent winner Rosie Ruiz was accused of taking the subway for part of the route, Tour cyclists have been accused of various indiscretions. Ruiz was stripped of her title, and Tour de France riders have likewise been expelled.

The first documented case of Tour cheating occurred in 1904, the race's second year. Ferdinand Ryan, who placed 12th in the inaugural race, repeatedly was caught drafting behind cars and was disqualified. Three other riders, according to Tour historians, were also disqualified for similar offenses.

Through the years, Tour cheating has been progressively creative. In 1911, rider Paul Duboc suffered miserably and collapsed about 60 miles into a stage that included the famous climb to the Tourmalet. It's never been proven, but Duboc's problem has always been linked to poisoning via another competitor.

Riders taking their own drugs have been the race's biggest problem. During the 1955 race, seven riders suspected of taking amphetamines collapsed. One of the race's darkest days occurred in 1967. British rider Tom Simpson collapsed while climbing and struggling up the barren ascent of Mont Ventoux. Simpson was flown by helicopter off the mountain, but died late in the afternoon of the stage. Amphetamines were discovered in the pocket of Simpson's jersey, and his autopsy revealed alcohol was present in his bloodstream.

In 1978, Belgian rider Michael Pollentier was caught with a contraption and tubes under his uniform that allowed him to produce fake, clean urine for drug tests following his apparent win in the stage to L'Alpe d'Huez. Pollentier, who had assumed the race leader with his stage win, was striped of the yellow jersey and his earnings, and he was disqualified from the race.

The Tour's most infamous cheating case occurred in 1998. Willy Voet, the team *soigneur* for the Festina team, was arrested three days prior to the race at the French border crossing for smuggling drugs. As the race began, the aftermath of Voet's arrest hung over the event. Festina team officials were eventually questioned, and the Festina team was expelled from the race. When police began to search other teams' hotel rooms, riders vocally protested, and then took more drastic action. With nine stages left, the *peloton* staged a two-hour, mid-race protest by stopping and sitting down on the course. Riders protested again several days later, too. Numerous teams left the race in disgust and disgrace, and when the *peloton* arrived in Paris on the final day only 96 of 189 starters finished the race.

Photo finishes and split seconds

Every rider in the same *peloton* receives the same finishing time, recorded by the race's timekeeper. A separate group of riders or an individual rider is given a new time as he crosses the line. Riders who finish outside the permitted time limits are also timed, and the timekeeper continues his daily task for the finish line until the broom wagon, the final official race vehicle, arrives.

Times recorded in Tour road stages are rounded down to the nearest second and used in overall standings. In time trials, stages in which several riders can finish within the same second, times are recorded to the hundredths of a second.

A photo is taken as the lead rider or riders cross the finish line. The image is required to identify stage winners in many sprint finish stages. Particularly in flat stages, when a large group of riders furiously sprints toward the finish, only a split-second image can determine the winner, who may be victorious by the width of a spoke.

During some photo-finish stages, a winner is easily determined. But it's not uncommon for Tour officials to consider a photo finish for several minutes before announcing some stage winners (see Figure 5-2 for an example). Sprinting specialists have an uncanny knack for knowing if they've won, even if the finish appears extremely close. But cyclists aren't always right. On more than one occasion, a sprinter in a group finish has, at the last split nano-second, thrust his hand into the air to acknowledge a win, only to discover, a few minutes later, that he hasn't won.

Staying in the know

Riders in the Tour wearing earpieces communicate with their team directors via two-way radios. Team directors tell riders what's happening in the *peloton* or give instructions to a team leader, another individual rider, or the team at large.

Radio communication between riders and their teams doesn't always work in mountains, and in some instances, riders don't listen or feign as if they can't hear a race director's instructions.

Starting orders and paying fines

No rider likes to be fined, but after every stage, the amounts of fines (in Swiss Francs) for individuals and teams are listed in the official results booklet. Riders' fines are levied for a multitude of infractions, from holding on to a team car too long to indiscreet bathroom breaks. Teams are also fined for improper passing in the race caravan and a host of other infractions with similar penalties. Fines range from 30 Swiss Francs ($25) to several thousand Swiss Francs and time penalties.

Figure 5-2: A photo finish from the 1998 Tour de France.

A lot of fines are levied because of marketing stunts. Mario Cipollini was famous for this and had it written into his contract that his sponsors pay for all his fines. One time, he showed up to the Prologue wearing a full body suit printed like a human muscular skeleton. Needless to say, this was not his team uniform, but he got a lot of publicity (and so did his sponsors!).

Chapter 6

Understanding Race Strategies

. . . .

In This Chapter

▶ Understanding that planning is paramount for success

▶ Doing the right thing — protecting the race leader

▶ Moving the riders en masse

▶ Watering sunflowers along the route

. . . .

*U*nlike some sports, when the strongest athlete goes to the front of the race and tries to stay there, the Tour de France is three weeks of strategy and nuance. Riders use and conserve their energies for appropriate moments — like when the hills are steep and their muscles quickly begin to burn. In that respect, cycling is ahead on the brains-o-meter when compared to some other sports. This is where cycling's team strategy comes in.

This chapter explains what's really happening when you see a rider take off alone, and then everyone calmly follows in a huge pack, or when a rider drops way behind. You will know exactly why and what they're thinking and doing. We also tell you the answer to the universal question, "What happens when they gotta go to the bathroom?"

Here's the Plan, Man!

One of the most often asked questions in the Tour de France is, "If Lance Armstrong is the best rider in the Tour de France, why doesn't he just win every day?" The answer is simple. If Armstrong or any other Tour de France champion tried to win every day, he would fail. In this way, team strategy is more important than individual race strategy. Although Tour de France strategy may seem odd, that's just the way the race works. The overall champion wins because he uses his strength and his teammates' strengths wisely. As such, the Tour de France is unlike any other sport.

Winning is still a good thing in cycling, but the simple equation of winning at all costs doesn't fit for a cyclist trying to win the overall title.

The Tour de France is like a chess game — that is, if the pawns, rooks, knights, bishops, and the king all had wheels, shaved legs, and wore Lycra/Spandex shorts. The riders, like chess pieces, all have places and responsibilities as they roam around a game board called France. And like chess, if they make a wrong move, the game can quickly end.

Michael Jordan is often considered the finest player in basketball history. But if he had no one around him to set screens, pass him the ball, or help him defend the other team's players, he would have accumulated exactly zero NBA championships. The Tour works the same way. Just as the Chicago Bulls had team plans during Jordan's six NBA titles, so, too, did Lance Armstrong's teams have race plans during his six Tour de France victories (at least it was six when this book went to print).

Peloton is a French word that means group, and in Spanish it means squad. The *peloton* is the entire group, or pack of racers (see Figure 6-1), usually numbering around 200 cyclists (sometimes a little more; sometimes less) each year in the Tour de France. Teams don't necessarily ride all together in the *peloton,* so you see a kaleidoscope of different colored jerseys charging down the race route. However, notice that the contender for the overall title usually has at least two, and maybe more, of his teammates riding protectively near him. The teammates' job is to protect the contender from crashes and from the wind and to lend a wheel or his own bike if the contender has a mechanical problem.

Each rider in the *peloton* starts out with a specific job to fulfill that has been assigned by the *directeur sportif,* also called just the *director,* who is the team manager (see Chapter 4). Each job description may also change as events or situations evolve throughout the race.

The *peloton* splinters into different groups during the stage; you hear them called a *chase group* or *pack.* On French National Television or on the Outdoor Life Network (OLN), you see icons for Chase Group 1 and Chase Group 2, and also see the time differentials shown between the groups and the leaders. During the difficult mountain stages, the *peloton* may be strung out, with groups of stragglers as much as 45 minutes or more behind. The stragglers, called the *gruppetto* by the Italians and the *autobus* by the French, risk being removed from the race under the official time-limit rules (see Chapter 5). Sometimes, if an important contender has a mechanical problem or if he crashes, teammates drop back to help bring him quickly back to the *peloton.*

Figure 6-1: The *peloton* charges down the *Champs Élysées* during the 2004 Tour de France, led by the U.S. Postal Service Professional Cycling Team.

As you're watching the Tour, you may hear the announcers refer to the *peloton* as if it has a mind and life of its own. They may say that the *peloton* doesn't seem to be interested, or that the *peloton* has finally decided to give chase. The *peloton* has certain acknowledged leaders who command respect and cooperation from all the riders. The strongest and most respected leader may be called *The Patron,* which is French for owner or boss. This leader may have a strong influence on where and when the *peloton* takes an action, or if it does not respond. The *peloton* is an awesome and goose-bump-inspiring sight to see 200 riders come thundering by you, at high speeds, with mere inches between each other's wheels.

Protecting the race leader

Drafting, which is illegal in some sports, is an integral part of cycling strategy — and it doesn't require pencils or paper. Cyclists use drafting the same way a defensive driver stays behind an 18-wheel truck in a rainstorm, or to put it into racing terms, the way NASCAR drivers draft off each other. By *drafting* (riding behind or close to one or more teammates), the team leader remains protected — and saves up to 30 percent of his energy — until it's time for him to strut his stuff en route toward his goal of winning the Tour de France.

Nowhere in recent years has the power of drafting been more apparent than with the U.S. Postal Service Cycling Team (now the Discovery Channel Pro Cycling Team). George Hincapie is the only rider who has been a teammate of Lance Armstrong's in all his Tour de France titles. More times than not, during stages (see Chapter 2), Hincapie has finished just ahead of Armstrong or just behind him. In many instances, much of Hincapie's job for a day was to escort Armstrong through the flats and over rolling hills and to provide a buffer for the champion when danger lurked. This approach is the same with other teams. When working for a team leader or in a group of riders from several teams, riders draft off other riders to help them fight against the wind.

Chasing down the competition

Each team must determine how best to protect its leader. Likewise, each squad and its team director also make an equally important decision almost every day: If another team's rider decides to pedal for the glory on a particular day, the other teams have to decide whether to let the rider pedal miles ahead of the field or respond furiously and make a concerted effort to track him down.

Each team's director monitors the race from a team car. If he makes a decision to tell the team to ride after the leader of the day's race, the move can occur swiftly. The riders' quick moves (see more in the "Attacking and breakaways" section later in this chapter) occur when a cyclist leading the day's race has such a big margin that he's threatening to take over the race lead or has already done so.

The race leader's teammates try valiantly, regardless of the situation, to keep him in the overall race lead. In doing so, each team has to decide which of its riders on any given day (or every day) sacrifice their individual performances, and use the synergy of strength in numbers to quickly narrow a stage leader's margin. (See Chapter 3 for more information on stage leaders.)

Pulling and sacrificing

When a rider *pulls*, he takes the front spot of the group and sets the pace. This move may actually increase the speed or provide only a *false speed* for a short period. *Taking a wheel* means tucking right behind another rider to gain the optimum draft, otherwise known as *sitting on*.

Pulling is used most effectively in the mountain stages. *Domestiques,* or helpers, are assigned to lead their top contender up the climb, setting a fast pace to make it difficult for the other teams to follow. These special *domestiques* are top-notch climbers themselves. They allow the team leader to conserve his energy by following closely on their wheel, drafting behind while they pull him along with their combined energy. (And no, they aren't allowed to physically push or pull him in any way.)

No team ever wants to see its leader completely alone near the top of a grueling climb, trying to fend off attacks and having no one to protect him or pull him along. A distinct psychological advantage occurs when the other riders in the *peloton* can see a team leader flying up the mountain, being pulled along by two or three strong climbers on his team. So, *domestiques* ride for their team leader until they have no leg strength and no energy left: They completely sacrifice themselves. Then another *domestique* takes over, or the leader has to continue climbing solo. The sacrificial *domestique*, completely spent, drifts to the back of the *peloton* and becomes part of the *gruppetto*, trying to make the time cut.

Sacrificing for the leader

Several riders may be directed to go full speed in a stage to pull and sacrifice for their leader. A good example in the 2004 Tour happened during Stage 13, from Lannemezan to Plateau de Beille. Johan Bruyneel, the *directeur sportif* for the U.S. Postal Service Cycling Team (now called the Discovery Channel Pro Cycling Team), sent his entire team out in front right from the start. The U.S. Postal team set a tempo that overwhelmed most other riders and they sacrificed themselves along the way, and then dropped to the rear of the *peloton* with the *gruppetto*.

The stage was 217 kilometers (135 miles) long, finishing atop the daunting 18.5-kilometer ascent to Plateau de Beille. This climb has a gradient of 6.4 percent. The stage included five other climbs, making for a grueling day. The Col des Ares was just a warm-up at 797 meters (about ½ mile) with a 3.4 percent gradient. Then, in succession, came the 1,069-meter (about ¾-mile) Col du Portet d'Aspet, with a 10-kilometer ascent and a 5.4 percent gradient, and then the 1,395-meter (nearly 1 mile) Col de la Core, with a 14.5-kilometer climb at a 5.8 percent gradient. The Col de Latrape was at the 139-kilometer (86-mile) mark in the race, presenting a long, grinding 18-kilometer (11-mile) ascent with a 3.3 percent gradient, followed by the 9.5-kilometer (nearly 6-mile) Col d'Agnes, with an 8.4 percent gradient.

Approaching the end, the front of the *peloton* had only about 30 racers, with five from the U.S. Postal Service Cycling Team. Jose Azevedo, Jose Luis Rubiera, Floyd Landis, and George Hincapie were pulling Lance Armstrong toward victory on the Plateau de Beille at an unbelievable pace. Azevedo brought Armstrong up the challenging ascent, while other top contenders, like Haimar Zubeldia, Tyler Hamilton, and Iban Mayo, dropped off. Only Ivan Basso could keep pace with Armstrong's group.

In the end, Armstrong gained his first stage win of the Tour. Thomas Voeckler remained in the yellow jersey in the General Classification (see Chapter 3), but Armstrong was on his way to his sixth Tour de France victory.

Attacking and breakaways

An *attack* is a rapid and often surprise acceleration by one of the riders in the *peloton.* The timing of the attack is crucial, and experienced riders have well-earned knowledge of the course, combined with an uncanny intuition, to know just when to take off. In an instant, the rider stands and accelerates, flashing by the leaders. If his attack is successful, he may be victorious. But, most often, the leading group chases him down (known as a *counter-attack*), or he realizes that he cannot maintain the pace, and slows down to await the inevitability of being swallowed up by the *peloton.*

The *directeur sportif* may send a rider out to attack on long, flat stages to set a high pace and try to exhaust other riders. Riders may attack in the mountains to try to wear out the leader and his *domestiques.* Short, repeated bursts of attacks are also used to challenge and test the overall contender, to test the *peloton,* or to entice another rider to form an alliance and go for a stage win. Different teams cooperate to constantly attack and exhaust the overall contender in the mountain climbs.

A *breakaway* is usually a small group of riders (sometimes a solo rider) taking off when the *peloton* is setting a relaxed pace along the route. Breakaways frequently happen early in a flat stage and usually do not contain any of the top contenders. A rider in a long breakaway gets lots of valuable television exposure and makes sponsors happy. Usually, the breakaway riders are low in the General Classification (see Chapter 4), perhaps 10 to 25 minutes back, and are not a threat. So the overall contender and his team, as well as the *peloton,* make the decision to not use up any effort or energy to chase a breakaway down. In the last kilometers of the stage, the *peloton* reels in, or chases down, the breakaways, and they drop back with the *gruppetto.* A breakaway rider is seldom victorious in the stage, but it does happen.

Miles to Go Before 1 Sleep

The distance of each Tour de France stage is measured in kilometers. All of the stages, added together, are known as the *course route,* which is announced the October before each year's event. The *Prologue* or prerace can be as short as approximately 5 kilometers (3.1 miles), while the event's longest days can approach 250 kilometers (155 miles). The longest stage of the 2004 race was the tenth stage from Limoges to Saint-Flour at 237 kilometers (147 miles).

The severe climbs of the Alps and Pyrenees take their toll on riders' legs, but the cumulative effect of long stages does damage, too. The 2005 Tour de France route included five stages of at least

200 kilometers (125 miles) long, including the longest of the race, the 239-kilometer (148-mile) 17th stage from Pau to Revel.

While high-mileage stages are hardly something riders look forward to, particularly in the race's waning days, a long stage can be a reprieve. A flat stage 50 percent longer than a mountain stage with a half-dozen climbs can be considered refreshing — especially for cyclists who have already ridden up steep terrain and negotiated harrowing descents for days.

The day's unique circumstances, the closeness of the overall title and the subtitles, the cumulative strength of the teams', and the weather conditions dictate stage strategy. Tour de France riders are accustomed to riding in strong winds, rain, and even snow. But in some ways, how the *peloton* approaches and endures a seven-hour ride across the French countryside is much the same as how a motorist considers negotiating a seven-hour drive. Driving through fields of sunflowers or vineyards on a clear, windless day, for example, can define a pleasant French holiday. But covering the same route in a rainstorm and into 60 mph winds isn't particularly appealing. The difference is that a motorist can make a choice. A Tour de France cyclist can opt not to make the journey on a miserable day, too. But if he does so, his Tour de France participation abruptly ends.

For the race leader and those seeking a top overall race finish, a long, flat stage often requires a minimal show of superior individual skills. It requires plenty of attentive riding, too. Ideally, several of each teams' support riders ride close to their team leader. Particularly on inclement weather days, the team leader can greatly benefit from riding behind his teammates. In short, the team riders are required to utilize vast amounts of energy to break through the headwinds and negotiate troublesome *crosswinds* (winds coming from the side).

Domestiques: Delivering news and other stuff

A stage distance may be changed in severe weather or because of a natural disaster. On rare occasions, mountaintop routes have been shortened in blizzard-like conditions. Announced routes have also been altered because of unexpected road construction, mudslides, and other catastrophes.

Delivering messages from the directeur sportif

Most teams in the race have two-way radio communications between riders and team directors, who follow their riders in team vehicles. But technology sometimes fails. And if a team director wants to tell his riders something, that leaves one surefire method. If the team director can get the attention of one his riders, the cyclist falls back and rides alongside of the team car while he's getting the instructions. This rider loses a good chunk of time, but the messenger returns to the main group and delivers the good — or bad — news. As such, that rider's potentially strong individual day could be easily nullified. That's the nature of cycling strategy — a team rider's job is done well when he sacrifices his potential glory for the good of the team.

Resupplying food and beverages

Each road stage of the Tour de France has designated areas for team personnel to deliver food and liquids to the riders. It doesn't always go smoothly and rarely are the scheduled resupply areas adequate, particularly on hot and long mountain stages.

In fact, team riders — and even team leaders on rare occasions — have to work like pack mules during a stage. It can happen once or several times during a stage. It likely may be the same rider who had just fallen back to the team car for instructions who again is called upon to fetch water bottles, fruit, and energy bars for his teammates.

It's common practice for the rider who's sent to the team car to carry back as much as he can. He'll stuff a half-dozen full water bottles into the pockets in the back of his shirt. He'll throw a few *musettes* (small bags of food) over his head and stuff bananas into the waistband of his cycling shorts. He'll even carry another water bottle in his mouth for a while if the route suddenly requires that he have two hands on his handlebars.

Bringing in replacement wheels

The most annoying delay for cyclists is a flat tire, and there's only one sure thing about a flat tire in the Tour de France — there's never a good time to get one. Team cars have replacement wheels, and the race provides a vehicle, called a *neutral support vehicle,* that can replace any rider's flat tire, regardless of his team affiliation.

Sometimes, it seems like a *domestique's* day will never end. Even if he has delivered water bottles and brought food to his teammates throughout the day, if the team leader has a flat tire, the same *domestique* stops and waits for the repair of the leader's tire and wheel. A *domestique* may even give his team leader his bike if the problem is more serious than a flat tire. Giving someone else your equipment is illegal in some sports, but giving up your bike to a teammate is perfectly legal in the Tour de France. It's not a strategy that anyone looks forward to, but when it happens, it means a team rider has done his job and done it well.

Pedaling into U.S. record books

Tyler Hamilton had ridden for two weeks with a fractured clavicle, but in Stage 16 of the 2003 Tour de France, he still felt like he had something to prove. After missing an early break on a misty and cool morning in the stage from Pau to Bayonne, Hamilton joined the lead group of riders, and then timed his strategy perfectly to become the sixth American in history to win a stage of the Tour. (With his stage win, Hamilton joined Armstrong, Greg LeMond, Andy Hampsten, Davis Phinney, and Jeff Pierce as the American winners of Tour de France stages.)

After riding for more than 113 kilometers (70 miles) with the lead group, Hamilton powered off the front of the *peloton* and built more than a five-minute lead while riding nearly 80 kilometers (50 miles) alone. His move occurred on the ascent to the Col de Bagargui. The lead group of 17 riders dwindled to 10 when Hamilton made his move.

Despite the collective strength of the riders in the chasing group, Hamilton maintained a four-minute margin as he neared the day's final miles and with his victory nearly secured. Considering his injury and his sudden move, Hamilton used the element of surprise strategy perfectly and successfully.

Hamilton, from Marblehead, Massachusetts, said afterward that he wanted to thank his teammates. "I wanted to pay back my teammates who had been there helping me every day since the crash," said Hamilton, who suffered a nondisplaced collarbone fracture in a crash near the finish of the first stage. "I'm exhausted; I gave everything. I'm still not 100 percent, but to win a stage is fantastic."

"To win a Tour stage is beyond my wildest dreams," Hamilton continued. "I've been a bit disappointed up to now, even though I was seventh overall, which I think is respectable if you consider my injury, but without it, I know I could have been even better. After my victory today, I can forget about all my grief."

The peloton: Stuck in the middle with you

Riding in the *peloton* with roughly 200 other racers requires skill, alertness, assertiveness, and just plain old guts. The competitors ride for hours with only a couple of inches between their wheels and the wheels of other riders. In front, in back, and on each side of them, a potential accident is waiting to happen — and frequently does. One fleeting moment of inattention, and a rider is on the ground. Swerving and braking unexpectedly, or someone having a mechanical problem, can cause several riders to fall like dominoes on wheels.

The *peloton* was nervous

During the 2004 Tour de France, the *peloton* was nervous about riding over a narrow cobblestone road in Stage 3 from Waterloo to Wasquehal. Even before the cobblestones in Wandignies, some of the riders panicked and began fighting to get to the front. The inevitable crash occurred, and the *peloton* split, leaving top contenders Iban Mayo and Haimar Zubeldia caught in the back. These unlucky riders lost more than four minutes getting back to the front of the *peloton,* and lost all chances of a top position in the General Classification. Their chance of winning the Tour de France ended with the crash in that early stage.

In the *peloton,* massive pileups occur in a flash. In a recent Tour, a huge crash occurred because the riders in the middle of a pack heard what they thought was someone braking in the front of the *peloton,* and instantly grabbed their brakes. What they heard was noise from a spectator. Still the panic response from the riders caused a huge pileup of riders and bikes. *Clavicle* (collarbone), shoulder, and wrist injuries are common, and the unfortunate rider is often out of the Tour. At that point, the team has to ride the Tour with the serious disadvantage of being one rider short. Less serious injuries, such as road rash, bloody elbows and knees, torn shorts, and raw fingers, are common.

Experienced riders are very aware of who is riding next to them, and they move away from reckless or inexperienced riders. Race commentators often say that "the *peloton* is nervous" in the beginning stages of the Tour. Constant chatter is ongoing in the *peloton:* talking, shouting, and arguing. Hearing a rider swearing and shouting at another rider to get away from him, and stay away, is commonplace in the *peloton.* Nobody wants to ride two inches away from an erratic racer.

Elbowing and jostling for position is a normal part of being in the *peloton,* as is giving someone the shoulder or the evil eye to intimidate them. On the other hand, cooperation and respect among riders is an absolute must and is an unwritten rule of the *peloton.*

The strategy for most team leaders is to stay in front, safely ahead of any crashes or screw-ups by other riders. On a rainy day, many teams move their leaders to the front. The team leader rides, surrounded by his *domestiques.* Lance Armstrong usually rides with two or three of his teammates beside him, and he's nearly always toward the front when riding in the *peloton.*

The exception to this tactic is when a bunch sprint is coming up; it's one of the most dangerous times in the *peloton*. Sprinters are traditionally the aggressive daredevils of the *peloton*. When the sprinters take off, everybody gets out of their way — even team leaders drop back and let sprinters fight it out. The team leaders sometimes drop all the way back into a separate, small pack behind the main *peloton*. Why then, would any rider stay in the middle of the *peloton?* Energy conservation is the answer. Riding in the *peloton* and being protected from the wind can save 30 percent or more of a rider's vital energy resources. This is energy saved for grueling climbs or for being sent out in front to chase down a breakaway. By riding in the *peloton,* riders save themselves for demanding assignments or weather conditions that they have to endure to finish the stage.

Heeding Nature's Call While Riding

A *peloton* of 200 riders ride for hours on a bike in front of thousands of fans. They're drinking gallons of fluids from water bottles to stay hydrated. They're sweating and they're . . . yes, this is the common question, "Hey, what do they do when they gotta go?"

French attitude toward heeding nature's call is different than many Americans' values. Along French roads, men commonly stand beside their cars, casually urinating. And although it's commonplace in Europe, Tour regulations don't permit riders to openly urinate in front of spectators. So, what's a rider to do?

Frequently, several riders in the *peloton* make a decision to stop along a less crowded stretch of road. They stop their bikes, put a foot down, and do their thing. The rest of the *peloton* has an unwritten, absolute obligation to not attack while these riders are watering the sunflowers. They mellow out and wait for the others to resume their places in the *peloton*.

Sometimes, racers ride three or four abreast, each with an arm on the shoulder of the rider next to him. This is not a spontaneous gesture of camaraderie: They're bracing and balancing the rider on the inside while he urinates. That rider discreetly adjusts the leg of his shorts to accommodate the process.

Whether in a small group or solo, the rider has to be cognizant of where the riders are when he urinates on the move. He gets a great deal of grief from the other riders if there's any overspray. In short, he has to make sure nobody is downwind.

Breaking the rules

The unwritten rule to not attack during a bathroom break was violated during Stage 6 of the 2000 Tour. Laurent Jalabert was wearing the yellow jersey and stopped along the road soon after the depart in Vitre. Jacky Durand attacked and took several riders with him and the group, ending up more than seven minutes in front. While Durand said he hadn't known that Jalabert stopped, the race leader lost the yellow jersey and was furious.

What happens if a rider needs a more serious bathroom break? He has to head out into the bushes just like Tour spectators. The *peloton* usually slows down and waits for him to finish, because they all know they may be the one who needs to stop next time.

The unwritten rule for press photographers used to be that cameras were turned away from riders heeding nature's call. In recent times, shots of riders standing along the roadside are pretty common, and often pretty funny. No close-ups, of course!

Part III
Loving the Ride: A Man and His Bike

"Listen, thanks. I'll return them as soon as I get the wheels fixed."

In this part . . .

Riding the Tour de France isn't easy. This part describes race cyclists and how they do what they do. Proper training, diet, rest, perseverance, mental toughness, and luck are all integral to Tour success. You discover what riders do to balance all the necessary racing components on a day-to-ay basis. And the last chapter in this part provides everything you need to know about riders' equipment — from helmets to bikes, jerseys to shoes.

Chapter 7

Who Are These Guys and How Do They Do It?

*R*acing at the highest professional level begins each year in January, so that, by the time riders begin the Tour de France, they've finely tuned their bodies for several months. Every Tour team has a season itinerary that includes numerous one-day races, shorter-duration stage races lasting as long as ten days, and three-week stage races called *Grand Tours*. Many of these European events are longstanding traditional competitions and are now part of the newly created ProTour.

Racing is highly competitive, and victories and top performances are well rewarded. Cyclists also know their results in these events may lead to selection to their team's Tour de France squad. Teams selected to participate in the Tour have a couple dozen riders on their respective rosters, yet only nine riders compete for each Tour team. Competition among most riders is fierce for only a few available roster spots. Teams usually begin to announce their Tour rosters in the days following conclusion of the *Giro d'Italia* (Tour of Italy) in late May or in early June. In some instances, teams' final roster spots aren't announced until a few days prior to the Tour.

Racing hard through the spring, potential Tour riders have a plan: Get into prime shape, stay healthy, avoid injury, and arrive at the starting line for the first Tour stage at the peak of condition — if they're selected. It's easier said than done. This chapter shows you how the nine riders who make each Tour team push their bodies to endurance extremes. They're training and competing hard while avoiding a wide variety of potential disasters waiting around every bend in the road.

Two Hundred Cyclists: Maintaining Their Bodies

To prepare for the season and maintain peak efficiency, Tour cyclists lead a finely monitored, balanced life. Proper training, nutrition, rest, massage, and general good health are all intertwined components of their competitive careers.

Nutrition and proper rest are paramount in most sports. And because cyclists use their legs like pistons day in and day out, their leg muscles (and the rest of their bodies) are regularly massaged. Manipulation of cyclists' muscles greatly enhances recovery from training and racing that can last seven hours per day — and for three weeks at a time.

Shaving legs and getting road rash

Like their counterparts in swimming and triathlons, cyclists shave their legs. It's part tradition, part comfort, and part medical necessity. It's why Tour riders shave their legs as part of the cycling lifestyle, not only for the Tour's three weeks. Some riders believe there's an aerodynamic benefit to riding hairless, but various tests in controlled wind-tunnel environments discount the theory. More relevant are the benefits of massage on hairless skin, and the ease of cleaning and treating wounds.

Hair can be an irritant during massage, and cyclists like the benefits of a smooth massage, not the potential scraping of their body hair. Also, without hair on their legs, cyclists who crash and suffer skin abrasions, commonly known as *road rash,* are fortunate. Abrasions and other skin problems (see typical bandages in Figure 7-1) are easier to manage when there's no hair in the way.

You are what you eat

Beyond intense racing, Tour cyclists face another difficult test on and off their bikes: eating enough food. Tour cyclists may consume up to 7,000 calories per day while on the Tour; they eat much less when competing in other races or not competing at all.

Figure 7-1: Bandages are a common sight on riders at the Tour.

Tour teams eat breakfast and dinner together at their respective hotels. A third pre-race team meal is part of the nutrition equation, if time permits, on late-starting stage days or on rest days. Riders also eat huge amounts of food during stages. Turkey and ham sandwiches, rice cakes, fruit, energy bars, and energy gels are standard fare. Tour cyclists may consume 400 calories — sometimes more — for each hour on their bikes.

Team *soigneurs* (masseurs and support staff) and chefs prepare riders' daily racing food. It's distributed by team personnel in *musettes* (small bags of food) in designated stage areas called *feeding zones*. Teams' *domestiques* (team riders) also make many trips back to team cars during road stages to resupply their teammates with snacks.

During the Tour, riders generally divide their food intake into three main groups: carbohydrates (70 percent), protein (15 percent), and fat (15 percent). During sit-down meals prepared by team chefs, popular carbohydrate sources include potatoes, rice, pasta, cereal, whole grain breads, fruits, and vegetables. Eggs, chicken, fish, some red meat, and yogurt are popular proteins. Butter, cheese, and carefully chosen cooking oils (olive oil) are regular fat sources.

When Tour riders eat is also important. Riders eat a breakfast that's heavy on carbohydrates, and they try to finish their meals about three hours prior to racing. Riders are handed chock-full *musettes* during and shortly after stages are over, plus recovery fluids. Team dinners, which have about the same number of calories as breakfast and are also heavy on carbs, are consumed just before riders retire to their rooms for the night.

Hydrating — or else

Tour cyclists need massive amounts of liquids to maintain proper body fluid levels. Riders usually carry two 20-ounce water bottles on their bikes during road stages. As temperatures increase and sometimes exceed 100 degrees, dehydration is an acute possibility. Riders drink two bottles of water every hour during the Tour, and in extreme heat, cyclists can drink three bottles (or nearly two quarts) of fluid per hour — that's as much as three gallons during a long stage.

Tour 2003: It was a very hot year

The 100th anniversary of the Tour in 2003 is often cited as among the greatest editions in race history. Lance Armstrong rode to his tightest margin of victory in the Tour's fastest-ever race. Nearly every stage included dramatic moments — crashes, surprising attacks, unique developments in the *peloton* (the pack of riders), and surprises in varied jersey competitions (see Chapter 3).

The 2003 Tour was also among the hottest in history. Temperatures reached into the high 90s (°F), and the heat took its toll in several ways. Numerous riders suffering from dehydration withdrew. Cyclists are not inclined to take water from fans because it could be contaminated, but the 2003 Tour was an exception. Riders often accepted water from spectators and used it to douse themselves in the scorching heat.

Extreme temperatures also could have easily foiled Armstrong's bid for his fifth consecutive title. Armstrong suffered from dehydration during the exceedingly hot and humid Stage 12 individual time trial stage from Gaillac to Cap Decouverte. Favored to win, Armstrong faltered in the second half of the 47-kilometer (29.2-mile) course and placed second, 1 minute and 36 seconds behind Germany's Jan Ullrich. Armstrong finished with large amounts of dried salt on his mouth and ended the day with only a precarious 15-second overall race lead over Ullrich, the 1997 race winner.

Because of dehydration, Armstrong's weight dropped from 72.5 kilograms (159.5 pounds) to 66.5 kilograms (146.3 pounds) during the 12th stage. But the next day, Armstrong was among favorites again in the 197.5 kilometer route from Toulouse to Plateau de Bonascre. The stage finished with two Category 1 climbs (see Chapter 3); Armstrong placed fourth and said it was impossible to recover fully from the effects of the previous day's bout of dehydration.

While consuming mass amounts of fluids, cyclists need to maintain proper levels of sodium, potassium, and calcium to coordinate bodily functions. Because Tour riders sweat profusely, their replenishment fluids include drinks with high electrolyte levels. In fact, it's common to see riders during and after stages with dried salt on their helmets, jerseys, shorts, and body parts. Keeping teammates supplied with enough fluid is among the primary jobs of *domestiques*. But on warm Tour days, *domestiques* can't always get enough water to teammates, and lack of proper hydration causes a share of riders to abandon the race.

 Cyclists must also be aware not to drink too much water. If they don't balance the equation of fluids and electrolytes properly, a rare but serious condition called *hyponatremia,* or water intoxication, occurs. Hyponatremia is the result of a severe dilution of the body's electrolytes. An athlete suffering from severe hyponatremia can lapse into a coma or even die.

What's Up, Doc?

Tour teams have physicians and other staff medical personnel who travel with the cyclists throughout the season. Because cyclists compete at the highest fitness level and put their bodies through incredible physical stress, their immune systems are susceptible and illness is common during the Tour. From bee stings to food poisoning, broken bones to saddle sores, team physicians meet cyclists' daily needs. In addition to team physicians, the Tour has staff physicians who monitor the race and who examine each Tour entrant prior to the race.

While it's part formality, every Tour rider undergoes an examination that includes weight, lung capacity, heartbeat, and verbal assessment tests. Heart rate and weight totals are documented in riders' profiles and conducted to detect any irregularities. Lung capacity evaluations are used to determine respiratory problems. Physicians also question athletes about any existing injuries or illnesses.

Team and Tour physicians do their best to keep riders racing. From broken bones to stomach viruses, physicians work long hours before, during, and after stages to keep riders healthy or mend them when they're not. It's not uncommon to see a team physician leaning out of a team car helping a rider during a stage. One of the only times a rider can hold onto a moving support vehicle during the Tour, without penalty, is when he is ill or injured.

Despite eating and drinking well and astute physicians' care, competing while sick is common at the Tour. Colds, flu, infections, and broken bones stop many cyclists' race participations. But many cyclists persevere with varying illnesses. Finishing the Tour is tantamount to success for many riders, and riding through various illnesses is a daily occurrence, if the team physician allows. Any rider with an infection that could spread to another team member is quickly quarantined.

Things That Go Bump in the Day

Tour crashes are unpredictable and dramatic, and they vary greatly. It's rare if a stage is held without at least one rider taking a minor spill. At times, a large group of riders may fall in a chain reaction and escape unhurt. Or one rider can crash by himself and suffer fatal injuries.

Crashes occur for many reasons. Tour riders often compete together while riding on thin tires, on varying road surfaces, and at speeds that can approach 97 kph (60 mph) during mountain descents. A pebble, twig, or a pothole; a slight mistake by a rider in a massive pack; or a momentary lapse of reason can bring down the entire *peloton*.

Crashes in furiously fast finish line sprints are the most common. If the *peloton* is together, it often approaches the line while pedaling around 73 kph (45 mph). If riders' wheels touch or cyclists otherwise bump, the entire field can fall, en masse, in a few seconds. What happens in a massive crash depends on how and where riders fall. The first riders down are likely to suffer more serious injuries, because they hit the ground harder and are susceptible to other riders and bicycles piling on top of them. Cyclists who fall later in the domino effect of crashes are often more fortunate because they fall on other riders, not directly on asphalt. But cyclists who fall later in crashes can also be hurt by other riders' bicycles.

Riders must finish a stage within a designated time of the stage winner to participate the next day, so riders who can continue to race, even with minor injuries, return to their bikes and do so. Riders who have suffered some type of injury, particularly in major pileups, get in communication with team directors to assess damage to themselves and their bikes and decide whether to proceed. If a team leader or key team member has been hurt, team members and directors may need miles to reassess team strategy. Of course, cyclists suffering serious injuries who are unable to continue are transported via ambulance to a local hospital or abandon the race in team vehicles or in the broom wagon (see Chapter 3 for more on the broom wagon).

Singing in the rain

Rain is a Tour de France curse. Riders are accustomed to wearing special jackets and pedaling for hours in inclement weather. But they never get used to slick roads and the dangerous ways of pedaling in shower storms, particularly while descending slick roads.

Just as drivers are warned of especially slippery roads, so, too, do Tour riders face the dangers of wet asphalt. On sharp corners and on steep descents, riders rely on superior bike-handling skills — and luck — to avoid catastrophe in wet conditions.

It's not always possible. Riders' brakes get wet and their bikes' thin tires can't get proper traction. Turning slightly too sharply on a descent or descending (see Figure 7-2) too quickly off a mountain can equate to potential disaster. Riders' support staffs can, however, make adjustments for slick roads — for example, change to tires that have a little more tread for traction or decrease tire pressure to give more surface/road contact.

The 1K rule

Several major crashes at the end of road races in recent years prompted *Union Cycliste Internationale* (International Cycling Union) to reexamine what's commonly known as the *1K rule.* Here's what the rule says: If a problem occurs within the final kilometer (0.62 miles) of a stage, riders who are involved in a crash, suffering a mechanical problem, or dealing with a tire puncture are given the same finish time as the rider(s) he was "in the company of."

As of Jan. 1, 2005, the distance of the rule was extended to 3 kilometers (1.8 miles). The change was made so that riders not seeking to contest sprints don't have to worry about losing finishing time and are, therefore, at less risk of crashing.

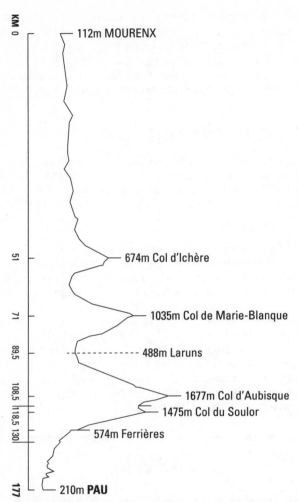

Figure 7-2: Profile of ascents in Stage 16 of the 2005 Tour from Mourenx to Pau.

Dealing with mechanical failures

Tour cyclists use the finest equipment, and Tour teams employ the sport's finest mechanics. But faulty gears, bad brakes, punctured tires, and bent rims are common in the Tour, and riders are at the mercy of mechanics' quick fixes and equipment changes.

When a rider notices a problem with his bike, he raises his hand or communicates via radio to his team. The Tour also provides mechanical support available to all teams. (More in Chapter 4.)

Tour tragedies: Death on the mountain

Fabio Casartelli of Italy was an accomplished young professional riding as a Motorola teammate of Lance Armstrong during the 1995 Tour de France. But on July 18 in the 15th stage, Casartelli suffered fatal injuries after crashing on the Col de Portet d'Aspet in the Pyrenees. Casartelli, the 1992 Olympic road race champion, crashed with several other riders on the descent and suffered severe facial and head injuries. He was traveling at more than 85 kph (53 mph).

Casartelli's death was the third Tour death in competition and the first since 1967. Three days after his teammate perished, Armstrong won the 18th stage to Limoges. As he crossed the line, Armstrong pointed his hands toward the sky to acknowledge and honor his fallen teammate. The Tour revisited Col de Portet d'Aspet in 1997 and stopped momentarily at the spot where a monument honors Casartelli. Future Tours will likely do the same.

Death first struck the Tour in 1935 when Spanish rider Francesco Cepeda suffered fatal injuries after plunging down a ravine on the Col du Galibier. British rider Tom Simpson collapsed and died on the climb of Mount Ventoux in the 1967 Tour. Amphetamines and alcohol were discovered in Simpson's bloodstream during his autopsy. Like Casartelli, a monument near the climb's summit honors Simpson, and the Tour has paid its respects on several stage occasions.

The first Tour rider's death occurred in 1910, but Adolph Helière of France didn't die in competition — he went for an ocean swim on a rest day and drowned. Several noncyclists have also perished at the Tour. Radio reporter Alex Virot and Rene Wagner, his motorcycle driver, were killed in 1957 after falling into a ravine during the Barcelona to Ax-les-Thermes stage. And in more recent years, spectators have died after being hit by race caravan vehicles.

In some instances, if a team leader's bike needs repair and the team mechanics or Tour mechanical support isn't nearby, a teammate gives up his bike — or a part of a bike, like a wheel — to the leader, so that the leader doesn't lose substantial time. (Of course, the riders have to be nearly the same size for this type of bike exchange to work.) The team rider then waits for repairs of another new bike. He usually loses substantial time, but that's the nature of cycling as a team sport.

Chapter 8

Spending a Day in the Life of a Rider

In This Chapter

▶ Eating well and sleeping well to win

▶ Getting ready, getting set, getting to the start

▶ Wondering whether this day is finished yet

▶ Resting, traveling, and talking

*W*atching the Tour de France on television, you see riders and their *entourage* (support staffs) arrive, and you see riders lining up at the start. As a spectator, you view bits and pieces of the race, and then you see the finish, complete with fanfare and awards on the podium.

But what about the rest of the day? What do these riders do in their spare time? Wait a minute — do they even have any spare time? A typical day for a Tour de France rider is filled with back-to-back scheduling: Rest is vital but elusive, and even time to rest has to be scheduled into a jam-packed day.

Morning, Noon, and Night

Teams at the Tour de France have similar daily routines and schedules. The lodging for all teams is scheduled by the Tour de France organization, so teams don't have any choice about where they stay. Team lodging may be scattered all over an area near the start or finish lines, so teams may have a drive of an hour or more to get to the race start or to get back to their hotels from the finish line. Usually, three or more teams stay at the same hotel.

Wherever they are, the riders are expected to participate as a team unit for their scheduled meals, training rides, and meetings with the public or press. Riders are rarely seen wandering around sightseeing or shopping solo, unless it's a rest day. Riders at the Tour de France have very little free time.

The Tour de France organization reserves 1,200 rooms every day to provide lodging for the teams and their staff, the press, and Tour personnel.

Rise and shine

Riders share a room with a teammate, and they all hope it's a compatible match. Riders are awakened each day by their *soigneurs* (masseurs and general support staff), and while riders may groan about the early hour, they know they have to be at the breakfast table on time. They shower, shave, and jump into their team sweat suits and hurry to the team breakfast table. Riders are often in a good mood in the morning (some may even joke around or play pranks on each other), and are psyching themselves up for the long racing day.

Team managers try to set up a separate dining room for the team, if the hotel is large enough. The staff also tries to set up large tables so six, eight, or more teammates can sit together.

Breakfast of champions

Healthy, adequate nutrition is an absolute top requirement to maintain the endurance and stamina required to finish the Tour de France. By the time a rider gets to this level of competition, he eats what works best for his body chemistry.

Some people think a hearty breakfast of eggs, bacon, pancakes, and syrup is what riders want for breakfast, but that's not the case. In fact, when European teams come to America to race and see what is offered for breakfast, they often buy their own breakfast foods to bring to the team dining room. Preferred breakfast choices include cereals, muesli, pasta, rice, bread rolls, eggs, yogurt, fruit, milk, juices, bottled water, jam, and honey. Sometimes, chicken is offered, too, along with olive oil for pasta.

Riders may drink coffee, but in moderate amounts because coffee can be dehydrating. Caffeine is not a banned substance at the Tour unless the caffeine concentration in the urine exceeds a certain amount.

Loving those boxes of cereal

Several European teams come to the United States to race the USPRO Championships in Philadelphia, and they all take their meals in the hotel dining room. During the 2003 race, one morning at the team breakfast, the hotel staff stood in awe as they watched a 125-pound, climbing specialist eat *nine* individual serving size boxes of cereal with milk, plus yogurt and fruit.

Mini-meetings in the morning

All teams have a meeting in the morning before the start of the Tour stage. For some teams, the meeting happens at the breakfast table, if breakfast is served in a private dining room. Other times, riders meet in a hotel room or on the team bus on the way to the start line. Pep talks, team strategy, and specific assignments for the day's stage are presented by the *directeurs sportif.*

Cleaning and packing up

After breakfast, on race days, the riders return to their rooms and quickly gather their racing kits and necessities for the day. In most cases, rooms look like disaster areas — tidiness is not a part of the plan.

The *soigneurs* usually have a day bag packed with each rider's gear to take on the bus. The *soigneurs* are responsible for packing up all the riders' belongings and loading it in the bus or team cars. While the riders are limited to small bags of team-issue clothing, the amount of team luggage transported by team personnel is amazing.

European hotels seldom have parking lots at the door, so drivers must double-park on the street and unload the luggage on the sidewalk. Curious crowds and autograph seekers often gather at team hotels.

Moving On Down the Road

When many of the teams leave the hotel for the start of a Tour stage, they travel in a luxurious team bus. These buses are complete with a shower, bathroom, kitchen, and washers and dryers.

Television(s), espresso machines, air conditioning, and GPS are standard fixtures. Snacks, coffee, juices, and water are also plentiful, so the team rides in luxury while they talk or plan strategies. The bus is followed by the team cars and a team equipment truck. (Note that some of these vehicles leave early, ahead of the bus, to scout out the route and stake their claim to a spot in the team parking area.)

Getting to the start of the stage on time is always a challenge. Team vehicles fight their way through thousands of cars — traffic jams are notoriously horrendous before the race. While the teams always leave appropriately early, they sometimes need a police escort with sirens and flashing lights to get them through the traffic jams.

As the team vehicles reach the Depart area, the crowds on foot and bicycles present another challenge. The drivers must inch their huge buses through swarms of fans with cameras and try to not run over fervent autograph seekers. (If you go to the Tour, be careful in these areas! Read more on attending the Tour in Chapter 11.) The bus finally reaches the designated team parking area, where there are barricades to keep out the crowds. However, sponsors, guests, and the press are allowed inside this area, so there's a large crowd.

Get Ready, Get Set, Go!

Try to imagine the scene: a chaotic mass of fans and media members pushing against the yellow tape or barricades and waving cameras or items for the riders to autograph. The riders come out to warm up on their bikes, trying to concentrate, while cameras flash and people yell their names, begging for an autograph. Still, the riders have plenty to do before the race begins. This section shares the details of the final pre-race preparation.

Fine-tuning the bikes

Bikes are lined up precisely in a row beside the team bus. At this point, mechanics (also called *wrenches* — see Chapter 4) have been setting up and fine-tuning the bikes since the team truck or bus arrived. The bikes are shiny clean, and every part, every setting, is precisely measured and adjusted.

The riders do, however, request last-minute adjustments on their bikes (see Figure 8-1) and their shoes as they are leaving for the start line. Some riders, such as Lance Armstrong, are known for their perfectionism about their equipment — the equipment has to be perfectly and precisely the right measurement.

Figure 8-1: Juan Lujan, mechanic for the U.S. Postal Service Cycling Team (now the Discovery Channel Pro Cycling Team), fine-tunes Viatcheslav Ekimov's bike.

Warming up

Riders warm up in their team's barricaded area before the start of each stage. Bikes are placed on stationary trainers (see Figure 8-2), where the back wheel rides on rollers and the front wheel is on the ground. Before time trial stages, riders work hard in their warm-ups, sweating profusely, feet flying on the pedals. For other stages, they're just trying to loosen up.

Last-minute instructions

The *directeur sportif* and his assistants watch the riders warm up and assess how the riders are feeling. The directors may also give riders individual instructions while they're on the warm-up bikes. When the entire team is back in the bus, the *directeur sportif* again reinforces the game plan and each rider's job for the day. He gives last-minute instructions to the team and/or to individual riders.

The riders hydrate, eat *energy gel* (like jelly, only a little more solid), and may make a final trip to the bathroom. Because of the importance of lining up at the start with the race number, *soigneurs* make sure riders have their numbers on and are in the right place.

Figure 8-2: U.S. Postal Service Cycling Team warms up in Cambria.

Signing in

Each rider is required to go individually to the *signature registration area* or *sign-in area* near the start line (see Chapter 5 for additional details). He must be there in person to sign his name on the start list. A signing-in ceremony is held, where the race leaders are announced, applauded, and celebrated.

The riders then return to the team bus to await the start time. It is another hectic, chaotic trip to and from the sign-in area for the riders. They ride their bikes through massive crowds, barely able to squeeze through the jam-packed people. Pencils, pens, scraps of paper, books, cameras — sometimes even babies — are thrust into their faces. Small children may be pushed out in front of riders, in the hopes that they won't say no to an autograph request from a child.

Lining up

A few minutes before the official start time, the riders make their way from the bus back through the crowds and start lining up. The race leaders and other well-known riders are placed at the front, and riders from each team generally group loosely together in the lineup. The credentialed press photographers, who wear identifying vests, are allowed out on course for a short time to take their photographs.

The Tour is filled with colorful ceremonies and pageantry at both the start and finish of a stage. Local dignitaries and Tour officials speak briefly before the stage begins.

Starting the Race

When the start gun sounds, the official cars and dozens of the elite French Republican Guard on motorcycles move out, followed by the 200 riders. Behind them are more official cars, police motorcycles, the 200-plus team cars, followed by numerous press vehicles and emergency vehicles. The race cavalcade has hundreds of vehicles.

Lunch for the Bunch

During Tour stages, lunch is handed to the racers as they ride through a designated area called the *feed zone,* or *zone de ravitaillement.* Food is packed in cloth bags, called *musettes,* each of which has a long, thin shoulder strap, like a purse.

Keeping the teams safe every day

The Tour de France is organized by the Amaury Sport Organization, or ASO, under the direction of Jean Marie LeBlanc. A major challenge for the organizers is providing for day-to-day safety and security for each rider. Each day in a rider's life at the Tour, he depends on the ASO security arrangements to keep him safe while he is giving his utmost for his team. The stage each day is fraught with potential minor and major dangers.

Who protects the rider every day? During the three-weeks of the Tour, the ASO has 13,000 *gendarmes* (French police), 45 *Guardes Républicaines* (the snazzy-looking gendarmes in tall black boots on the motorcycles), 9,000 police staff and CRS (companies for Republican security — units of the national police), hundreds of *sapeurs-pompiers* (national volunteer emergency and fire personnel), 3,000 government officials, and dozens of well-trained Tour security guards.

Each rider knows that, every day, their safety depends on these well-trained security forces.

The team *soigneurs* stand beside the road holding the *musettes* at arm's length. The riders slow their speed to each grab a *musette.* The riders put the *musettes* around their necks while they transfer lunch to the back pockets of their jerseys.

Riders receive small packets of high carb, easily digested items, like little sandwiches filled with honey and banana slices, sweet cakes, pastries, energy bars, energy gels, and water or a sports drink. They discard the empty *musettes* along the side of the road (see Figure 8-3), sending the fans into a grabbing frenzy. The *musettes* and water bottles (called *bidons*) are highly sought after by the fans lining the road along the feed zones.

Figure 8-3: This musette was tossed onto the mirror by Lance Armstrong as he rode by, enroute to Saint-Dizier.

It Ain't Over 'Til It's Over

By the time a stage of the Tour de France is finished, the teams have been riding for as long as six hours of intense concentration, always on the alert to avoid crashing. Riders are constantly chasing, pulling, or protecting their team leader. But crossing the finish line doesn't mean the day is over for the riders. There are hours and miles to go before they can rest. They are only halfway to slumberland.

Soigneurs waiting at the finish line

Teams have their *soigneurs* standing just past the finish line, waiting with towels, drinks, and jackets. The riders are exhausted, sweaty, and depleted, some of them just barely hanging on. In fact, sometimes, a *soigneur* has to literally hold up a rider to keep him from falling and help him climb off his bike because his legs have no strength left (see Figure 8-4).

Figure 8-4: The *soigneur's* job starts at the finish line. Head Masseur Freddy Viaene runs protectively with Jose Azevedo after the Stage 16 finish on L'Alpe d'Huez.

Winners at the finish are required to go directly to the medical area for drug testing, and then give interviews in the press area. Both of these areas are barricaded off from the public and are zealously guarded by Tour security forces. The area behind the podium is also barricaded off, and only a few people are allowed to enter. Most of the press is prevented from entering, causing tensions to elevate. The big television companies are allowed to enter, along with a few select photographers.

The victorious riders are delayed for nearly an hour from getting to their team bus to clean up and replenish their bodies. As fatigued and drained as these riders are, they must fulfill Tour requirements.

Getting crushed by the cameras

For many of the riders, crossing the finish line means getting crushed by the media. Hordes of press, carrying cameras and microphones, descend upon them (see Figure 8-5). Pushing and shoving and jostling for position, the press is relentless in getting the story.

Figure 8-5: The media swarms the riders as they finish at L'Alpe d'Huez in Stage 16 of the 2004 Tour de France.

Media coverage of the Tour is awesome: More than 2,300 accredited journalists, plus 1,200 photographers, camera operators, and TV directors follow the Tour each summer. In addition, according to the Tour organization, an entourage of 1,100 technicians or drivers, and more than 500 other journalists are given credentials.

Surviving the crowd: Getting to the bus

A long stretch of the road after the finish line is barricaded to prevent the crowds from rushing out on the course. Riders may finish 30 minutes or more after the winners cross the line. For safety reasons, fans are prevented from swarming out onto the *arrivé,* or finish line area.

A favorite spot for fans to gather is right past the final barricade on the road. Riders slowly make their way through a shoulder-width path on the way to the team bus. Race leaders usually have a staff person to run road-blocking for them, but the rest of the riders struggle their way through the crowd. It's not unusual to see riders with pen marks on their jerseys from people grabbing them, pen in hand, trying to get a signature.

The crowd estimate for the 2004 Tour de France was 15 million spectators from more than 22 countries. The ASO estimates 76 percent of French residents have attended the Tour at least once.

Replenishing the calories

The first thing riders do when they enter the team bus is begin restoring their energy balance. Their depleted bodies must be cared for immediately. Carbohydrates are metabolized quickly, so high-carb snacks are available. Energy drinks restore the electrolyte balance, so riders hydrate their bodies. Each team has its own kind of easily-digested sandwiches.

Traveling to the Next Hotel

Each team bus pulls out immediately after the last rider boards. It may be a long drive to the night's lodging, but even if the distance is short, race traffic is usually bumper-to-bumper for miles. Bus drivers are experts in this kind of traffic, but thousands of other vehicles leave the finish area at the same time, and many of those drivers aren't experts.

While their bus is heading out, riders are eating and cleaning up — getting out of their dirty, sweaty clothes. Keep in mind that staying in their sweaty Lycra/Spandex shorts can cause sores that can be a problem to heal. Team physicians immediately treat any injuries, including road rash, sore muscles, cuts, and any other tender areas.

No Fun-Filled Evenings for the Riders

When the team bus arrives at the hotel, riders go to their rooms and settle in. Showering and organizing their gear comes first, and then the nightly routine begins. Nobody talks about a night on the town, partying, or hanging out at a local pub. Instead, the Tour is serious business and all forms of recreation are on hold till the last night of the Tour, when some serious partying goes on all night long.

Getting a rub: Massage is a must

Most teams have two or three *soigneurs* who give massages. A massage is an absolute must for tired, sore, and/or injured muscles. Skilled massage therapists are a god-send for aching legs, arms, and backs. The *soigneurs* know each rider's body and are skilled at working out the areas of stress and injury. Because even a small injury or sore spot can become a major problem, a well-maintained body is the best injury prevention.

A little nap time

After the massage, riders head to their rooms for a well-earned nap. The old saying that the Tour is "won in bed" may bring a sly grin, but what they are talking about is rest. Rest is a vital ingredient for a winning team, or for just being able to finish the Tour at all. One team's *directeur sportif* is so adamant about resting that he wants his team to be horizontal when they are not riding!

Dining together

A team always sits together at dinner, which is usually served about 8 o'clock at night, depending on when the riders are finished racing.

Burning calories

The adage that an army lives on its stomach is true for Tour de France teams. There's nothing more vital than adequate nutrition and hydration for each rider. Staying in top performance shape to endure and finish a Tour means consuming an enormous amount of calories on an almost constant basis. Most riders burn about 4,000 to 6,000 calories on flat stages and up to 8,000 calories on grueling mountain stages. In spite of this level of calorie consumption, riders lose as much as eight pounds by the time they cross the finish line on the Champs Élysées in Paris. During the last mountain stages, the *soigneurs* sometimes find it difficult to give massages to the depleted riders. Body fat and some muscle are almost impossible to maintain with the enormous energy and power output of the riders.

Bringing your own chef

The only American team at the Tour, the Discovery Channel Pro Cycling Team (formerly the U.S. Postal Service Cycling Team), brings its own chef along. Swiss chef Willy Balmat supervises and/or prepares all the team meals to insure quality and proper nutrition. He prepares special egg-white omelettes for breakfast, and often a special risotto (rice dish) for dinner. He prepares boiled potatoes with olive oil and salt for the team as post-race snacks; he even makes his own olive oil, using it to cook for the team. Willy cooks special requests from the riders and tries to provide variety in their meals, and he celebrates all rider and staff birthdays with a special cake during the Tour.

Meals are prepared by the hotel chef and staff, which can make the team and staff somewhat nervous. No, it's not because they worry that the riders won't like the menu — it's the possibility of eating tainted food. Food preparation at little-known hotels leaves riders at risk for food poisoning, which can take a horrendous toll on racers in the Tour. Food preparation is one of the variables that the team management can't completely control, so they can only hope that the food has been prepared under sanitary conditions and has been properly refrigerated.

All teams eat a certain meat on a certain day; for example, everyone may have chicken on Tuesday. How it's prepared and served is up to each team. Salad, soup, vegetables, and enormous amounts of bread and butter are offered. Pasta is always a staple, usually doused liberally with olive oil and Parmesan cheese or sauce. Rice may be served, but not as often. Chicken, fish, or lean meat is usually simply prepared. A cheese board or dessert may be offered at the end of the meal, but teams usually eat yogurt or fruit. Most teams don't drink alcohol, using it only for celebrations.

Riders consume astonishing amounts of food. Getting adequate calories in a day to maintain strength and energy is the goal. Riders on the teams must input enough calories to balance the enormous caloric output for each day's stage in order to sustain power and energy. This is why teams set up tables in the hotel hallways with high-carb food that riders can eat at any time during the evening, night, or early in the morning before breakfast. Snacking is encouraged, and energy bars are everywhere.

Rooming together

Sharing a room with someone for three stressful weeks isn't always a pleasant experience. Team management does its best to put two friends together, but that is not always possible. Small annoyances like loud music, talking on the phone, and snoring can become major problems, and because teams often stay in very small hotels, which means tiny rooms, the two riders can get on each other's nerves. Overall, however, there is great camaraderie, tolerance, and friendship among teammates. They know they depend on each other during the Tour.

Listening to music or reading a magazine

When riders aren't giving press interviews in person or on the phone in the evening, they have free time. Most of riders listen to music or read magazines and newspapers. Riders have the latest high-tech music storage and players, and some are known for their traveling music collections. If their rooms have a television with more than one channel, they may try to catch clips of Tour events of the day.

Calling home and cybersurfing

Many riders bring their laptops or PDAs to stay in touch with friends and family. It's up to the *directeur sportif* whether they're allowed to spend time surfing the Internet at night, though. Johan Bruyneel, *directeur sportif* for the 2005 Discovery Channel Professional Cycling Team, bans Lance Armstrong from using a laptop for the entire Tour.

Riding and writing

A few riders write daily journals or reports for Web sites. Propping their laptops on their hotel beds and typing away, they give us the scoop about what really goes on in the *peloton.*

Frankie Andreu (see Chapter 4) was one of the first riders to write a daily report from the Tour. His daily reports were very popular: People loved to read what really happens in the *peloton* from a rider's perspective. Now retired from cycling after finishing nine Tours, Andreu still writes Tour reports and does television coverage for OLN during the Tour.

Riders are known for their cellphone use — the phones seem to be attached to their ears during their free time. Cellphone service is decent in Europe, but not in remote areas.

Early to bed, early to rise

Many teams have a lights-out time, and the riders are expected to adhere to that rule. No problem — the hard-working riders are exhausted at night and often fall asleep very early. Nobody wants to let their team down by running out of energy during a stage because they didn't get enough sleep the night before.

No Rest for the Weary on Rest Day

The Tour organization designates two *rest days* during the Tour, usually near the ninth and 16th stages. Theoretically, the day is spent relaxing and recovering. In practice, these are some of the busiest days for the teams. If nothing else, fans mob team members more on rest days than on other days (see Figure 8-6).

Figure 8-6: Crowds of fans and the press mob the teams during the two rest days of the Tour.

Le Grand Boucle (the Big Loop), as the Tour is affectionately called, circles around the countryside in France. But there are gaps in the race route where the teams and the entire Tour organization must travel long distances to get from one stage to another. The only available time to move the thousands of vehicles, teams, and staff is on rest days.

Taking the A train: Traveling

The riders and *directeurs sportif* may fly or take a train on a rest day to travel to a stage start in a distant town. Using public transportation means little rest for riders, because they have to deal with crowds of fans and unending requests for photos and autographs. When traveling, all riders hope for is to rest or read, undisturbed.

Soigneurs, wrenches, drivers, and other staff must transport team vehicles to the next hotel. (See Chapter 4 for more on these team members.) They drive hundreds of kilometers to the next start location, which means there's no rest for the team staff, either.

Practice makes perfect, even on rest days

When teams arrive at their destination, they head for the hotel and change into their kits (see Chapter 9). Wrenches set up the bikes, and riders head out on a training ride to stay in top condition. They have to ride every day to keep their legs fresh and ready to go on race morning.

The Armstrong chronicles

During the 2004 Tour de France, the Outdoor Life Network sent camera crews that were dedicated just to filming Lance Armstrong's quest for his record-breaking sixth victory. Wherever Armstrong went, OLN followed. OLN reporter Craig Hummer was assigned specifically to cover Armstrong. Spectators always saw Hummer and his crew at every start and finish of every stage.

OLN's television coverage of the Tour drew record ratings for the month of July in America. According to an OLN press release, on July 25, 2004, gross viewership for the day was 2.2 million.

Press conferences and interviews

Rest days are also the days when the riders meet with the radio, television, and newspaper reporters. Interviews are usually scheduled by team press agents. Race leaders receive dozens of requests for interviews.

Sponsors also schedule time for guests, dignitaries, and celebrities to meet and be photographed with teams on rest days. Guided tour groups who are affiliated with sponsors also arrange for their entire group of guests to meet and have photo sessions with teams.

Chapter 9

Having the Best Equipment in the Bunch

*E*quipment rules at the Tour de France, where riders use state-of-the art bikes, accessories, and apparel. In some instances, the Tour is the groundbreaking platform for new technology, but it's also a race for time-tested technology traditions.

This chapter describes the equipment that teams use. Sponsors' names may differ, but from wheels to heart rate monitors, frames to helmets, Tour cyclists are at the forefront of the sport's cutting edge of technology.

Using High-Tech Bikes

From a technology standpoint, the Tour is divided into two eras: 1936 and the years before, and 1937 and the years that followed.

> ✔ **Before 1936:** Throughout the event's first 34 years, riders were prohibited from using any system that automatically changed a bike's gears. If a rider wanted his equipment to help him more efficiently go up or down a mountain, he had to get off his bike and manually change gears.

> ✔ **After 1936:** In 1937, innovation prevailed. Since then, Tour cyclists have been allowed to change gears while riding via a bike's derailleurs. Located near the pedals and outside of the rear wheel, front and rear derailleurs allow easy changing of gears via a cable system.

The accepted use of derailleurs is one of the Tour's major technology advancements. But event pioneers would likely have been taken aback by many other technology advancements — from lightweight bicycle frames to helmets, carbon saddles to disc wheels.

Weighing in on those bikes

According to *Union Cycliste Internationale* rules, Tour riders, for safety reasons, must ride bikes that weigh no less than 6.8 kilograms (14.96 pounds). To ensure adherence to this rule, riders' bikes are weighed periodically during the Tour. If a rider's bike is too light, his mechanics scamper to add weight so that the cyclist can participate.

Bike weight minimum limits aren't popular among cyclists or among manufacturers, who attempt to outdo each other by introducing increasingly lighter bikes and components.

Not so heavy metal

Steel was the metal of choice in early Tour bikes. As the heaviest of all bike frame metals, steel is still used in many frame tubes because it's durable and stiff. But manufacturers' penchant for lightness has prompted many new options. Aluminum, titanium, carbon fiber, and *metal-matrix* (that is, metal and nonmetal) frames are readily available and increasingly popular. Titanium alloy is a popular lightweight option, and it's corrosion-free but more expensive than other metal choices. Carbon fiber is also lightweight, wears well, and is more reasonably priced; when manufactured properly, it can be stiffer than most metals.

Armstrong, the lightweight

Just prior to perhaps the most highly touted stage in Tour de France history, Lance Armstrong had a problem. It was Stage 16 of the 2004 Tour, the uphill time trial to L'Alpe d'Huez, and Armstrong couldn't start. The reason: His bike, a Trek Madone, was 10 grams too light. Somehow, the U.S. Postal Service Team mechanics had to find the best way to add weight, the equivalent of about ten paper clips.

After various quick but unsuccessful attempts, a bicycle computer and some ballast was added to the pending race winner's bike. Armstrong's bike made its weight, and he rode to the stage victory en route to his sixth consecutive Tour title.

All equipment on the bikes is also designed to be as lightweight as possible. Bottle cages are measured in grams, and water bottles are lightweight, as are a rider's sunglasses. Bike computers, handle tape, and all bike components are as light as possible.

Ordinary or specially made bikes?

Tour de France riders compete on both specially made bicycles and bikes available to the general public. Teams use bikes of manufacturing sponsors; Trek, Giant, Look, Colnago, Specialized, Cannondale, and Pinarello are among more than a dozen manufacturers supplying bikes to Tour riders.

Some teams' and riders' bikes are specially made and aren't available to the public. Trek, however, supplied bikes to the U.S. Postal Service Team (now the Discovery Channel Pro Cycling Team) during Lance Armstrong's sixth Tour title run, and the company promoted its Madone model as the bike Armstrong used in the 2004 Tour de France.

Although most riders use a specific manufacturer's model, they also use different bikes within a category. Armstrong, for example, used a slightly heavier, more durable bike during early stages of the 2004 Tour that included rough, cobblestone sections. In road stages that included climbs, Armstrong switched to a lighter road bike, which television commentators sometimes referred to as *Lance's mountain bike.*

Time trial bikes

Because time trials are individual races timed against the clock, riders use more aerodynamically constructed bikes than they do in the rest of the Tour. Each team still uses its sponsoring manufacturer's equipment, but construction of time trial bikes and road bikes is vastly different.

Cyclists are positioned closer to the front of a time trial bike, via a shorter wheelbase, for pedaling power. The frame and handlebars are designed to enhance aerodynamics. Time trial bikes are also ridden while equipped with solid disc or spoked wheels. Most riders use spoked wheels (with as few as three carbon-made spokes), but on short time-trial courses with little or no wind, riders often use a rear disc wheel along with a front spoked wheel. It's rare for a rider to use two disc wheels, because potential windsail effect could increase control problems and, consequently, affect his finishing time or even his ability to finish.

If time trial bikes are so much faster, why don't riders use them in all the stages? The answer lies in the rulebook. The *Union Cycliste Internationale* has rules that limit the technology and geometry of frames for different types of races, so a time trial bike can be used only in a time trial.

Wheels Go Round and Round

Every Tour bike has two wheels, but what wheels riders use is as diverse as cyclists' personalities. Like bike frames, cycling shoes, attire, and various other equipment, riders use wheels provided by sponsoring manufacturers. Rims, tires, and spokes are far more advanced than they were during the Tour's infancy; in fact, because of rim strength and new technology, wheels no longer need as many spokes for support as they used to.

What wheels riders use is determined by weather conditions and, to some degree, by team and rider preference. Tour cyclists primarily use two types of wheels:

- **Spoked wheels:** Depending on weather conditions and course terrain, riders use traditional spoked wheels with as many as 20 spokes. But cyclists can also use spoked wheels with three carbon spokes (see Figure 9-1) to help with aerodynamic efficiency. Spoke wheels are lighter than disc wheels, so they're also used in uphill time trials.

- **Solid-disc wheels:** These wheels are reserved for use during individual time trials and team time trials. The discs are made of carbon fiber, and they're the best way for riders to reduce resistance in low-wind conditions.

Figure 9-1: U.S. Postal Service Cycling Team time trial bicycles with Hed wheels.

A windless day is a perfect time trial day. Solid disc wheels provide ideal aerodynamics for time trials. But on windy days, solid disc wheels often prove ineffective, because they act like sails. Cyclists opt for tri-spoke wheels or traditional spoke wheels during windy time trials.

Shifting Gears

Like driving a manual-transmission car, cyclists shift their bike gears depending upon terrain, the speed they're trying to achieve, and their preferred *cadence* (pedal strokes per minute). This section explains how shifting works.

A rider uses a low gear to increase his cadence and a high gear to decrease his cadence. A higher gear at the same cadence increases speed.

Cogs, cassettes, and cranks

Seemingly as many varieties of cogs, cassettes. and cranks are marketed as there are riders in the *peloton.* Tour bikes generally have ten cogs, and they are collectively known as the *cassette.* A *cog,* also known as a *chain ring,* is attached to the *crank,* the shafts attached to the pedals.

Each cog has *teeth;* the smallest cog has 11 and the largest 27, which is used for extremely steep mountains. The chain ring on the front of the bike has from 39 to 53 teeth.

Lance Armstrong often opts to use a 39×21 (which means 39 teeth on the front cog and 21 teeth on the rear cog) while climbing; Australian sprinting specialist Robbie McEwen uses a 53×11 combination in mass sprints at the end of flat road stages.

Cranks, also available in different metals and sizes, are two arms to which pedals are attached. They're particularly important because power from rider' legs is directly transferred to the bike via cranks.

What gears do they use?

Depending upon a rider's size and weight and the terrain he's riding, gear ratios can vary greatly. Riders like Jan Ullrich, the 1997 Tour winner, enjoy *pushing* gears to sustain a slow, steady cadence, particularly while climbing. Lance Armstrong, who has climbed Tour mountains with Ullrich in many Tour stages, prefers smaller climbing gear ratios by spinning, which means he's pedaling at a faster cadence.

While there are several preferred gearing standards, how big or small gears riders shift into is a personal choice. Tour riders can switch into cogs with gears with a low rating (the number of teeth) and into the mid-50s. The higher the number of the front cog and the lower the number of the back cog, the more the difficult the pedal stroke.

Use a triple, be a wimp?

Most Tour bikes are equipped with two front chain rings, which is the same as the two front cogs. Occasionally, riders have added a third ring — a *triple* — in the Tour of Italy and Tour of Spain. But those two Grand Tours include mountain stages with more severe gradients than the Tour de France. Adding a third chain ring can increase the possibility of mechanical problems, because it further complicates gearing.

A Helmet Is a Helmet — Not!

Designing and engineering helmets for Tour riders is serious business. Designers are hoping to save a gram or two of weight, offer a sleek aerodynamic design, allow for excellent extreme ventilation, and protect the rider in the event of an accident. Teams work closely with their helmet sponsors, getting helmets as close to perfection as possible. What you may think of as "just a helmet" is actually the work of skill and art to a team that wants a cutting-edge advantage.

Looking back at helmet history

In the 1880s, when cyclists rode high-wheel bicycles, their head protection was sometimes a pith helmet. Protective headgear evolved into beanies, called *hairnets,* made of padded leather strips that protected mostly cyclists' ears.

Bowl-shaped polystyrene foam helmets and helmets with hard shells and foam liners were the next phase of helmets marketed. Rounded, bowling-ball shapes allowed helmets to skid along paved surfaces, minimizing impact. In the mid-1980s, manufacturers such as Giro began experimenting with aerodynamic designs and hi-tech materials. A new era in bicycle helmets emerged, with strong advocates for and against using helmets for cycling safety.

Dude, you gotta wear 'em!

Wearing a helmet is no longer an option or riders. As discussed in Chapter 5, in 2003, *Union Cycliste Internationale* set mandatory regulations for wearing helmets during races. Many riders disagree with this rule, which was imposed after the death of a racer during Paris-Nice, a renowned spring classic race.

Andrei Kivilev, of Kazakhstan, riding for Cofidis, fell about 40 kilometers (24.8 miles) from the second stage finish. It was a slow-speed crash: Some said it was caused by touching wheels; others thought he was looking down while adjusting his earpiece or sunglasses. It was sudden, swift, and unexpected, with not one second to react or prepare. The crash didn't seem serious, and the *peloton* raced on. But Kivilev fell, taking full impact on his face. He wasn't wearing a helmet, and he eventually died from his injuries, leaving a young wife and six-month-old son. The *peloton* was devastated by his loss, and many riders wept openly before starting the next morning. Riders decided to neutralize the third stage in the rider's honor. A moment of silence was followed by a solemn procession along the race route to the finish line. Physicians have speculated that Kivilev may have lived if he had been wearing a helmet, and his death further continues the Tour de France helmet controversy.

Union Cycliste Internationale also tried in 1991 to initiate a compulsory helmet rule. Ironically, riders at that time staged a protest during the Paris-Nice race, so the sport's governing body backed off from the issue.

Even with the new rule, there are a times when helmets can be removed: Riders, at their own risk, can remove their helmets for the final climb, in order to remain cool, if the finish is on an uphill section or at the top of the hill, under the following conditions:

- ✔ The uphill section is at least 5 kilometers (3 miles) long.
- ✔ The helmet is not removed before the start of the uphill section

While watching the Tour, take notice of who's wearing his helmet and when. You don't often see a rider tossing away his helmet; instead, the team car guards expensive headgear. Helmets may be custom fit, and a team may not have many extra helmets in the team truck.

Protection versus ventilation

A major challenge in helmet design is providing maximum protection as well as maximum ventilation. A racer sweating along roads in France in sweltering heat needs maximum ventilation from his helmet. Airflow is critical to carrying away body heat in summer temperatures and moisture in cold temperatures. In fact, research by the Bicycle Helmet Safety Institute shows that a well ventilated helmet is cooler in summer heat than a bare head. This is why many helmets are advertised by the number of vents they contain.

But a rider also needs maximum protection from crashes. A sleek, 240-gram, 18-vent helmet provides excellent ventilation, but it also needs to have maximum impact performance. A helmet has to be designed to manage the crash energy and protect the head and brain. Having larger vents and lighter helmet shells doesn't always provide maximum protection.

 Ask a pro rider what he wants in a helmet, and he'll likely say he's looking for a model with minimum weight and maximum ventilation. But riders wear sponsor helmets, regardless of ventilation or weight.

Time trial helmets: Aerodynamics is everything

Polycarbonate shells, painstakingly designed and tested in wind tunnels, are standard for time trial helmets. Sculpted designs, experimentations with materials and textures, and lab testing at every stage all help to produce a helmet that can claim a time trial win.

Ventilation is not usually a priority for time trial helmets, given the short length of the races, nor do helmets offer much impact protection. Because micro-thin shells aren't lined, ventilation comes from air circulating under the shell, but it's in lieu of impact protection.

Doing the daily laundry

Riders are issued only a minimal amount of team clothing. They don't have an unlimited number of jerseys and shorts. As soon as riders return to their hotel, they put dirty laundry into mesh bags and place the bags outside their room doors. A *soigneur* picks up bags and heads for the nearest Laundromat. All clothing and mesh bags are labeled with each rider's name. You won't see an exhausted, hungry rider with a hectic evening schedule washing his socks in a motel bathroom.

For non-riding occasions, each rider receives casual pants, shirts, sweat suits, and tennis shoes with sponsor logos.

The town of Saint-Flour, in the south-central part of France, welcomes the 2004 Tour de France with this painted mountainside.

Tour supporters canvas the start/finish lines, handing out everything from yellow wristbands from the Lance Armstrong Foundation to food.

Tour sponsor Crédit Lyonnais warms up the crowd before the riders finish Stage 3 in Wasquehal in the 2004 Tour de France.

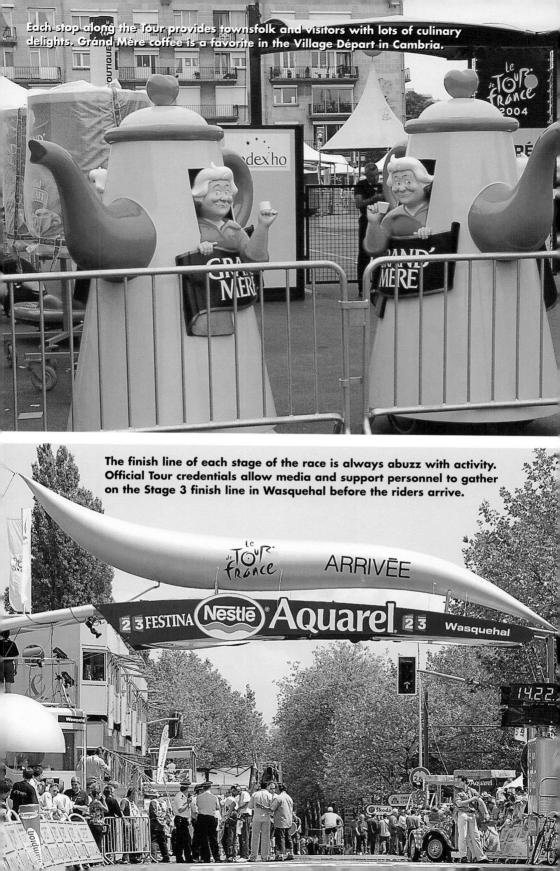

Each stop along the Tour provides townsfolk and visitors with lots of culinary delights. Grand Mère coffee is a favorite in the Village Départ in Cambria.

The finish line of each stage of the race is always abuzz with activity. Official Tour credentials allow media and support personnel to gather on the Stage 3 finish line in Wasquehal before the riders arrive.

Lance Armstrong talking with Johan Bruyneel, Directeur Sportif -- cycling's equivalent of a head coach -- before a time trial in the 2004 Tour de France.

The handlebars, brakes, and gear shift levers, along with the rider's arm positioning, are all optimized to take advantage of the aerodynamics needed to gain speed and shave time.

Riders bunched together like Jan Ullrich (left), Alessandro Petacchi (center), along with others, form the peloton, the main group of riders.

Riders can achieve speeds of up to 30 mph on the Champs Élysées in Paris, the final stage of the Tour.

Lance Armstrong on the podium in Paris for his historic sixth consecutive win at the 2004 Tour de France.

Sleek, aerodynamic designs with minimal wind profile and wind drag are optimal time trial helmet benefits. Time trial helmets weigh about 8 ounces. Their design includes an aerodynamic tail that extends in the rear to provide unfettered air flow over riders' backs, and their unique shape looks like an outer-space creation (see Figure 9-2). These newfangled shapes are excellent for time trials and are standard in European races. But engineers in the United States are working on new models, because they believe tear-dropped-shaped helmets can snag on roads in crashes and cause severe head and neck twists. Louis Garneau and Shain are companies offering time trial helmets approved for use in U.S. racing.

Figure 9-2: Time trial helmets hanging in the U. S. Postal Service Cycling Team truck.

Wearing a Kaleidoscope of Kits

A *kit* is a rider's uniform. A rider's full kit, that is, the entire ensemble of clothing he'll wear during the year, includes the following:

- **Jersey:** A *jersey* is a top that riders wear. Riders wear team jerseys (adorned with numerous sponsor logos) that are form-fitting, so that nothing flaps around to cause wind resistance.

Jersey material is breathable, wicks moisture away from the body, is soft and supple, and doesn't chafe. A jersey usually has three back pockets to hold food, a water bottle, a rolled-up vest, jacket or gloves, or whatever else the rider needs to carry.

✔ **Shorts:** Shorts are made of Lycra/Spandex for flexibility and comfort, with padding that wicks moisture away from the skin. Riders are particular about the fit and comfort of their shorts. A rough seam can feel like a saw blade after hours in the saddle, and resulting sores can jeopardize a rider's ability to remain in the race.

✔ **Bib:** A *bib* is a one-piece top/short combinations. The top portion looks like a tank top, while the bottom is just like cycling shorts. Bibs are made of moisture-wicking mesh; that is, material that draws moisture away from the skin.

✔ **Jackets and vests:** Jackets and vests are made of windproof, water-resistant, breathable fabrics and can be either *thermal* (warm) or just wind-proof. They're always covered with sponsors' logos. Jackets are often vented with mesh under the arms. *Rain jackets* are (you guessed it) windproof, waterproof, and breathable. Arm warmers and leg warmers are used for cold weather riding and are made of similar high-tech materials.

✔ **Caps (riding and knit):** In cold weather, a rider may wear a knit cap or a headband made of thermal fabric that insulates and wicks away moisture. A knit cap has to fit snugly under the helmet. *Riding caps* are beanies with mini-visors, plastered with sponsor logos. Considering recent helmet regulations, riders mostly wear caps on training rides, but some riders occasionally wear caps under their helmets.

✔ **Thermal undershirt:** Riders wear layers of clothing for warmth; most riders prefer exterior layers that they can easily remove while riding, given the extreme weather changes during Tour routes. So, if a rider chooses to wear a thermal undershirt, he wears it for the entire stage — that's why a fabric that's breathable, moisture-wicking material, such as CoolMax, is essential. Riders generally wear a thermal undershirt when they know the entire racing day will feature cold weather.

✔ **Gloves:** Gloves are for crash protection, for warmth, and to avoid having sweaty hands slip off the handlebars. Most riders wear traditional, fingerless (called *half-gloves*) when riding. But in extremely cold weather conditions, riders wear weatherproof, full-finger gloves.

Gloves are designed and manufactured using innovative technology, such as carbon infused leather, thermal windproof fabric, breathable mesh, and/or moisture-wicking microfibers.

Many gloves offer padding against vibration and have nonslip material on fingers and palms.

✔ **Shoes and socks:** Cycling shoes are made with lightweight, high-quality materials, such as carbon fiber. Quality workmanship and utmost attention to fit is essential for performance and comfort. State-of-the-art, high-tech engineering provides perfect design and fit. Shimano, one well-known cycling company, believes cycling shoes are the most critical interface between rider and bike.

Socks worn by each team vary, based on the team sponsor's product and personal preference. In general, cycling socks are made of breathable fabric, like CoolMax, Micro Denier, or Micro Supreme, that wicks moisture away. Cycling socks need to be soft, form-fitting, and with no friction that could cause sores.

✔ **Booties:** *Booties* (sock-like boots that fit over the top of a rider's shoes) have two functions: aerodynamics and warmth. Booties are almost always used in time trials, and they're lightweight, sleek, and help minimize wind resistance. Riders all wear booties with unified color and sponsors' logos. Cold weather brings out team booties, too, even during non-time-trial races. Booties come in different thicknesses and materials for various weather conditions.

But when you hear someone refer to a *rider's kit,* it usually means team attire he's wearing. All team members wear the same kit, in team colors. Shoes are the exception. A cycling shoe manufacturer usually sponsors an individual rider, not an entire team, so you may see George Hincapie wearing Carnac shoes, while his teammate Lance Armstrong is wearing Nike shoes.

Sponsors' logos usually provide basic color schemes for team kits, and often become part of team nicknames. For example, Team Saeco was known as the Red Train and the U.S. Postal Service Cycling Team (now the Discovery Channel Pro Cycling Team) was known as *Le Train Bleu,* or the Blue Train.

Cap frenzy

During the Tour de France, Europeans, especially French and Belgian cycling fans, covet little beanie-like team caps. If you in any way look like you might be with a team or sponsor, you may be asked, *"casquette? casquette?"* Casquette means cap, and a new team cycling cap is a prized possession for fans.

Lots o' stuff

What do riders do with all the stuff — from jerseys to booties — when they change teams or get new gear? A group of professional riders in Boulder, Colorado, decided to band together and sell their old stuff. You probably won't find any Tour de France goodies on this site, but check out www.theprosstuff.com for bargains and up-to-date news and gossip.

Weightless is the goal

From jerseys to shoes to water bottle cages, one goal and obsession for a rider is to reduce weight. Decreasing weight and wind resistance for a rider's kit may give a few seconds' advantage and result in a spot on the podium.

Given that some Tour de France wins are measured in seconds, a lightweight, form-fitting, minimal-wind-drag jersey can give a 30-second advantage during a 140-kilometer stage. It sounds trivial for a three-week race, but 30 seconds can give a winning margin between two riders. So designers create lightweight microfiber materials that wick moisture away from rider's bodies and fit tightly to reduce wind resistance. Three pockets are placed strategically on the jersey's lower back to avoid wind drag. Jersey collars are designed to zip for a close, tight fit. Placement of seams is vital — preferably, there are no seams at all. And always, it's essential that moisture be carried away from the body.

Hundreds of thousands of dollars and thousands of hours are spent researching materials to provide perfect form, function, and performance. Nike, Trek, Specialized, Descente, Nalini, Vermark, and Giordana are all well known cycling research companies. These companies power the research and innovation in cycling clothing, manufacturing it with advanced product technology, including microfiber polyester materials that provide warmth, cooling, and windproof moisture control.

Riders are particularly concerned about engineering and materials for their shorts. Shorts (and jerseys, too) must be stretchy and comfortable for hours of wear, with no areas that bind or chafe. Shorts are lined with a soft padding known as *chamois* (pronounced shammy) to prevent chafing and irritation and to provide some padding for the long days in the saddle. A great variety and quality of chamois is available, and riders are constantly trying to find the perfect one. Riders also smear *chamois cream* on both their shorts and their bodies to prevent painful saddle sores. Keep in mind that the pain from saddle sores and boils can force riders to abandon the Tour.

Wearing time trial skinsuits

Time trial kits are special aerodynamic, one-piece skinsuits made with innovative, ultra-lightweight fabrics in varied textures. Some skinsuits have a dimpled texture that provides surface turbulence in certain areas of the rider's body, which increases speed. (This technique is also used for competitive swimmers' skinsuits, because research shows a skinsuit moves faster through air and water than bare skin does.) Skinsuits are seamless, or they have as few seams as possible that are strategically placed to prevent wind drag. Lightweight mesh may be used in some areas of the skinsuit for ventilation and cooling.

The goal is always to minimize weight and wind-drag. A standard team kit, no matter how form-fitting, creates substantial wind-drag: Seams, pockets, zippers, thick elastic at the bottom of the shorts all create wind-drag and weight for the rider. A skinsuit, on the other hand, weighs up to 30 percent less than a regular team kit.

When talk turns to time trial kits, it's inevitable the Nike–Lance Armstrong partnership comes up. Nike, as a major sponsor of the U.S. Postal Service Cycling Team (now called the Discovery Channel Pro Cycling Team), researched and engineered a skinsuit for Armstrong's 2004 Tour de France win. Nike's goal was an extremely lightweight, cooling, breathable suit with minimal wind drag. The skinsuit was almost 22 percent lighter than a standard Tour-issue skinsuit and was made available for all Tour classification leaders to wear, if they chose.

Getting that layered look

Tour cyclists have an advantage over recreational cyclists: Pros have a team car, so they can discard or add clothing as weather dictates. But even pros wear multi-layered kits. Advanced technology allows riders to wear layers of warm, lightweight clothing that can be easily removed while riding.

A fascinating sight is seeing a rider cruising along at 30 miles per hour while removing his *leg warmers* (tube-shaped pieces that slip over tights or bare legs) or *booties* (sock-like boots that fit over the tops of shoes). Another rider may lend a helping support hand, but more often than not, you see quite a one-man, one-leg balancing act.

Adding pizzazz to a skinsuit

Great Italian sprinter Mario Cipollini is known for his flamboyant style. He's famous for wearing outrageous attire, resulting in fines from race officials for violating uniform regulations. But Cipollini's sponsors, who've received massive additional publicity for Cipollini's style choices, gladly pay those fines.

Zebra stripes and an anatomically correct skeleton — both printed on aerodynamic skinsuits — and a king outfit, complete with cape and crown, are among Cipollini's most more famous Tour apparel selections.

In the 2004 Tour de France, the length of Cipollini's skinsuit violated official rules. But race photographers took plenty of images, and Cipolllini's sponsors' logos were prominently displayed. Still, in order to compete, the legs of Cipollini's skinsuit had to be shortened with scissors just prior to the day's stage.

Part IV
Watching the Race

The 5th Wave   By Rich Tennant

Tour de Living Room

©RICHTENNANT

Awesome move, Mom.

In this part . . .

We give you everything you need to know about attending the Tour or watching it at home. You find out how to book hotel rooms, travel with tour groups, and follow the race via Internet sites.

Chapter 10

Perfecting the Art of Spectating from Home

In This Chapter

▶ Being a TV couch potato

▶ Surfing for Tour information

▶ Impressing your friends with your knowledge of the Tour

*A*maury Sport Organization, the company that owns and organizes the Tour, estimates that, during the 2004 Tour, two billion people watched 2,400 hours of Tour television coverage on 78 channels in 170 countries. In addition, 7.7 million people visited the official Tour Web site. Live Tour coverage on the Internet is available on several sites, as are riders' and fans' Tour diaries, photos, and chat rooms.

This chapter gives you information and resources for watching the Tour at home and staying on top of all the news and results. From the printed word to cyber cycling, you find out how and where to get your Tour de France fix each day.

Watching in Your Pajamas

Maybe you're already hooked on the Tour de France, but have you tuned in to your favorite television channel to get your daily Tour fix? If not, tune in to a live broadcast on TV or on the Internet while you're in pajamas. Everyone else is fast asleep and you're wrapped in blankets, cheering on your favorite team in the wee hours of the morning. You're not jammed elbow-to-elbow at the finish line (see Figure 10-1), nor are you fighting crowds and traffic. Instead, you're just fighting sleep. Welcome to the world of a Tour de France couch-potato fan!

Figure 10-1: Crowds at the finish line in Namur during Stage 2 of the 2004 Tour de France.

Television coverage in the United States: Outdoor Life Network

Many cycling fans in the United States are fairly recent recruits to Tour television coverage. Television popularity has grown tremendously, though, thanks to the Lance Armstrong phenomenon. Armstrong's amazing cancer survival and his multiple Tour de France victories have captured the interest and enthusiasm of the American public.

The Tour seen 'round the world

Coverage of the Tour de France is worldwide; over two billion cycling fans have access to Tour de France television broadcasting. Here are the countries and channels listed by Tour de France organizers. Be aware that this list for your location may change over time. Always consult your local listings.

North America

✔ OLN (via cable or satellite)

✔ CBS, United States

✔ Canal Evasion, Canada

✔ TV Azteca and Televisa, Mexico

Central and South America

✔ ESPN International (via cable or satellite)

✔ TV 5 (via cable or satellite)

✔ Canal 4, El Salvador

✔ Globo TV, Brazil

✔ TVN, Chili

✔ Senal Columbia, Columbia

✔ Meridiano TV, Venezuela

Europe

✔ Eurosport (via cable or satellite)

✔ France Télévision 2/3, France

✔ RTBF and VRT, Belgium

✔ ARD and ZDF, Germany

✔ ITV, Great Britain

✔ TVE, Spain

✔ TV2 and Denmark TV, Denmark

✔ TSR, TSI, and DRS, Switzerland

✔ NOS, Holland

✔ RAI, Italy

✔ RTP, Portugal

✔ TV2, Norway

✔ ATV, Austria

✔ 7 TV, Russia

✔ Nova TV, Croatia

✔ 3 Program TV, Slovenia

✔ OBN, Bosnia

✔ TV 5 Riga, Latvia

Asia

✔ ESPN Star (via cable or satellite)

✔ Ten Sports (via cable or satellite)

✔ TV5 (via cable or satellite)

✔ Fuji TV and J Sky Sports, Japan

✔ CCTV, China

✔ TVB, Hong-Kong

✔ SCV, Singapore

✔ VTV, Vietnam

✔ SBS and Fox Sports, Australia

✔ Sky TV, New Zealand

Africa

✔ ESPN International (via cable or satellite)

✔ Supersport (via cable or satellite)

✔ CFI TV (via cable or satellite)

✔ TV5 (via cable or satellite)

✔ M-Net, South Africa

Outdoor Life Network (OLN) is the best source of television coverage in the United States for cycling fans. OLN provides some 300 hours of coverage during the three weeks of the Tour, plus additional Tour-related programming. OLN is seen via cable and satellite systems in the continental United States.

OLN Tour coverage begins in early morning with a pre-race show, and then switches to Live Tour coverage. Each day's stage is also shown in the prime time of evenings — a repeat of the morning show with additional coverage, a recap of the previous Tour stage, interviews, and Tour-related programming.

OLN also provides commentary from some of cycling's greatest names and personalities, who explain race strategies and nuances in an easy-to-understand manner. You get an analysis of events, find out about riders' personalities, and hear fascinating stories and facts about Tour history. Great graphics and a virtual map of the Tour route also keep you right on virtual sidelines.

During rest days, OLN may also offer a live chat room for cycling fans. You sign in, type in your Tour questions or comments, and read live responses from cycling personalities.

OLN has the schedule for Tour coverage on its Web site (`www.olntv.com`), but be sure to check your local listings for programming schedules for your time zone.

In addition to OLN, on Sunday mornings during the Tour, CBS broadcasts a one-hour recap as part of its weekend sports telecast.

Nearly constant television coverage in Europe (those lucky dogs)

Any American Tour de France fanatic would be in heaven to have the television coverage that's available in many European countries in July. France Télévisions, a huge conglomerate, is the voice and eyes of the Tour de France through television stations: France 2, France 3, and France 5. France 3 broadcasts directly to the Tour de France organization and provides live feeds syndicated to hundreds of television stations throughout the world, including the Outdoor Life Network (OLN) in the United States.

France 3 Television broadcasts every Tour stage, from start to finish. Hours-long programming for pre-stage activities and post-stage podium awards, plus interviews, satisfy even the most rabid cycling fan. France 3 race coverage is broadcast directly into the media room at the Tour, where it's combined with detailed race information and statistics displayed on dozens of television monitors. This race transmission is the source for a great deal of press coverage from the Tour de France.

Tour de France coverage is broadcast to over 170 countries via radio, television, streaming media on the internet, and mobile phone updates. France 3 also has a call-in 900 number with a poll for fans viewing the Tour.

Motorcycle units: Speeding down twisting roads

France 3 Television production and camera crews look like a small army as they move into action each day. Several France 3 production trucks, with thousands of feet of cables and wiring, assemble in the media technical parking area. Dozens of technicians swing into a chaotic, yet efficiently organized, plan to ensure that filming the day's stage will work flawlessly. France 3 has six to eight motorcycle units (called *motos*) with cameras and commentators that shoot close-ups of racers.

Riders often descend narrow, twisting mountain roads at such speeds that it's impossible for most vehicles to keep up with leading racers, so motorcycle units are the only source of live action transmission for television. Each camera person has to be really gutsy, because she or he sits or stands in these fast-moving motorcycles. It is extremely risky for drivers to maintain control with weighty camera equipment and an extra rider, even more so on wet roads.

Motorcycle units transmit race action to low-flying helicopters, which relay the footage to France 3 production units at the finish line. Hundreds of other radio and television trucks and equipment are parked in the technical area, all using the same live global feed.

Cybering the Tour

Easily accessible at all hours, the Internet provides a wealth of information, news, and history about the Tour de France. Some Internet sites featuring the Tour de France come and go, yet many sites run by newspaper or magazine corporations are steady and consistent. So although information, news, and gossip are at your fingertips, remember that everything you read is not necessarily accurate or true. Cross-checking with several internet sources is always a good idea.

Web sites listed here are valid at the time of this writing, but sites disappear without notice. Unfortunately, you may find that some links are now nonexistent.

Fan sites

Cycling fans are no different than fans of any other sport. They're fiercely loyal and supportive of their favorite riders and teams. In Italy, fans are called *tifosi*. They're fervent in their adoration of favorite racers. *Tifosi* are everywhere in the world for their favorite cycling heroes. A half-million fans lining along the road to L'Alpe d'Huez are the best (and sometimes, the worst) examples of *tifosi*.

You can find dozens of Internet sites for many great cyclists, both present and past, by using an Internet search engine. Again, a warning that fan sites can be very transient, so you may receive a "Page Not Found" message, but many sites are owned by teams or riders and are long-lasting.

Here is a listing of Web sites for the cyclists (listed alphabetically) who placed in the top ten of the General Classification at the last Tour (as of the writing of this book). If a cyclist doesn't have an individual site, the team site is listed.

- ✔ **Lance Armstrong:** www.thepaceline.com and www.lancearmstrongfanclub.com
- ✔ **Jose Azevedo:** www.discoveryproteamfans.com
- ✔ **Ivan Basso:** www.ivanbasso.it
- ✔ **Andreas Kloden:** www.andreas-kloden.com
- ✔ **Levi Leipheimer (team site):** www.rabobank.nl
- ✔ **Francisco Mancebo (team site):** www.illesbalears-banesto.com
- ✔ **Oscar Pereiro (team site):** www.phonak-cycling.ch
- ✔ **Carlos Sastre (team site):** www.team-csc.com
- ✔ **Georg Totschnig:** www.totschnig.cc
- ✔ **Jan Ullrich:** www.janullrich.de

Team sites

Most professional teams have complex, lush sites produced by major sponsors. Sites give a bio for all the riders on the team, show a team photo gallery, give the team racing schedule, and offer the latest team news. Sites have links to their sponsors or other related links.

Their hearts are beating for you

Polar Heart Rate Monitors sponsors several teams at the Tour de France. During the Tour, you can log in to the Polar Heart Rate Web site http://tdf.polar.fi/tdf/heartrates.html and follow heart rates of selected racers on teams like T-Mobile, Liberty Seguros, and Rabobank while they're racing stages in the Tour.

Cybering in other languages

Some of the best Tour sites are in languages other than English. Have a linguistic adventure by visiting sites from other nations using these translation tools:

- Newspaper translation: www.newstran.com
- Text or Web page translation: www.google.com/language_tools or www.babelfish.altavista.com
- Text translation: www.dictionary.com

Many team sites offer a guest book, where you can give congratulations or leave messages for team members. Team sites may also offer great diaries by their team riders. Some team sites may offer the option of purchasing team items or memorabilia. You can even sign up for latest news with an e-mail list on some team sites.

Here are links to team sites of the top teams, in order of their finish at the last Tour (as of the writing of this book).

- **T-Mobile:** www.t-mobile-team.com
- **U.S. Postal Presented by Berry Floor:** www.thepaceline.com
- **Team CSC:** www.team-csc.com
- **Illes Balears-Banesto Santander:** www.illesbalears-banesto.com
- **Quick-Step Davitamon**: www.quickstep-davitamon.com
- **Phonak Hearing Systems:** www.phonak-cycling.com
- **Rabobank:** www.rabobank.nl
- **Credit Agricole:** www.credit-agricole.fr
- **Brioches La Boulangere:** www.brioches-laboulangere.com

Tour blogs: Here today, gone tomorrow

Tour *blogs* (Web logs) are a fun way to see what other people think about Tour happenings. A blog is basically somebody's journal or diary, posted on the Internet. A few writers are pretty consistent with their Tour blogs, but as always, blogs come and go. Blogs are free, so you can sign up for one and do your own Tour Blog!

Here are a few blogs that have been around for a while — some are really good, with news clips and explanations about events and strategies. Also included are some Tour diaries that are entertaining and have first-rate information. Will they exist when you try to find them? Who knows, but it's worth taking a look.

- ✔ **Tour de France 2004:** www.tdfblog.com. This is a well-done, first-class blog by Frank Steele.
- ✔ **Scott Daubert's diaries:** www.trekbikes.com/diaries/ scott.jsp. It's not exactly a blog, but there's good stuff here!
- ✔ **Mike Jacoubowsky Tour diaries:** www.chainreaction.com/ tdf.htm. This site gives you great Tour diaries from a bike shop owner and Tour fan.
- ✔ **Logos Tour 2004:** www.w3os.nl/logos/tour/tour2004. Gives lots of info and links to resources.
- ✔ **Velogal's Race Blog:** www.velogal.blogspot.com. Offers postings during cycling season.

Forums and chats: At your own risk

Finding a forum or chat room for the Tour de France is easy in July — cyberspace is filled with Tour talk. Many sites that deliver cycling news also offer forums.

While both forums and chat rooms tend to be user-friendly and welcome newbies, some chat rooms and forums can be pretty rough on newcomers. Check 'em out first before you sign up. You'll find one that's right for your Tour questions or comments.

Here are a few sites that have interesting and active forums about the Tour de France during cycling season. There are many more.

- ✔ **Active.com:** www.active.com
- ✔ *Bicycling:* www.bicycling.com
- ✔ **Cyclingforums.com:** www.cyclingforums.com
- ✔ **Cycling Plus:** www.cyclingplus.co.uk/forum (United Kingdom)
- ✔ **Daily Peloton:** www.dailypelotonforums.com
- ✔ **Eurosport:** www.eurosport.com
- ✔ **France 2 Television:** www.forums.france2.fr/tdf
- ✔ **Outdoor Life Network:** www.olntv.com

  ✔ **Sportal.com:** `www.sportal.com.au` (Australia)

  ✔ **Velo Club du Net:** `www.velo-club.net` (France)

  ✔ *VeloNews:* `www.velonews.com`

E-mail updates

Want to get Tour information and results on your laptop or PC? How about signing up for e-mail updates at the following Web sites, which are either e-zines, newsletters, or some combination of the two.

  ✔ **Tour de France Times:** `www.byjamesraia.com`

  ✔ **Tour de France News:** `www.tourdefrancenews.com`

  ✔ *Procycling Magazine:* `www.procycling.com`

  ✔ **Sport.fr:** `www.sport.fr`

  ✔ **Eurosport:** `www.eurosport.com`

  ✔ *L'Equipe:* `www.lequipe.fr`

Searching for Tour info and photos

Searching the Internet for news and images about the Tour de France will result in thousands and thousands of listings. Remember to enclose the phrase **"Tour de France"** in quotations, and your results will be more specific.

Getting the picture

Graham Watson is a legendary Tour de France photographer who received his first Tour press credential in 1981. He has numerous Tour photography books, merchandise, and beautiful images on his site (`www.grahamwatson.com`). Other famous Tour photographers include Cor Vos (`www.corvos.nl`) and Sirotti (`www.fotoreporter.sirotti.it`).

Seasoned Tour reporters and authors include Samuel Abt, Frankie Andreu, Graeme Fife, Rupert Guinness, Andrew Hood, Phil Liggett, James Raia, Bob Roll, Sal Ruibal, James Startt, and John Wilcockson. (Okay, two of those names are your friendly authors of this book, so we're tooting our own horns just a bit!) Read articles by these writers for entertaining, well-written Tour information.

The following are some major search engines on the Internet:

- **Google:** www.google.com
- **Yahoo!:** www.yahoo.com
- **KartOO:** www.kartoo.fr
- **Dogpile:** www.dogpile.com
- **AltaVista:** www.altavisa.com

In addition, you can also sign up for free Tour de France Google news alerts at www.google.com/alerts. Or sign up for free Yahoo! news alerts via cellphone, instant messenger, text messaging, or your PDA at www.yahoo.com.

Hearing Tour news live

Radio coverage of the Tour is extremely popular in France and other Tour-friendly countries. At the finish press area, one hears a cacophony of languages, as commentators from several countries are watching television monitors and broadcasting live feeds to radio stations in their countries.

Here's a sample list of radio stations offering live broadcasts or updates from the Tour:

- ABC: Australian Broadcasting
- BBC: United Kingdom
- COPE: Spain
- Der Speigel: Germany
- Europe 1: France
- Europe 2: France
- Radio 1: Netherlands
- Radio e Televasio de Portugal
- Radio MARCA: Spain
- Radio Netherlands
- Radio Vlaanderen: Belgium
- RAI: Italy
- RCN: Columbia
- RTE: Ireland
- RTVE: Spain

Internet sites for up-to-the-minute Tour race news include the following:

- ✔ **Official Tour de France site:** `www.letour.fr`
- ✔ **Cyclingnews:** `www.cyclingnews.com`
- ✔ *VeloNews:* `www.velonews.com`
- ✔ **Eurosport:** `www.eurosport.com`
- ✔ **Daily Peloton:** `www.dailypeloton.com`

These sites carry live feeds with minute-by-minute updates from the Tour at every stage. You get race details and results as they happen. For Tour de France headlines and stories, try `www.topix.net/cycling/tour-de-france`.

You can also sign up for news alerts on your cell phone. *SMS updates,* short for *Short Message Service,* are text messages that arrive on your cellphone. For example, both the T-Mobile team site (`www.t-mobile-team.com`) and the Paceline team site (`www.thepaceline.com`) offer SMS updates through different cellphone service providers. Eurosport also provides SMS updates, as does OLN, Fox Sports, RadSport-News, News24.com, ARD/ZDF, and France Telecom. Many news sites offer SMS service, too. You sign up for free, but you incur usual cellphone charges for minutes used.

Finally, check out these sites for live streaming video coverage: OLN Television (`www.olntv.com`), Eurosport (`www.eurosport.com`), and the Official Tour de France Web site (`www.letour.fr`; note that you can choose the English version by clicking a small flag icon on the bottom right of the screen).

Sounding Like an Expert

Watch out — you may really get hooked on this Tour stuff. If you do, you'll want to find out as much as you can and talk with people about the Tour. Maybe you've been in a chat room or forum or out on a club ride, and you want to sound like a seasoned Tour fan. This section gives you tools you can use to impress the gang.

Classic, unknown, and weird cycling movies

When cycling movies are mentioned, it's usually the classic 1979 film *Breaking Away.* Along with *American Flyer,* these two movies offer a limited choice for cycling-starved fans during winter months.

Googling around a couple of years ago, one of your authors discovered a Web site treasure that lists over 100 cycling films. You'll need to Google the phrase **cycling films big list** to find this site by Séamus King (the URL is too long and ugly to list here). The site is well worth the Google search.

Looking for a charming film? *Belleville Rendez-Vous,* also called *The Triplets of Belleville,* is a film by Sylvain Choumet. Also explore the Web site for this movie at www.bellevillerendezvous.com.

Cycling magazines

Glossy cycling photos and insightful interviews, right in your hands, are just a subscription away. Here is a listing of only a few print magazines of many that are available:

- ✔ *Bicicletta:* www.cycling.it
- ✔ *Bicycling:* www.bicycling.com
- ✔ *Cycle Sport Magazine:* www.cyclesportmag.com
- ✔ *Cycling Plus:* www.cyclingplus.co.uk
- ✔ *Cycling Weekly:* www.cyclingweekly.co.uk
- ✔ *Cyclisme:* www.cyclismag.com
- ✔ *L'Equipe:* www.lequipe.fr
- ✔ *Pedal:* www.pedalmag.com
- ✔ *ProCycling:* www.procycling.com
- ✔ *Rad Touren:* www.radtouren.de
- ✔ *Ride Magazine:* www.ridemedia.com.au
- ✔ *Road Magazine:* www.h3publications.com
- ✔ *Velo Magazine:* www.velomag.com
- ✔ *VeloNews:* www.velonews.com

Getting maps and marking the route

Getting into fine details about routes for each stage of the Tour is another way of knowing what's happening. Many fans who attend the Tour mark routes for every stage of the Tour, even if they're viewing from only one spot along the road. Try it — get a road map of France and a marker pen, and trace the route map (see Figure 10-2) as if you were going there yourself. That way, even if you can't be there in person, you can still map out the Tour and be in the know about where the race is going.

Figure 10-2: Route map of the 2005 Tour de France.

Speaking the language

Knowing a few key words and phrases in French is helpful, even if you're spectating from home. And spending some fun time to learn a few basics goes a long way toward increasing your enjoyment of the Tour.

We highly recommend *French Phrases For Dummies* by Dodi-Katrin Schmidt, Michelle M. Williams, and Dominique Wenzel (Wiley). Pick up a copy and you'll be in the know, translating those French explanations and race cartoons on your screen with flair.

Knowing about the publicity caravan

Watching the *publicity caravan,* or *caravane publicitaire,* on television gives you a taste of what it's like to be there in person. (See Chapter 11 for more on making the trip.) Basically, what spectators see is a gigantic parade of sponsor vehicles that precedes the race by an hour or so. Take a look at Figure 10-3.

Figure 10-3: The publicity caravan lines up under threatening skies.

Madness and Mardi Gras mixed together

Slowly winding along the route, this bizarre caravan of some 200 sponsor vehicles travels the entire stage route each day, including steep and winding mountain roads. From tiny one-person cars to semi-trucks, this collection of Mardi Gras–like floats stirs fans into a frenzy.

Looking like a Rose Bowl parade without flowers, floats are giant icons for Tour sponsors. It's an onslaught of bigger-than-life sponsor representations: huge fiberglass PMU (Paris Mutuel Urbain, a French off-track betting system for horse-racing) jockeys riding horses, a giant Michelin doughboy, the 10-foot-tall Crédit Lyonnais lions, music blaring from loudspeakers, and nonstop dancers tethered to floats for safety.

Nestlé Aquarel, a major sponsor, has a fire truck float with "firemen" who spray the crowd with fire hoses and dangle bottles of water from fishing poles to tantalize hot, thirsty crowds. Aquarel distributes about 14,000 water bottles a day to teams and fans.

Wanting tacky things

Crowd frenzy is generated by trinkets that sponsor floats throw to pleading fans. Key rings, tiny packets (containing candy, sausage, or cheese), *musette* bags (bags given to riders containing food), rain hats, plastic trinkets, pens, red-checkered caps, and bottles of water are randomly thrown to crowds. People are delighted to catch these trinkets, grabbing and shoving to grab items mid-air, and they display their prizes with glee.

Knowing sponsor factoids

Crédit Lyonnais, a humongous international banking and financial institution, is a major sponsor of the Tour, sponsoring the *maillot jaune,* or yellow jersey (see Chapter 3). The company distributes signature yellow caps and goodie bags everywhere along the Tour route. Crédit Lyonnais also has a traveling bank that accompanies the Tour, and it's the only bank in France open on Bastille Day, a French national holiday.

Supermarché Champion is an enormous supermarket chain in France that sponsors the red and white polka-dot jersey awarded for the best climber classification (see Chapter 3 for information on the various jerseys).

Nestlé Aquarel supplies the bottled water for the Tour (roughly a million bottles in three weeks), while Skoda is the official supplier for hundreds of official Tour vehicles. Skoda sponsors the white jersey, awarded to the Tour's best young rider.

PMU (Paris Mutuel Urbain) is the French national horse betting monopoly, in business since 1930, and sponsors the green jersey. PMU distributes giant green hands that fans love, but riders and photographers hate. Fun for fans, but riders get cuts and bruises from being pounded with the green hands during finishes. Photographers moan when dozens of giant green hands are blocking their perfect finish shot.

All of these sponsors participate in the publicity caravan, have a presence at the Village Départ, and are visible everywhere at the Tour. Millions of Euros flow into the Tour organization from sponsors, a necessity to keep the Tour thriving.

Chapter 11

Going to the Tour: A Brief Guide

The Tour de France organization estimates that 15 million spectators line the route each year as the Tour starts, winding around the countryside and in the mountains of France. Spectating at the Tour is an art as well as an exercise in assertiveness, endurance, and tenacity. Map-reading skills, driving skills, and language skills are a prerequisite to survival as a spectator.

The exhilaration of seeing the publicity caravan (see Chapter 10) and *peloton* (main group of riders) flashing by brings fans back year after year. For many cycling fans, it is the experience of a lifetime. This chapter is a brief overview of choices and options for planning a trip to the Tour.

On Your Own or with a Tour Group

Deciding how you're going to see the Tour de France is a decision you have to make months before the Tour starts in July. Reservations with Tour groups for the next year's Tour fill up almost immediately after the current Tour de France ends. Lodging in France is booked as soon as the following year's Tour route is announced at the end of October.

However, if you're adventurous and flexible, it's quite possible to head over to France at the last minute and view the race with last-minute lodging and travel arrangements. First-class or budget, with a tour group or on your own, the Tour can be your summer destination.

Picking it up fast

Enhance your Tour experience and lessen stress by doing your homework before you leave. Learning about France and its history, traditions, and customs will vastly increase your comfort level.

For example, July 14th is Bastille Day, a French national holiday. Nearly all businesses close to celebrate the holiday. Along the Autoroute, gas stations with convenience stores may be open, but in small villages, all business stops. Gas stations and shops are closed, and owners are on holiday. If you need to buy anything, you're probably out of luck.

In addition, memorizing a few key French phrases also facilitates your Tour de France experience, and a smiling "bonjour" (good day) goes a long way toward helping with communication difficulties.

Be sure to pick up a copy of three key *For Dummies* books as must-have travel resources:

- ✔ *France For Dummies* by Darwin Porter, Danforth Prince, and Cheryl A. Pientka (Wiley)

- ✔ *French Phrases For Dummies* by Dodi-Katrin Schmidt, Michelle M. Williams, and Dominique Wenzel (Wiley)

- ✔ *French For Dummies* by Dodi-Katrin Schmidt, Michelle M. Williams, and Dominique Wenzel (Wiley)

Selecting packaged tours

Letting someone else take care of all the details may be your idea of Tour heaven. If so, a tour package may be just right. If all you want to do is get your passport, change dollars to euros, and pack your luggage and bike, then signing up for a tour group is the way to go.

First, decide what kind of guided Tour experience you're looking for, because many tour groups allow you to ride for part of the trip (see Figure 11-1). Do you want to take your bike or travel totally on four wheels? If you're a cyclist and you're not going solo, is your companion a cyclist, or does he or she need non-cyclist accommodations? Do you want only a brief look at a stage or two, or do you want to see the entire three-week race? (If nothing else, your budget may make some decisions for you.)

Figure 11-1: Tour group bikes are parked after riding up La Mongie.

Finding a tour group that has space available may be more of a challenge — many groups fill up soon after the Tour de France finishes at the end of July. Do a little Internet research and ask friends or folks in your bike club. Word-of-mouth recommendations about tour packages are good, but try to get at least one second opinion, too.

Here are some questions to ask when looking at options at tour group options:

- How long has the company been in business and how many Tours has it done? Is the Tour de France its specialty? What is the specific route, and how much of the Tour will you really see? How many starts and how many finishes? Will you be viewing in villages or along the road in the mountains?

- Who will be leading the group and how many staff people does the company have? Are the guides experienced cyclists, and how many times has your particular guide done the Tour?

- What are the reservation and cancellation policies? What currency is required for payment? Are credit cards accepted? (If the company accepts credit cards, it may give you a little more protection.) When are deposits and balances due? What is the policy on return of deposits?

- Will the company provide you with contact info for references? Will they connect you with other guests in your area before the trip begins?

✔ What specifically does their tour package include, and what's not included? (Airfare is usually not included, but most companies do pick you up from the airport. Some meals may be included, and most lodging in France also includes a small breakfast.) Are snacks and water provided during the travel day?

✔ What is the form of transportation? Will it be motor coaches or passenger vans. Who will be driving and how are those drivers qualified?

✔ What about lodging? (Three-star hotels are standard for most tour groups.) Is it shared rooming? (Most groups are based on double occupancy.) What is the cost of a single room? How often will you change hotels during the trip?

✔ How many people will be in the tour group? How many bus or van loads of people? Will it be all adults or will there be families? Does the company make provisions for non-cyclists in the group? Will the tour be canceled if not enough people sign up?

✔ If you're cycling, what is the fitness level expected? How long will the rides be? Is there a support vehicle that will follow you, and will staff be riding along with you?

✔ Does the tour operator provide specific schedules, maps, and meeting points for each day? If you're cycling, will you receive a clear and detailed route sheet to your destination, as well as mechanical support?

Selecting a tour group that best fits your requirements and your budget can be time-consuming, but it is vital, so start early and choose carefully.

If you plan to cycle during your trip, make sure you choose a tour group that accommodates your level of cycling. For your enjoyment and safety, you want to ride at your level of skill and training. Make sure the tour operator understands your cycling experience and your training plan. And yes, you need to follow a training plan well in advance of cycling with a group at the Tour.

Cycling with celebrities

Many tour groups offer the opportunity to travel with a cycling celebrity who has ridden the Tour de France. Hearing first-hand stories, analysis of strategies, and getting the scoop on Tour riders adds fun and excitement to your experience.

Finding tour groups for le Tour

Searching for a tour operator for Tour de France guided trips can be a daunting task. The following list of well known tour groups is not all-inclusive, but it will help you get started.

- The Adventure Travel Company: www.tourdefrance.com.au
- Bikestyle Tours: www.bikestyletours.com
- Breaking Away: www.breakingaway.com
- DuVine Adventures: www.duvine.com
- Erickson Cycle Tours: www.ecycletours.com
- Graham Baxter Sporting Tours: www.sportingtours.co.uk
- Inside Track Tours: www.insidetracktours.com
- Marty Jemison Cycling Tours: www.martyjemison.com
- Steve Bauer Bike Tours with Chris Carmichael: www.stevebauer.com
- Trek Travel Cycling Vacations: www.trektravel.com
- Vélo Classic Tours: www.veloclassic.com
- Velo Echappé Cycling Trips: www.veloechappe.com
- Vélo Sport Vacations: www.velovacations.com
- Yellow Jersey Tours: www.yellowjerseytours.com

Former Tour cyclists Steve Bauer, Frankie Andreu, Kevin Livingston, Phil Anderson, Neil Stephens, and Marty Jemison offer tour groups. Having an opportunity to get first-hand tips from Chris Carmichael, Lance Armstrong's coach, while you ride could be the pinnacle of your Tour trip. If cycling with celebrities appeals to you, check out trips listed in the "Finding tour groups for le Tour" sidebar to see which tours offer a cycling star.

Doing the Tour on your own

Many cycling fans prefer to make their own travel plans or even head over to France without formal plans or reservations at all.

If you're the type who just throws jeans, T shirts, a toothbrush, and sleeping bag into a backpack and takes off, read no further. Grab your maps and head over to France for a great adventure! You'll meet many people doing spontaneous traveling and also seeing the

Tour. France is hospitable and generous to free-spirited Tour visitors, if you're polite and respectful of customs and traditions.

Planning your own trip takes many hours and includes determining your route, deciding where you want to view each stage, and finding lodging that will be compatible with your viewing plans and budget. Be sure to take into account your driving times and distances in kilometers from stage starts to finishes.

You can find the Tour route on the official Tour de France Web site at www.letour.fr. Click on the country flag for language options. There, you find a map of France, with town-to-town stage routes, a flash version of the route map, and detailed information about towns along the route.

You absolutely must have at least one detailed map of France; many folks use a large folding map and also a road atlas of France. We recommend Frommer's Road Atlas France, with detailed road mapping and town plans. Get out some highlighting pens and draw every stage of the Tour route in one color, and the route that you will drive or ride in another color. Spending time and paying attention to details at this stage pays off when you're driving the roads in France.

The first task is to get your flight reserved as soon as you can — start searching early in the calendar year, if possible, for the best deals. If you wait until the last minute, many airlines are booked for the day before the Tour begins and for the day after the Tour ends. If you decide to travel a few days before the Tour starts or after it ends, check online for better deals.

Don't put anything of value into your checked-in luggage. Unfortunately, items like expensive digital camera batteries, memory cards, or other items that you may not necessarily think of as "valuables" can end up missing from suitcases or backpacks. One American rider had his jersey, worn during a stage win (never washed and with his number still on it), stolen out of his backpack after his baggage was checked.

Ted Arnold's Self-Guided Tour de France

How about an expert helping hand with your Tour planning? Ted Arnold, an experienced guide for the Tour de France, writes a how-to-do-it-yourself book every year, and it's a gold mine of information.

To order this invaluable guide, go to www.velotainment.com. There, Ted also has an interesting and informative blog that you may want to check out.

If you're flying into Charles de Gaulle International Airport in Paris, and it's your first time, plan on a hectic, confusing, and chaotic experience. Allow extra time to ask questions, get lost, and stand in long lines with passport in hand at Customs. And be sure to grab a free luggage cart, because you may be walking a long way to the rental car area. Relax — you'll figure it all out and find your way.

Details, Details, Details

Taking care of all the major details — as well as the nitty-gritty ones — before you leave pays off when you've driven for hours and are stuck in traffic somewhere along the Tour route. Teams at the Tour have everything planned down to the nth degree, and so can you. This section shows you how.

Transportation details

Choosing your form of transportation is an important detail. Will you drive a vehicle while following the Tour route? If so, you may choose to rent a small economy car, a luxurious sedan with GPS, a camper van, or a large recreation vehicle.

If you're staying three weeks or longer, you may want to look at a *buy-back arrangement* (also called a *short-term lease*). Renault and Peugeot have programs where you "buy" a brand-new vehicle, drive it for unlimited miles, and then the company buys it back from you on your return date. What are the advantages in buy-back over renting?

- ✔ You have many choices from economy to luxury, depending on your budget.

- ✔ Your vehicle is also brand-new, and you can specify the model and even the color.

- ✔ The vehicle is fully insured with no deductible, and it's tax-free, which means no VAT (value-added tax) is charged.

This arrangement involves more paperwork, which is mailed to you and completed ahead of time, but the pick-up and return process is the same as for a rental vehicle. Auto Europe (www.autoeurope.com) handles the online or telephone reservations for Peugeot. Renault USA (www.renaultusa.com) handles the arrangements for the Renault buy-back program.

When you're seeing only a couple of stages that begin or end in a town with a train station, you'll find that traveling via rail is simple, fast, and efficient. SNCF is the French national railway. Trains run frequently and they stay on schedule; station attendants are helpful and speak some English.

You can take your boxed bicycles on designated trains in France (TGV and Corail are two French railroad companies), loading them into the luggage area. Porters or baggage carriers are available only in main stations like Paris, however, so what you take, you carry.

While hitch-hiking is a common form of Tour viewing, because of the inherent risks of hopping into cars with strangers, we don't recommend this. But during the Tour, standing along the route at an intersection or road junction with a handwritten sign telling where you're heading will almost always get you a lift. Use caution, exercise good judgment, and be aware that hitching is not a good idea for solo traveling.

Cyclists number in the thousands along Tour routes, so if you decide to bike to the stages, you'll have good company and great support. Choose your riding distance carefully and leave early. Maps that you purchased previously and highlighted (see the preceding section) will be your best friends now.

Race routes are often closed to cyclists very early by Tour security forces. When they say no, listen up — they mean it and won't hesitate to use force if you challenge them by continuing on your bike. Get off your bike and start pushing. It's a good idea to stick an extra pair of walking shoes in your daypack for unexpected hikes like this.

Lodging details

Another major detail is lodging — where, what kind, what price? Do you want to stay in hotels or motels, in hostels, in private homes, or campgrounds? Do you want to be as close as possible to the race start or finish or close to a viewing location that you have selected? What is your price range? How particular are you about your accommodations? (You get what you pay for in terms of lodging in France. Most reservations staff speak English in major motel chains.)

Hotels like Novotel, Sofitel, and Ibis are usually reliable choices for lodging. Hilton, Hyatt, Holiday Inn, Marriott, Best Western, and Choice Hotels International also have locations in France that are familiar to Americans. Most of these hotels are located along the Autoroute and are easy to find, and some of these places offer wi-fi or high-speed Internet access. You can make your reservations online for all these lodging choices.

You have many options for making reservations for lodging, but your best bets are via telephone or the Web. You can always start with a motel chain (for example, www.novotel.com). or you can use online sites like Orbitz (www.orbitz.com), Travelocity (www.travelocity.com), Expedia (www.expedia.com), and Yahoo! Travel (www.travel.yahoo.com). You may want to first check out an online lodging information site such as About.com (http://gofrance.about.com/od/lodging) or Lonely Planet (www.lonelyplanet.com). Frommer's is also a great place to start (www.frommers.com). Or perhaps you just want to kick back and have a travel agent do all the planning and make reservations for you.

Camping is a popular choice for cycling fans during the Tour de France. Campgrounds are plentiful, but they're usually packed full along the routes. You can try camping along roads, in front yards, anywhere you can find — anything goes during the Tour. But asking permission from the owner is always a good idea.

Finding more information

For more transportation and lodging info, check out the following:

Transportation: Many options are available for renting or leasing vehicles. Here is a short list of rental agencies:

- ✔ Auto Europe (rent, lease, buy back Peugeot or rent motor homes): www.autoeurope.com

- ✔ Renault EuroDrive (rent, lease, or buy back Renault): www.renaultusa.com

- ✔ Europecar (rent or lease): www.europecar.com

- ✔ Avis Car-Away (rent motor homes): www.aviscaraway.com

American auto rental companies also rent vehicles in France. Check online for rates and availability with Alamo, Budget, Dollar, Hertz, National, and Thrifty.

Lodging: Check online for the major American hotel chains that provide lodging in France. Many of the larger hotel groups can be found in France. English is spoken and be sure to call if you're arriving late.

Accor Hotels (www.accor.com) gives you many French hotel and motel options for reservations: Sofitel, Novotel, Mercure, Ibis, Etap, Red Roof Inns, and Formula 1 are all part of the Accor group. Tour de France teams stay in many of these hotels, so you may see team trucks and cars in the parking lots, and plenty of riders coming through the doors.

People set up campsites anywhere, but be aware that folks who are there first can be territorial. Be sure to ask whether they mind if you set up near them, and it's a good idea to make friends and allies so you can jointly protect your viewing spot.

Camping usually means partying — loud, boisterous drinking and partying into the wee hours for many folks. If you have a problem with noise or midnight revelry, perhaps camping won't work for you. It's difficult to find an isolated camping spot anywhere near a good viewing location, especially in the mountains.

Hostels are numerous in France, and if a Tour route goes near a hostel, you have an inexpensive option for lodging. Most rooms are shared, with two to four beds in a room, but some hostels have family rooms available. Check with Hostelling International at www. hiayh.org for international locations and membership information.

Other lodging options include bed and breakfast lodging or renting an apartment or villa. If you're staying in one location and want to spend time in a town or village, you can check out the official Gîtes de France Web site at www.gites-de-france.fr for lodging options. Note that you can view this Web site in English.

Where to Watch

Deciding where to watch each stage is a big deal, because it also impacts where you'll stay and how far you'll travel in a day. Everyone has his or her opinion about the most exciting viewing location. Seeing the race start, watching riders along the way, or being at the finish (as in Figure 11-2) — what's your ideal spot? How about what many cycling fans consider the ultimate spot — in the mountains?

Checking out the Village Départ

The Village Départ (vee-laj day-par) is the morning mecca for sponsors, celebrities, media, and select honored Tour guests. It's the place to be seen and to be a part of the in-crowd. Situated close to the start line, the Village is enclosed with a 7-foot-high wire fence. Unrelenting Tour Security Guards check every person who walks through. No credentials, no entry, no exceptions.

Figure 11-2: Crowds starting to arrive at the finish on La Mongie.

You may enter the Village only if you have proper credentials. VIP or sponsor guests have a certain color wristband that must be worn tightly enough to not allow it to be slipped off and handed through the fence to someone else. Other folks, like Tour staff members and Press, have credentials with a photo, worn around their necks on a lanyard.

Appearing like magic every morning near the start line, the Village is located in an adjacent field or park (see Figure 11-3). If there are statues and water fountains, all the better for some semblance of elegant ambiance. This one-day village usually covers an area about the size of a football field, but size varies depending on the town or village that's hosting the Tour start festivities.

In reality, parts and pieces of pointy-top white tents and the fencing are trucked in and assembled during wee hours. Construction may not be a miracle, but it's a well-planned daily project assembled like pieces of a Lego game. Tents, tables, chairs, banners, electrical equipment, cooking equipment, telephone, Internet access, a mini beauty salon, a Tour merchandise boutique, a news stand, a coffee shop, and a bar (yes, a bar in the morning) all pop up and are mobbed when the gates open. Food, freebies, and schmoozing are magnets for the rich and famous, and particularly for mooching media. Local specialties are cooked on-site for the hungry celebs.

Figure 11-3: The reception area of the Village Départ in Châteaubriant.

Imagine a few thousand very important, hungry people having to line up and individually show their access passes. It's quite the mob scene, and cutting in or crowding in front of other folks is the norm. Even celebs try to sneak in or bluff their way in. Tour security officers have seen and heard it all before. Nice try, but no dice.

Starts and finishes

Do you want to head out early to watch the teams arriving for the stage start? Seeing a cavalcade of buses and team cars laden with bicycles, waving to riders on the bus, and watching cycling heroes come down bus steps to fiddle with their bikes is a treat. You may be able to see your favorites warming up, and they may pass within arm's reach on their way to signing in.

Very often, though, the team area is off limits to crowds, so you may be standing behind fences and viewing from a distance. Other times, fans are only a few feet away. A few lucky people may get autographs when they're in the right place at the right time. Hearing the crowd roar when they see Lance Armstrong or Jan Ullrich can be worth being jammed in crowds so thick you can hardly move.

Do you want to arrive early and try to grab a spot right near the start line? An area immediately near the start is barricaded off for guests, sponsors, and press. But hanging on the fence as the huge *peloton* (main pack of riders) and hundreds of vehicles head down the course is thrilling. Riders in the *peloton* start slowly, so you may be able to spot your favorite rider in the melee.

If you want a good spot at the start line, allow traveling time to arrive about three hours before the start time. Parking is always a time-consuming nightmare. Be prepared to sit in traffic jams and walk a long way to the start line area.

You need to immediately grab your spot along the start line fence and not leave, or someone will instantly take over your place. If you head over to the team area to see the teams arrive without leaving someone to hold your spot, you'll likely end up standing behind a huge number of people when you return.

Maybe you want to catch a glimpse of the race passing by from a small village with some sharp turns on the route. You can then run into a nearby cafe or bar to view the remainder of the race. Shop owners are used to being jam-packed with Tour viewers and are pretty mellow about customers sitting for a long time at tables. Buy some food, snacks, or a *Coca* (Coke) to drink fairly often while you're taking up space. Cokes are expensive — maybe 3 euros, with no ice. But hey, you're watching the Tour courtesy of the owner's television.

Getting to the finish, or *Arriveé,* has the same logistics as getting to the start. Leave hours early and allow time to get through traffic jams, park, and make your way through the crowds early enough to find a choice spot. Time trial finishes, sprint finishes, and mountain finishes are so popular that folks take up their viewing spots hours — or even days — before race day.

The same rule applies to the finish line viewing as to watching starts — stay in your spot or someone will take it over. Even if you don't move, someone may elbow right in front of you, so you'll have to be assertive to stand your ground.

Some shop owners put televisions in their windows, so fans can stand on the sidewalk and watch. Folks in smaller villages will put a television on their windowsill to share the race with passersby. Chasing the Tour is a bonding experience, and the French love to share their Tour stories.

Partying and painting in the mountains

The ultimate viewing spot for many cycling fans is in the mountains. Spectators in recreation vehicles or who've been camping arrive three or four days early to grab choice spots on the slow, steep, elbow turns. Fans of certain teams stake out large territories, and woe be to anyone who tries to move in on their spots. For example, turn 7 on L'Alpe d'Huez is known as the *Dutch corner.*

If you want a viewing spot near the top, you need to drive up at least one night before, squeeze into a parking spot, and spend a cold night camping or sleeping in your car. But remember, it's usually an all-night party in most areas.

If you're arriving the morning of the mountain stage, you'll find roads closed hours early by Tour security. Only hikers or cyclists are allowed, so you may need to hike long distances to the best spots. Leave early — hours and hours early — park at the bottom, and start walking. Be sure to take clothing for all kinds of weather, plus sunscreen, rain gear, snacks, and plenty of water.

Tour de France mountain stages, whether Alps or Pyrenees, are a combination of Mardi Gras and mayhem. Huge national flags and signs, urging favorite riders to victory, float in the wind. Large groups of fans wearing orange, pink, or polka-dot T-shirts gather by team color along the roadside. Loud and proud is the name of the game for cycling fans.

Alcohol use is endemic to mountain stages — kids drinking wine is not an unusual site. Killing time by partying and boozing is par for the course, and by the time the race arrives, the crowds can be rowdy.

Painting the roads on the route, especially mountain stages, is a Tour tradition. One can see the history of the Tour by old, faded names on the pavement. Names, slogans, and epithets are painted on the roads, covering the pavement in some cases. Fans work diligently the day before with paint cans and brushes in hand. If you're painting, beware: Paint that doesn't dry can be a slippery danger to racers. And if you want your sign televised, keep it appropriate.

Surviving sleepovers and takeovers

Staking out your claim to a small piece of viewing real estate in the mountains can be tricky. You have this great spot, but when you wake up in the morning, someone has quietly moved in, right in front of you. Even worse, they are holding the spot for a huge group of other fans. What happens? Unless you've made an alliance with other neighbors, you either fight 'em or join 'em, usually the latter.

The Devil and other weird characters

You'll see folks in all varieties of dress and undress at the Tour. Men mooning their backsides and women flashing their breasts, Basque men dressed as busty women, people dressed as giant Stetson hats, guys carrying an inflated whale, cyclists wearing stuffed kiwis on their helmets, people in polka-dot outfits riding polka-dot painted horses, women slowly cycling by in halter tops and thongs. You'll see it all at the circus mountain stages of the Tour de France.

Probably the best known and most pungent character is Didi Senft, best known as the Devil, and he jumps around beside the riders in any area that's likely to be covered by television cameras or print photographers. Senft has appeared every year since 1993. He has sponsors, wears a devil outfit, and carries an oversize pitchfork. And an oversized bike that is about 15 feet high — and rideable! He's popular with fans, but most riders avoid him.

Early bird gets the front row

Sleeping late will not get you a good view of the race, unless you've found a room overlooking the race course. Waking up and leaving early is what you do to get great views of the action. For example, watching the final stage on the Champs Élysées means heading to the course very early. Racers don't arrive until late afternoon, but most fans are holding their spot before 9:00 in the morning.

Getting photos and autographs

The most sought-after signature in recent Tours is Lance Armstrong's. He's mobbed the minute he walks out of the team bus (see Figure 11-4). He can't possibly accommodate every request, though, so only the lucky few receive that prized autograph.

Figure 11-4: Autograph seekers swarm the U.S. Postal Service Cycling Team bus in Wasquehal.

Other riders may be more accessible, but the best time to ask for autographs is at race start. Riders are fresh, relaxed, and rested — they are more likely to stop and give autographs on their way to or from the sign-in. But not many riders stop to pose for pictures — it takes too long and they get bombarded with too many other requests.

Many fans besiege the riders at the finish line, but that's really bad timing. Riders are exhausted, hungry, dirty, and sometimes injured. They may ignore fans, who may get hurt or angry at perceived rejection. But think about the hardest work day you've ever had — would you want to stop for autographs or photos on your way to shower, dinner, and rest?

Grabbing that bidon (water bottle)

Team water bottles are prized possessions, and fans scramble for ones thrown by riders. Because bottles are thrown randomly, it's mostly a question of being in the right place at the right time.

Fans often line up at feed zones, hoping to grab a discarded *musette* (food bag) or water bottle. In rare instances, a rider will reward a cheering fan with a bottle tossed right into his or her hands. The chance of getting a bottle signed is pretty slim, but what a souvenir if you do!

The Thrill of Finishing on the Champs Élysées

Even racers admit they always get a thrill from riding on this venerable final stage of the Tour de France. Starting at the Place de la Concorde, with the Arc de Triomphe towering at the far end, the *peloton* (main group of riders) thunders around its final laps — see Figure 11-5. The speed of the *peloton* is amazing. Racers and vehicles are a blur; a kaleidoscope of colors.

Racing on the Champs Élysées is tougher than it appears. The street is rough and cobbled, and it's steeper than it looks. Given the surface and the speed, the yellow jersey contender runs the risk of falling and losing his Tour victory during the last stage. The excitement builds with each lap, ending with a sprint finish.

The crowd roars so loudly that racers can't hear. The intensity is unbelievable: the *peloton,* team cars, official cars, and motorcycles flashing up one side of the Champs Élysées and back down the other side for eight laps. These sounds and sights bring fans back year after year to the Champs Élysées for the legendary Tour finale.

Figure 11-5: L'Arc de Triomphe at the top end of the Champs Élysées in Paris.

What you don't see on television

Crowds are packed 12 deep around the final kilometers of the course (see Figure 11-6), which is why fans in the know bring stepladders to stand above crowds. Fans are vying for spots where they can see the final laps on the billboard-sized television screen. Everyone is trying to figure out how to sneak into the restricted areas for a better view. Tour security guards are checking passes and throwing people out of these restricted areas.

Vendors are everywhere, selling everything from cigarette lighters to Tour Eiffel scarves to umbrellas to earrings. The Official Tour de France boutiques are swamped with hordes of people buying anything Tour de France.

Where the elite meet and greet

Along the prime area of the finish line, Tour sponsors offer hospitality areas. These grandstand seats are off-limits for anyone who doesn't have a sponsor pass. Sponsor guests are given royalty treatment and seating for prime viewing. Sponsor hospitality areas take up grandstand seating from the lower end of the Champs Élysées to way past the finish line.

Figure 11-6: Crowds milling around on the Champs Élysées.

Standing on the balcony of the Hôtel de Crillion is an elite viewing area for a few select visitors. Lance Armstrong stays in the Crillion, so it's a prime and coveted area. The Hôtel de Crillion flies the flag of Texas to honor Armstrong (see Figure 11-7).

Figure 11-7: The Lone Star flag of Texas flies atop Le Hôtel de Crillion to honor Lance Armstrong.

Tour security guards

Amaury Sports Organization (ASO), the organization that's responsible for putting on the Tour each year, has an expert team of security guards who return every year. They are efficient and relentless
about keeping people without credentials or passes out of
restricted areas. It's almost impossible to fool one of these guys
into believing that you belong where you don't. They're professional and courteous, but when they say no, you'd better go.

Hordes of ecstatic spectators

Estimates of a million spectators pouring into Paris for the finish of
the Tour de France seem true when you're trying to push your way
through shoulder-to-shoulder crowds. The excitement is contagious,
and the event provides the thrill of a lifetime for cycling fans. It's def-
initely worth standing in your viewing spot for hours to experience
this event. If you're somehow lucky enough, or early enough, to see
the podium ceremonies (see Figure 11-8), you'll have the ultimate
Tour de France experience.

Figure 11-8: 2004 Tour de France winners on the podium (left to right): Robbie
McEwen, Lance Armstrong, Richard Virenque, and Vladimir Karpets.

Part V
The Part of Tens

The 5th Wave   By Rich Tennant

In this part . . .

Like all *For Dummies* books, this one ends with a Part of Tens that provides lists of ten unique things about the Tour de France. You find our choices for the best Tour riders, the Tours that have had the most impact on the cycling world, ten unique statistics from the race's more than 100-year legacy, the most dramatic moments in the Tour's history, the most well known mountains and climbs, and ten other important cycling events.

Chapter 12

Ten Greatest Riders in Tour History

*E*quipment changes, weather changes, course changes, and strategy changes — all are part of the Tour de France. Great Tour champions all have different styles, too. But through the race's more than 100-year history, the best cyclists have all been the same in some respects. They've had great individual skills and one intangible quality — a focused desire to win.

This chapter, in alphabetical order, acknowledges the ten cyclists we've chosen as the finest in Tour de France history. Five riders are easy choices, because they dominated the event during their past or current tenures. Lance Armstrong has a record six consecutive Tour titles as of the writing of this book. Jacques Anquetil and Bernard Hinault (both Frenchmen), Eddy Merckx of Belgium, and Spaniard Miguel Indurain all captured the race five times.

Great champions like Gino Bartali, Fausto Coppi, Greg LeMond, Jan Ullrich, and Joop Zoetemelk are listed for diverse reasons — longevity, perseverance, and their ability to overcome personal tragedy. Plenty of other great bicyclists competed in the Tour, but here's our list of the ten finest.

Jacques Anquetil

Contrary to the regimented training of many champions, Jacques Anquetil became the Tour's first five-time winner with a unique, playboy lifestyle, a profound swagger, and tremendous skill as a time trialist. Raised in the country, Anquetil's career curiously involved number 17. He won the Grand Prix des Nations, and then the unofficial time trial world championship, at age 17, and he raced for 17 years.

Anquetil claimed his first Tour title in 1957 with nearly a 15-minute victory over Marc Janssens of Belgium. Anquetil celebrated his notoriety with as much vigor as he rode. He led a party lifestyle and fit the part of a southern California surfer: Anquetil had blond hair and blue eyes and often drove a sports car to races. Anquetil was infamous for smoking and drinking, and he uttered among the most often cited quotes in Tour history: "You can't ride the Tour de France on mineral water."

Four years elapsed before Anquetil claimed his second Tour in 1961, and he then won three more consecutive titles. Following his cycling retirement, Anquetil was in poor health for many years and died of stomach cancer in 1987.

Lance Armstrong

Brash and explosively talented, Lance Armstrong was age 21 in 1993 when he became the youngest cyclist to win the World Championship road race. But youthful confidence doesn't always mean much in the Tour de France.

Armstrong completed the event only once in his first four attempts, a 36th place overall finish in 1995. It was the same year his Italian friend and teammate Fabio Casartelli died during the race following a tragic hillside crash.

Armstrong's two-year absence from the Tour following his 1996 race abandonment was largely spent in recovery from his well-documented battle against testicular cancer. Armstrong returned to the Tour in 1999 more than 20 pounds lighter, and he began his still-in-progress race domination.

Much to the surprise of the French media, Armstrong won the Prologue. He also captured three more stages en route to the first of his six Tour titles, with more than a 7½-minute margin over Alex Zulle of Switzerland.

During his record-setting 2004 Tour victory, Armstrong won three mountains stages and both individual time trials en route to a nearly 6½-minute win over Germany's Andreas Kloden.

Armstrong is a dominating individual rider, a masterful tactician, and a consummate team rider. Many of Armstrong's stage wins have occurred in epic battles against the sport's finest, including German Jan Ullrich, the 1997 race winner, and deceased 1998 race titlist Marco Pantani of Italy. Armstrong has withstood numerous crashes. He has also spoken out in response to numerous drug accusations.

Gino Bartali

Many Tour de France riders' careers are fleeting. An ill-timed, split-second decision has stopped more than one cyclist's career. But not even WWII stopped Gino Bartali of Italy.

After winning his first title in 1938 — the first year individual riders weren't allowed to race (that is, they had to be part of a team) — Bartali returned a decade later and won again. While his doomsayers thought the 34-year-old was too old, Bartali's fans remembered his dominating pre-war mountain performances.

Bartali logged huge chunks of training miles and was devoutly religious. He didn't get along well with his equally famous countryman, Fausto Coppi. In fact, the two argued as the 1948 race approached and, in disgust, Coppi refused to participate.

Bartali remained unfazed. He attacked early and won the first stage in 1948, but faltered the next day. At the end of the first week, Bartali trailed Frenchman Louison Bobet by more than 20 minutes in the General Classification. When the race entered the Pyrenees, Bartali responded, knowing the seventh stage ended in the faithful city of Lourdes. He claimed the stage, won two more stages in succession, then crushed the field in the Alps.

Bartali eventually won seven Tour stages in 1948. With descending skills as strong as his climbing abilities, he claimed more than a 16-minute win over Belgium's Brik Schotte. Bartali's second Tour win placed him in a one-member fraternity. He's the only Tour rider to win overall titles a decade apart. Bartali also finished the Tour in second (1949), fourth (1951 and 1952), and 11th (1953), and he completed his Tour career with 12 stage wins.

Fausto Coppi

Gino Bartali entered the 1949 Tour as defending champion. He and Fausto Coppi reconciled, and the two Italians were ready for a much-anticipated battle. Coppi had already won the Tour of Italy three times, but at age 29 — six years younger than his compatriot — he was ready to claim his first Tour.

The two Italians often rode near each other in the second week in the Pyrenees. When the race entered the Alps, Coppi showed his still-youthful strength. He left Bartali as the race arrived in Italy and claimed a mountain stage and time trial en route to an 11-minute overall win over his aging countryman.

Swiss riders Ferdi Kubler and Hugo Koblet, respectively, won the 1950 and 1951 Tours. Coppi returned in 1952 after overcoming two sub-par racing years and the 1951 death of his brother during a road race. Coppi, 33, was in superior shape, and he won his second Tour by nearly 30 minutes over Belgian Constant Ockers. Coppi won five Tour stages in 1952, including the inaugural ascent of L'Alpe d'Huez, the event's most famous climb.

Coppi participated in the Tour only three times. His career was interrupted by war, numerous injuries, family tragedy, and his feisty temper. He won nine Tour stages, but when he left the sport, his life crumbled. Coppi divorced his wife for a girlfriend, a scandal that shocked Italy at that time. Coppi's untimely death at age 40 from Malaria only further added to his legend.

Bernard Hinault

Like Fausto Coppi, Jacques Anquetil, and Eddy Merckx, Bernard Hinault — the last French rider to win the Tour — made a stunning debut in the controversial 1978 race. Riders felt the route was too difficult, and they dismounted their bikes at the end of one morning stage to protest.

Michel Pollentier of Belgium won the stage to L'Alpe d'Huez and claimed the yellow jersey. But Pollentier was quickly disqualified from the race. During the post-stage drug test, he was caught using a contraption that held fake urine.

That's when Hinault capitalized on Pollentier's departure. He won three stages in his race debut, including two time trials. He claimed his first title by nearly four minutes over Dutchman Joop Zoetemelk. With a defending French titlist, the host country was overjoyed. Hinault won in dominating fashion in 1979, claiming seven stages and further displayed his determined, sometimes harsh nature. His demeanor and gritty facial expressions earned him the nickname "The Badger."

Hinault's only weakness was tendonitis. Suffering from severe knee pain, he abandoned the 1980 race as it entered the Pyrenees. Hinault won again in 1981 and 1982, but he missed the 1983 race when his tendonitis returned. Hinault was determined, and after finishing second to compatriot Laurent Fignon in 1984, he claimed his fifth title in 1985. American Greg LeMond was Hinault's team-mate and appeared in position to outshine the French star. Hinault was weakened by crashes, but Hinault hired LeMond as a support rider, not a race winner. LeMond was upset, but he relented. Hinault, who wore the yellow jersey for 78 days in his career, con-cluded his Tour efforts in 1986 when he finished second to LeMond.

Hinault had 28 stage wins in eight Tour appearances, and he is now part of the Tour organization and greets podium finishers after every stage.

Miguel Indurain

Greg LeMond was favored as defending titlist in the 1991 Tour. Former race winners Pedro Delgado of Spain, Laurent Fignon of France, and Ireland's Stephen Roche were also in the field. The sur-prising rider was Miguel Indurain of Spain. Indurain had finished 10th in 1990, the highest finish of his first six Tour attempts that included three abandonments.

Indurain was considered a good team rider, but no one predicted his early mountain attacks, strategic defensive riding, and final time trial dominance. A cyclist of little bravado and few words, Indurain won the first of his then-record five straight titles with a 3½-minute victory over Italy's Gianni Bugno. LeMond placed sev-enth that year in his last Tour finish.

For the next four years, Indurain dominated the Tour, all with little fanfare, little controversy, and no boastful predictions. Indurain respected his rivals and was respected by fans. He smiled often and remained quiet and powerful. Indurain never won more than two stages in any of his Tour titles, and he never won a mountain stage during his five titles, but after his initial race title, Indurain's overall margin of victory was never less than 4½ minutes.

Indurain sought a sixth straight Tour title, but his triumphant years ended abruptly in 1996. Indurain suffered in the Alps, and his con-trolled, rarely changing smile was suddenly replaced by a look of someone in panic. Indurain lost more than three minutes in the stage and eventually finished 11th overall in his final Tour attempt. Indurain's career included 12 stage wins in 12 Tour participations. He wore the yellow jersey for 60 days, fourth most in race history behind Eddy Merckx, Bernard Hinault, and Lance Armstrong.

Greg LeMond

Unlike Indurain and other Tour champions, Greg LeMond, the first of only two American race winners, showed his potential early. He finished third in the 1984 Tour and second overall in 1985 to his aging and injured team leader, Bernard Hinault.

In 1986, LeMond made history as the first American to win the Tour. With Hinault concluding his career, LeMond finally got his time in the Tour spotlight. He captured his second career win in Stage 13 and took the yellow jersey in Stage 17. By the end of the race, LeMond claimed the first of his three titles by more than 3 minutes over Hinault, his valiant and defiant teammate.

Like Lance Armstrong, LeMond's career was interrupted by life tragedy. On a 1987 hunting trip in northern California, LeMond was accidentally shot by his brother in law and suffered near-fatal wounds. While recovering, LeMond missed the 1987 and 1988 Tours. He triumphantly returned and took his second Tour title in 1989.

Always personable, LeMond won three stages during his second title year. His final-day time trial win and eight-second race margin over Laurent Fignon was the closest race finish in history. It's often considered the Tour's finest moment.

LeMond's gunshot recovery and his 1989 final-day dramatics bolstered the sport's popularity in the United States. LeMond uniquely captured his third and final title by 2 minutes 16 seconds over Italian Claudio Chiappucci of Italy in 1990. LeMond didn't win a stage, providing ideal proof the Tour is a race of three-week strategy, not single-day wins.

Like other champions, LeMond's Tour reign ended abruptly. He was favored in 1991, but LeMond began to suffer suddenly while approaching the summit of the Tourmalet in the Alps and finished seventh. LeMond withdrew in his final two Tour attempts, in 1992 and 1994. Besides his three titles, LeMond concluded his Tour career with five stage wins in eight Tour appearances.

Eddy Merckx

More than any other cyclist, Eddy Merckx had an uncanny ability to intimidate competitors. The Belgian cyclist is considered by many to be the finest rider in history. When he appeared at a race start, the rest of the field often knew it was riding for no higher than second place.

Merckx made his Tour debut in 1969 and predicted he would win, but about a month before the Tour, he tested positive for amphetamines during the Tour of Italy and was expelled from the race. Merckx protested vehemently, and after not competing for 18 days, he was cleared of charges based on "flawed test procedures." He kept his promise to win, despite the inauspicious pre-race publicity.

Merckx rode unchallenged en route to the finest debut in Tour history. He claimed six stages, plus the best climber and points competitions, and won by nearly 18 minutes over Roger Pingeon of France, the 1967 titlist.

Merckx was nicknamed *The Cannibal* for the way he "ate up" miles and "devoured the competition." Throughout his Tour career, Merckx's moniker was rarely inappropriate. He claimed eight Tour stage wins in 1970 and 1974 (the record for stage wins in a single year), six stages in 1969 and 1972, and four stages in 1971.

Like Bernard Hinault, Jacques Anquetil, and Miguel Indurain, Merckx valiantly tried to claim a sixth title, but he failed. His victory over Raymond Poulidor of France by 8 minutes 4 seconds in 1974 was his smallest overall margin of victory. In 1975, race observers said Merckx wasn't at his best as the Tour began. Several other contenders emerged in the mountains, but Merckx persevered, only to succumb to a fan's antics: While grinding his way toward a mountainous stage finish, a fan jumped into the road and punched Merckx in the lower back about a half-mile from the line.

Merckx stumbled across the finish, vomiting. The incident marked the beginning of the end of Merckx's career. He won two stages of the 1975 Tour, but finished second overall to Bernard Thevenet of France by 2 minutes and 47 seconds. Merckx didn't compete in the 1976 Tour and finished sixth overall in 1977. He completed an unequaled Tour career. In seven Tour appearances, Merckx claimed 34 stages and wore the yellow jersey for 96 days — both race records.

Jan Ullrich

Following the retirement of Miguel Indurain, the Tour was ripe for a new champion. Bjarne Riis of Denmark was the surprise 1996 winner. But lurking in his near shadow was a young German teammate named Jan Ullrich.

Ullrich was nearly born a cyclist. He learned the sport from a young age in regimented East German training camps. By age 22, he advanced through the ranks and claimed his first Tour stage and finished second overall in 1996. The following year, with defending champion Bjarne Riis faltering, Ullrich rode to his first and only Tour title, claiming a mountain stage, a time trial, and the first Tour title for Germany.

As defending champion in 1998, Ullrich began one of the Tour's unique wonderments. After struggling to lose weight in the winter months following his Tour triumphant, Ullrich won three stages. But he couldn't overcome the skills of one of the event's great pure climbers, Marco Pantani of Italy, who prevailed over Ullrich by 3 minutes 21 seconds. Nearly every year, Ullrich works his way into shape as the Tour progresses. He's usually at his strongest in the final week after overcoming his life's pleasure and obstacle — he loves to eat.

Ullrich missed the 1999 event because of injury, but he returned to finish second to Lance Armstrong in 2000, 2001, and 2003. In each of those years, Armstrong predicted Ullrich would be his primary competitor and in each year, it was true. Ullrich, still racing in his prime, is a superior climber and time trialist, and he's often considered the most talented rider in the *peloton* (pack of riders). His battles with weight and less-than-superior team support have proven costly. In seven Tour years, Ullrich has seven stage wins, seven race finishes, and five second-place overall place finishes, with a career-lowest fourth overall in 2004.

Joop Zoetemelk

After nine Tour finishes, including five second-place campaigns, Dutchman Joop Zoetemelk captured his only Tour overall title in 1980 with a 6 minutes 55 seconds margin over countryman Hennie Kuiper.

Zoetemelk was a strong time trialist and climber. But his ascension to the top of the Tour podium occurred after unusual circumstances. Zoetemelk won three stages in 1980, but Bernard Hinault withdrew while in the lead and with the race just reaching the mountains.

A prideful rider, Zoetemelk refused to wear the yellow jersey via default. But his fifth-place finish in the first mountain stage moved him into the race lead, and he wore the yellow jersey to the finish.

Zoetemelk finished second overall again in 1982 — his sixth runner-up finish — and he continued competing in the event through 1986. Zoetemelk finished all of his 16 Tour de France attempts — the most in race history — and claimed ten stages to complete the most enduring career in Tour history.

Chapter 13

The Ten Most Important Tours in History

*E*ach Tour edition has its own feel. Riders pedal along country roads for hours in strong winds, heavy rain, snow, and bright sunshine — sometimes all on the same day. The landscape, standings, and mood of the *peloton* (the main pack of riders) can remain unchanged for days. But in an instant, it can all change. Crashes, injuries, illness, a young rider's surprising attack, or a veteran cyclist's sudden failure all make the Tour unique every year.

Two World Wars interrupted the Tour, but since the event's inception, 91 Tours have been held in 102 years. Choosing the ten most important Tour editions is subjective. Just like in the Super Bowl, NBA Championship, Winston Cup, Stanley Cup, or World Series, cycling fans have favorite Tours for different reasons.

From great individual performances to hot technology, from race innovation to personal triumph, this chapter details our selection of the ten most important Tour editions.

1903: Publishing Wars and Garin Make History

Henri Desgrange was a newspaperman, marketing whiz, and cyclist, and he was competitive. Combining his various talents, Desgrange, publisher of *L'Auto,* and his colleague Geo Lefevre devised a bicycle race around France. The idea was for *L'Auto* to outdo its rival *Le Petit Journal,* the newspaper that promoted a vastly popular French cycling event, Paris-Brest-Paris.

Six-day track cycling events were popular at the time, so promoters of the new event staged a six-segment race around France. The idea wasn't well accepted at first, but entry fees were lowered, prize money was increased, and 60 cyclists were at the starting line for the first stage.

Maurice Garin, a native of Italy who became a naturalized French citizen in 1901, was favored. Stages were monumental, and Garin was victorious in the 467-kilometer (290-mile) inaugural day from Paris to Lyon in nearly 18 hours. Exhaustion took its toll, however. Only 21 cyclists completed the 2,428-kilometer (1,506-mile) journey (see Figure 13-1). Garin claimed the fifth and concluding sixth stage and defeated runner-up countryman Lucien Pothier by 2 hours and 47 minutes.

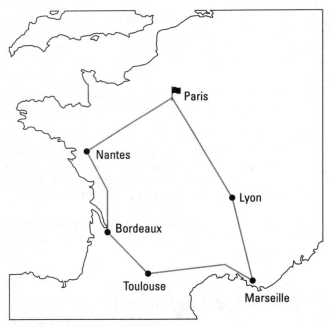

Figure 13-1: Map of 1903 Tour route.

Desgrange's plan worked perfectly. Circulation of *L'Auto,* published on yellow newsprint, doubled during the race, and *Le Petit Journal* eventually folded. The Tour de France was born.

1913: Time Changes, Tour Reverses

Throughout its tenure, Tour organizers have kept the race fresh. New routes, new jerseys, and the addition of time bonuses have enticed cyclists and kept race fans interested. So, it's no surprise that, a decade into the event, two monumental changes occurred.

✔ For the first time, the direction of the Tour route was reversed (see Figure 13-2).

✔ More importantly, the race leader was determined via total shortest accumulated time, not total points.

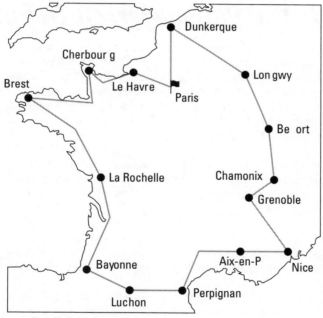

Figure 13-2: Map of 1913 Tour route.

Despite its constant innovation and growing popularity, the Tour had detractors. In 1913 , saboteurs put nails and glass on the route of the first stage, and 29 riders ended their journeys en route to the finish at Le Havre.

The 1913 Tour was also significant because of cyclists' ingenuity. In one instance, Eugene Christophe, riding in the lead, shattered part of his bike frame. Christophe carried his bike for two hours, arrived at a local blacksmith's shop, and spent an hour repairing his bike. He persevered, but didn't win the race.

Also that year, Belgian Marcel Buysse and Frenchman Lucien Petit-Breton were in the hunt for overall victory, but both suffered flat tires early in a stage to Geneva. Other race favorites seized the moment and attempted to leave Buysse and Petit-Breton permanently behind. Strategy prevailed. Buysse and Petit-Breton made their repairs and caught the leaders by working together. Philippe Thys of Belgium claimed the first of his three overall titles with more than an 8½-hour margin over Gustave Garrigou of France.

1919: The Yellow Jersey Debuts

World War I interrupted the Tour for four years, and the race wasn't the same when it returned. Former winners Lucien Petit-Breton (1907), Francois Faber (1909), and Octave Lapize (1910) were killed in battle. As the Tour start approached, many cyclists were in poor shape, and many roads of France weren't in great shape, either (see the map of the Tour route in Figure 13-3). In the end, only 11 of 69 starters finished.

But race organizer Henri Desgrange was insistent the race resume, and he had a plan. To match the color of his newspaper, *L'Auto,* Desgrange introduced a new marketing tool — the *maillot jaune,* or yellow jersey.

At the point in the race when the jersey débuted, Eugene Christophe hadn't yet won a stage, but he took the *maillot jaune* after assuming the race lead in the new jersey's 10th stage debut.

Christophe was among the unluckiest cyclists in Tour history. While leading the race, his bike frame broke (again!), and he lost the race lead while walking to a local bicycle factory. Christophe eventually placed third, 2 hours and 16 minutes behind Belgian Firmin Lambot, who claimed the first of his two titles.

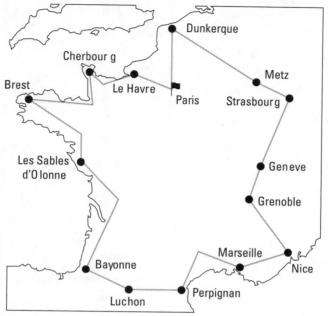

Figure 13-3: Map of 1919 Tour route.

1938: Le Tour: A Team Sport

In 1938, only teams were allowed to enter the race on that year's route (see Figure 13-4); individuals were no longer allowed to participate. If a cyclist didn't make his national squad, groups of *cadets* were grouped into B teams.

Gino Bartali of Italy captured the first of his two overall titles and best climber jersey in 1938, the final Tour before World War II interrupted the event for nearly a decade. The race also showcased cycling sportsmanship at its finest. Frenchmen Andre Leducq and Antonin Magne, both participating for the last time, pedaled away from the *peloton* in the final stage and put their arms around each other as they reached the finish. Race organizers called the final stage a tie, and the two veteran cyclists ended their respective careers with co-stage wins. Sylvere Maes of Belgium won the race by 30½ minutes over Rene Vietto of France.

Figure 13-4: Map of 1938 Tour route.

1969: Eddy Merckx Arrives and Dominates

When he wasn't winning, Eddy Merckx of Belgium was down in the dumps. Given his druthers, Merckx set out to claim every race he entered, including his Tour debut in 1969. Merckx wasn't the youngest rider to triumph at the Tour, nor was he the first boastful pending champion. But at age 24, Merckx said he'd win the race in his first attempt, and he did.

Like many great champions, Merckx had few weaknesses. He won the Tour with superior climbing, with his excellent time trial skills, and by intimidation. He attacked when he didn't have to, and he often left strategy as a concern for other cyclists.

Merckx's Tour debut in 1969 (see Figure 13-5) was nothing short of astonishing. He won the points and best climber competitions, six stages, including three time trials, and he captured the overall title by nearly 18 minutes over Roger Pingeon of France. The career of the cyclist considered the greatest in history had just begun.

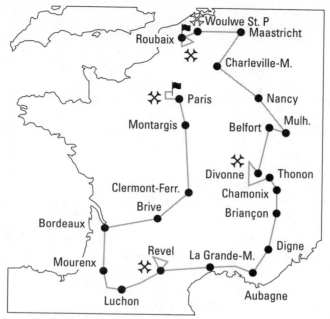

Figure 13-5: Map of 1969 Tour route.

1986: Greg LeMond and Other Americans in Paris

Greg LeMond should have won the 1985 Tour, but that year was still teammate Bernard Hinault's time as team leader. But after a third place in 1984 and second place in 1985, LeMond continued his career as one of the race's great riders with the first of his three titles.

Hinault didn't give up easily. He attacked often, but LeMond eventually wore him down on mountains (see Figure 13-6), and Hinault conceded by grabbing and raising LeMond's hand into the air as the two rode together in one late-race mountain stage. LeMond, world road champion three years earlier, defeated Hinault by 3 minutes and 10 seconds, and the Tour was again transformed.

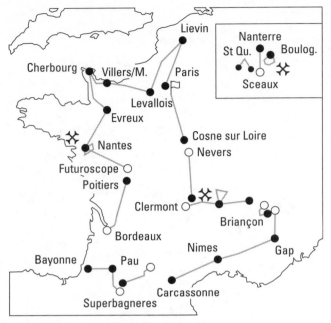

Figure 13-6: Map of 1986 Tour route.

LeMond became cycling's first million-dollar rider, the sport's popularity grew substantially, and LeMond brought the Tour into the collective U.S. consciousness. LeMond's win was also part of a bigger breakthrough year for U.S. cyclists in Europe. Team 7-Eleven, primarily composed of Americans, became the first U.S.-based team to participate. Davis Phinney, one of many U.S. pros based in Colorado, became the second American to win a Tour stage.

1989: LeMond Dramatically Wins Again

By 1989, the Tour had been held 75 times with countless dramatic stages, but nothing had approached what happened on the final day of the 76th Tour. Greg LeMond, two years removed from his near-fatal accidental gunshot wound, assumed and lost the yellow jersey twice. He trailed two-time French winner Laurent Fignon by 50 seconds entering the final stage, a 25-kilometer (15½-mile) individual time trial that finished on the Champs Élysées in Paris (see Figure 13-7).

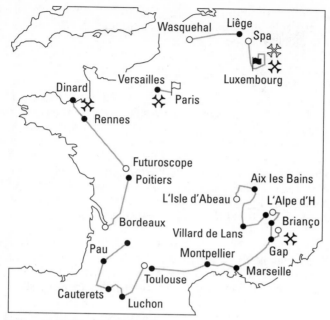

Figure 13-7: Map of 1989 Tour route.

LeMond, the second-to-last rider on the course, quickly narrowed his deficit. Purposely avoiding hearing his split times or knowing his overall status, LeMond crossed the line with an average speed of 54.55 kilometers per hour (33.84 mph). All LeMond could do then was wait. Fignon, the French hero and last cyclist on the course, finished 58 seconds slower than LeMond. The American leaped into the air, hugged his wife, and exalted for all of France to hear and see. Fignon, devastated, collapsed near the finish line.

LeMond's 8-second title margin remains the closest in race history, and his final stage speed remains the fastest in Tour history. LeMond also changed cycling forever in his dramatic final-day win. He was also the first cyclist to use aerodynamic handlebars in competition. The newfangled bars allowed him to race in a tucked position, a strategy that has been used since.

1999: Armstrong Shocks the World

Lance Armstrong had two stage wins and finished the Tour once in his first four attempts. But in 1999 (see the route in Figure 13-8), he returned to the race after two years from his well-documented recovery from cancer.

The French doubted Armstrong could participate, never mind contest the title. But when Armstrong claimed the Prologue over Alex Zulle of Switzerland, skeptics were still not convinced; they became more vocal. How could a cyclist return from near-fatal cancer, look so drastically leaner, and win?

Armstrong answered his critics verbally and on the bike. He claimed the 8th and 19th stages, completing a sweep of the race's time trials. He also won the 9th stage to Sestrieres, his first Tour road win in four years. The U.S. Postal Service Cycling Team (now called the Discovery Channel Pro Cycling Team), particularly George Hincapie, Tyler Hamilton, and Frankie Andreu, rode strongly and became known as *the Blue Train*. (Because of its blue uniforms and strategic close-grouped formation, the USPS team received the nickname from *L'Equipe*, the French daily sports newspaper.)

Armstrong rode to more than a 7½-minute win over Alex Zulle. The French remained skeptical, but they were also embarrassed. For the first time, a U.S. team won the team title and for the first time in more than 70 years, a French rider failed to win a single stage.

Figure 13-8: Map of 1999 Tour route.

2003: Armstrong and Ullrich Pedal in Fast Company

With entry into the exclusive five-title fraternity at stake in 2003, battles between Lance Armstrong and Jan Ullrich highlighted one of the most riveting Tours in history. The pace was fast, and the long-awaited celebration of the race's 100th anniversary couldn't have progressed with any more excitement.

The Tour visited several original host cities amid huge celebrations (see Figure 13-9). Armstrong overcame dehydration, several crashes, and an unplanned brief ride through a mowed field of hay to claim his closest overall victory.

Figure 13-9: Map of the 2003 Tour route.

Largely pushed by Ullrich and Kazakhstan's Alexandre Vinokourov, Armstrong was victorious over Ullrich by 1 minute and 1 second. He became the Tour's fifth five-time winner and joined Miguel Indurain as the only riders to win five consecutive Tours. The race's average finishing speed of 40.94 kilometers per hour (25.39 mph) was the fastest in history.

American Tyler Hamilton, riding most of the race with a fractured collarbone, claimed a stage after a long solo breakaway and finished fourth overall.

2004: Armstrong Rides Into History

What many predicted would be Lance Armstrong's hardest Tour was his easiest. Eight years in recovery from the cancer that nearly took his life, in 2004, Armstrong increased his Tour de France career stage win total to 21 with five more stage victories.

At age 32, Armstrong used the strength of his team when required and then rode off into the mountains, rarely challenged. In each of his titles, Armstrong has had one surprisingly strong rider at his side, and in 2004, that rider was Floyd Landis of San Diego, California. Armstrong handpicked Landis to the surprise of many onlookers as a Tour team member in 2002. Landis has finished three straight Tours, including his 23rd place overall in 2004, when he often joined Armstrong on steep mountains. The U.S. Postal Service Cycling Team also claimed the team time trial.

Early in the race, Armstrong accused a French television crew of entering his vacated hotel room. In other stages, Armstrong was spit on, and he raced past derogatory handmade fans' signs. But Armstrong's riding overshadowed any doomsayers. Armstrong accumulated a 6-minute and 19-second margin over German runner-up Andreas Kloden.

With his sixth title, Armstrong has accumulated a career-winning margin of 35 minutes and has ridden approximately 13,100 miles in 127 days in his Tour titles. His 2004 triumph included a victory in the Tour's most anticipated stage, the uphill time trial to L'Alpe d'Huez in which more than a half-million spectators lined the course (see Figure 13-10). Armstrong also added drama with a rare sprint triumph in Stage 17, the race's longest and most difficult day. Armstrong completed his 2004 title fifth among career stage winners (21) and third (65) in career days in the yellow jersey, behind Eddy Merckx (96) and Bernard Hinault (78).

Figure 13-10: Map of 2004 Tour route.

Chapter 14

Ten Unique Tour de France Statistics

Throughout its long history, unique riders, epic stages, bizarre occurrences, devastating crashes, heroic rides, and hard-to-explain scandals, the Tour de France boils down to statistics. Before, during, and after every stage, race organizers distribute reams of information. From riders' particulars to climbing gradients, accumulated kilometers to finishing time margins, the race is a huge, all-encompassing calculator of people, places, and things.

After 100 years or so of adding it all up, even basic Tour statistics are impressive. One example: In its 91 editions leading into the 2005 race, 53 different cyclists from 11 countries have won the Tour.

This chapter looks at the Tour de France by numbers. How many French riders have won? Who are the youngest and oldest riders to claim victory? What are the fastest stage and fastest Tours, along with the slowest stage and slowest Tours? What are the shortest and longest Tours? Every kilometer, every attack, and every sprint provides more statistics. But here's our list of the ten most interesting Tour statistics.

Young, Restless, and Champion

Frenchman Henri Cornet didn't have the best ride among the 27 cyclists who finished the 1904 Tour. But Cornet, only age 20, had the fastest legal time and became the race's youngest winner.

Cornet finished three hours behind apparent winner and defending title holder Maurice Garin. But Garin, his brother Caesar, and other top finishers Lucien Pothier and Hippolyte Ancouturier were disqualified for various rule infractions.

So, four months after the Tour ended, Cornet was declared the winner in what for a while seemed like not only the second but last Tour de France. Riders were ambushed and held hostage, and disgruntled spectators threw nails on the course. Riders cheated, and angry race director Henri Desgrange said the race would never be held again.

Cornet didn't know he was riding for the win, but he participated with a champion's spirit. He rode the final 35 kilometers (21.7 miles) with two flat tires.

While never again winning the Tour, Cornet nevertheless rode well. He abandoned the Tour in 1905 and 1907, and he wasn't able to start in 1906. But he finished eighth overall in 1908 and concluded his Tour career with a 28th place finish in 1912. Cornet died in 1941 with an enduring legacy — he was the youngest Tour de France champion.

Old and Leading the Pack

Firmin Lambot participated in the Tour for almost a decade. He first won the race in 1919 and claimed six career stages. But in 1922, Lambot's nickname, "Lucky," paid off with a career highlight and two Tour milestones.

Lambot, 36, didn't win any of the Tour's 15 stages. But as he was throughout his career, the Belgian rider was opportunistic. When several race favorites faltered, Lambot assumed the race lead after the 13th stage, and he cruised to more than a 41-minute race victory over France's Jean Alavoine.

The 1922 event marked the introduction of climbs to Vars and d'Izoard, two of the famous mountain ascents in the Alps. The 16th Tour de France also provided the race with new dynamics. It was the first time a rider won the overall title without claiming a stage, and Lambot became the oldest race winner — a designation that still remains.

Will You Still Need Me When I'm 32?

Like many pro sports, the Tour is a young riders' game. Only 12 riders age 32 and older have claimed overall titles. In chronological order, they are:

- ✔ 1902, Maurice Garin, age 32, France
- ✔ 1919, Firmin Lambot, age 33, Belgium
- ✔ 1921, Leon Scieur, age 33, Belgium
- ✔ 1922, Firmin Lambot, age 36, Belgium
- ✔ 1923, Henri Pelissier, age 34, France
- ✔ 1926, Lucien Buysse, age 34, Belgium
- ✔ 1929, Maurice Dewaele, age 33, Belgium
- ✔ 1948, Gino Bartali, age 34, Italy
- ✔ 1952, Fausto Coppi, age 33, Italy
- ✔ 1980, Joop Zoetemelk, age 33, the Netherlands
- ✔ 1996, Bjarne Riis, age 32, Denmark
- ✔ 2004, Lance Armstrong, age 32, United States

Winning, French Style

Considering their lack of victories in the last 20 years, it doesn't seem feasible French riders have dominated the Tour de France winner's podium. But with 36 Tour titles, French cyclists have claimed more than one-third of the overall titles. Belgium (18) has the second most Tour winners, followed by Italy and the United States, both with nine titles.

French titles have come in spurts. The first six editions (1903–1908) were all claimed by French riders as well as in several other time spans: 1930–1934, 1954–1957, 1961–1964, and 1981–1985.

As the race progresses every year, French cycling enthusiasts would like nothing more than another compatriot's victory. But a Frenchman hasn't won the Tour since Bernard Hinault's fifth and final title in 1985. Since Hinault's last title, three French riders have finished second: Hinault (1986), Laurent Fignon (1989), and Richard Virenque (1997).

Taking the Long Way Home

There's no such thing as an easy Tour de France. Some years have been longer and easier; other years have been shorter and more difficult. The 1926 Tour finally provided Belgian Lucien Buysse his time at the top of the podium. After placing third in 1924 and second in 1925, Buysse claimed the longest Tour in history. The 1926 race began in Evian, ended in Paris, and included 17 stages, totaling 5,745 kilometers (3,569 miles). That's an average of 209 miles per stage.

Buysse rode extremely well in the mountains and claimed the second stage in the Pyrenees among his three stage wins. Defending race titlist Ottavio Bottechecia, the first Italian winner, was so discouraged when he had to abandon because of illness he abruptly announced his retirement. Bottechecia competed in the Tour four times, won twice, and captured nine stages. But he was emotionally fragile, and shortly after he left the sport, Bottechecia was found dead in an Italian vineyard. The cause of his death was never determined.

It has been nearly 80 years, but Buysse's more than 22-minute victory over Nicolas Franz of Luxembourg in the 20th Tour remains the longest Tour on record. And none of today's Tour stages comes close to the average Tour stage length in 1926.

Pedaling Short, But Not So Sweet

In 1904, the race was new, and France both loved and hated its new national cycling event. Race director Henri Desgrange created something monumental and it was so successful in its 1903 debut that the route wasn't changed in 1904. But by the second year, not all was well. Rampant cheating and fans' outrageous behavior nearly ended the event for good.

The Tour survived, and among many legendary occurrences, one statistic from its first two years is sometimes overlooked. The routes were identical, included six stages and totaled 2,428 kilometers or 1,508 miles — the shortest Tours in history. The first year, 60 cyclists began the race and 21 finished. Eighty-eight riders began the Tour's second year, with 27 riders finishing.

Humbling Experience: 300 Miles of Torture

The debut of the yellow jersey overshadowed most everything else in the 1919 Tour. French rider Jean Alavoine didn't get the jersey, but his runner-up overall finish to Firmin Lambot was eased by his five stage wins. Alavoine's forte was his straightforward belief — longer is better.

 Alavoine never won the Tour, but his victory in the fifth stage from Les Sable d'Olonnes to Bayonne covered 482 kilometers (300 miles), the longest in Tour history. The severity of the stage took its toll in two ways. Only 11 of 69 race starters finished the race, and those who arrived in Paris had the slowest average race speed in Tour history, 24.05 kilometers per hour or 14.94 mph. The Tour's crawling average speed remains a dubious record. But in 1924, the same 300-mile route was covered again in the fifth stage. Omer Huysse joined Jean Alavoine as winners of the longest Tour stages.

Speeding Over Hill and Dale

Lance Armstrong's statistics are among the most impressive of any Tour rider. His six consecutive titles top many lists of all-time great athletic career accomplishments. But in 2003, en route to tying the mark of five straight titles, Armstrong, along with compatriot Tyler Hamilton, Jan Ullrich of Germany, Joseba Beloki of Spain, Frenchman Richard Virenque, and Kazakhstan's Alexander Vinokourov, among others, rode at a pace never before seen at the Tour.

Celebrating the Tour's 100th anniversary, riders visited numerous course sites from the inaugural Tour. Armstrong's team, nicknamed *le Train Bleu* (the Blue Train), powered their team leader over mountains, and he powered himself through time trials.

 Armstrong won the mountain stage to Luz-Ardiden, and the U.S. Postal Service Team captured the team time trial. When Armstrong crossed the finish line in Paris, his winning average speed was 40.94 kilometers per hour (25.43 mph), the fastest in Tour history.

Knowing Your Neighbors: An American in Paris

By the time he was a teenager, Jonathan Boyer of Carmel, California, knew Europe held his cycling future. Beginning in 1973 at age 17, Boyer spent four years riding on French amateur teams, and then turned professional. Boyer became severely ill with a stomach virus contracted in Venezuela during the 1978 World Championships. He took nearly two years to recover, but he returned in grand fashion as a member of the French Renault-Gitane squad led by Bernard Hinault, then a two-time Tour winner.

Hinault recruited Boyer to help him win the third of his five Tour titles in 1981. But Boyer's inaugural race presence was also a milestone: It had taken more than 75 years of race legacy, but Boyer was the first American to compete in the Tour de France. Four years later, Greg LeMond became the first American to claim a Tour stage.

Boyer, who still lives in Carmel, finished 32nd overall in his Tour debut and completed the event five times, finishing as high as 12th in the General Classification. He participated in the Tour of Italy three times and won the U.S. National Road title and placed fifth in the Road Race World Championships in 1980. Boyer retired from pro cycling after finishing 98th in the 1987 Tour. He owns a wholesale cycling component distribution company and retail bike shop near this hometown — and he still competes as an amateur rider in regional events.

Climbing Into the Clouds: The Great Peaks of the Tour

Four years into the Tour's legacy, the race changed forever. The race's first climb, Ballon d'Alsace, was part of the 13-stage, 26-day 1906 edition. Near the city of Belfort, the summit of Ballon d'Alsace is 1,247 meters (3,990 feet). It's short by modern Tour standards, but it did its damage as the race's first grand peak. Eighty-two riders began the 1906 Tour and 14 finished.

Since then, epic climbs have been part of the Tour every year. Through the years, five climbs have become the event's most well known and demanding:

✔ **L'Alpe d'Huez, 1,860 meters (5,952 feet):** Fausto Coppi won the inaugural ascent in 1952 while Joop Zoetemelk (1976), Bernard Hinault (1986), Gianni Bugno (1990 and 1991), Andy Hampsten (1992), Marco Pantani (1995–1997), and Lance Armstrong (2001–2004) have all been victorious on the mountain. L'Alpe d'Huez extends 13.8 kilometers (8.6) miles with an average grade of 7.9 percent. It's not the most difficult Tour climb, but it's the most storied. Spectators camp for days in anticipation of watching cyclists negotiate the route's 21 switchbacks.

✔ **Col d'Izoard, 2,361 meters (7,744 feet):** First used in 1922, the Alpine climb extends 19.3 kilometers (12 miles) at an average grade of 5.9 percent. Greg LeMond and Laurent Fignon staged an intense battle on the climb in 1989. But its reputation was established in early Tour years by three-time race winner Louison Bobet and two-time Tour victor Fausto Coppi.

✔ **Col du Galibier, 2,645 meters (8,675 feet):** Among the Tour's oldest climbs, the Galibier joined the Tour in 1911, when it was still a dirt road. Often combined with the Col du Telegraphe (1,566 meters, 5136 feet), the ascent, shown in Figure 14-1, lasts 29.5 kilometers (18.3 miles) with an average grade of 6.8 percent. Jacques Anquetil dominated the climb in 1957, and many others helped build their legends on the climb, including Charley Gaul (1959), Eddy Merckx (1969), Joop Zoetemelk (1972), Tony Rominger (1993), and Marco Pantani (1998).

✔ **Col du Tourmalet, 2,360 meters (7,552 feet):** When it was first included in the Tour in 1910, the stage was nicknamed the *Circle of Death*. The Tourmalet extends 15 kilometers (9.3 miles) at an average 5.7 percent. It's also known as La Mongie, the name of the ski resort near the peak of the mountain. Like other famed Tour climbs, this Pyrenees ascent has provided many monumental Tour memories, including the words of Octave Lapize. He called race officials *assassins* as he endured the peak's inaugural ascent. Eddy Merckx, Claudio Chiappucci, and Richard Virenque, along with many others, have powered to victories on the Tourmalet. A monument to Tour founder Henri Desgrange is positioned on the top of the summit.

✔ **Mont Ventoux, 1909 meters (6,261 feet):** The most recent addition to the Tour's epic climbs, Mont Ventoux debuted in 1951 and has been included only 13 times. It extends for 21 kilometers (13 miles) at an average grade of 7.5 percent. It's sometimes called the *Tour of the Moon* because its summit is barren — frequent strong winds have blown away trees and other plant life. The climb has been infamous since the 1967 death of British rider Tom Simpson. While trying to catch the breakaway of popular rider Raymond Poulidor, Simpson collapsed, and he died while being transported by helicopter to a hospital. There's a memorial marking the place where Simpson fell and became the first Tour fatality in 40 years.

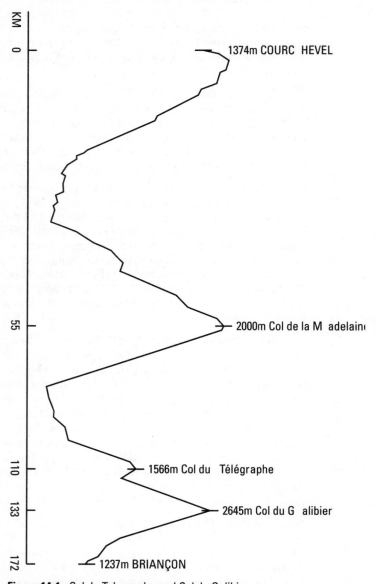

Figure 14-1: Col du Telegraphe and Col du Galibier.

Chapter 15

Ten Dramatic Tour de France Moments

Sudden, spectacular moments make the Tour de France what it is. Racing can change in an instant, whether from a rider's quick acceleration, an unseen obstacle in the road, or a cyclist's unscripted emotional finish-line reaction. Great Tour moments are etched in race lore, and they occur in an instant, year after year — always when least expected.

Countless epic battles, horrific crashes, furious sprint finishes, and curious split-second oddities have occurred in the race's century-plus history. It's impossible to choose the best moments, but here is our selection of ten dramatic Tour moments.

Assassins Among Us (1910)

Who could have known that the introduction of the first mountain in the Tour de France in 1905 would five years later lead to perhaps the race's most famous quote? And who could have known some Tour peaks encountered for the first time nearly 100 years ago would become today's race monoliths?

It was race founder Henri Desgrange, the person responsible for many Tour innovations, who added several climbs in the Pyrenees to the 1910 race. His goal was simple: increase race excitement to increase circulation of his daily newspaper, *L'Auto,* which gave vast coverage to the race.

During a two-day stretch, riders in Stage 8 in 1910 endured the rigors of climbing obscure, mountainous dirt roads. Ascents like Aspin, Tourmalet, Aubisque, and Peyresourde were included. Many riders walked with their bikes on some of the difficult sections. Octave Lapize of France got angry. As he progressed past the halfway point of the Col d'Aubisque, Lapize noticed race officials and he spoke his peace in their direction: "You're assassins! All of you!" said Lapize en route to his overall race win.

Lapize's abrupt words have stood the test of time as the race's mountain mantra. Tour riders have a love-hate relationship with the famous and infamous race peaks, and nothing speaks to the severity of the climbs (and to the race directors who devise their ascents) like Lapize's outburst.

A Tour First: Death in the Peloton (1935)

As the Tour approached its 30th birthday, the race was well established, offered monumentally long stages, and was constantly tweaked with new innovation. French riders often showed their dominance and, beginning in 1930, they won five straight years. Belgian Roman Mais ended the France dominance, but his win in 1935 was overshadowed by the Tour's first racing death.

Stage 7 was the race's key day. Progressing from Aix-les-Bains to Grenoble, the stage included ascents over Telegraphe, the Galibier, and the Lautaret. First, defending champion Antonin Magne of France was struck by a car on the Telegraphe, badly hurt, and transported to a hospital in a farmer's cart, where he died from internal injuries. Soon after, on the descent of the Galibier, Spanish rider Francisco Cepeda crashed and fractured his skull. He died from his injuries three days later — the Tour's first racing victim.

Poulider Versus Anquetil (1964)

Raymond Poulider of France may have been the most well-liked rider in Tour history. He won 189 races in his 18-year career, but he never won the Tour de France. Frenchman Jacques Anquetil and Eddy Merckx of Belgium, both five-time Tour winners, dominated the race during Poulidor's tenure, but because Poulidor kept trying in spite of injury and illness, he finished the Tour second or third overall a combined eight times. He was affectionately known as "Pou-Pou."

Poulidor's most memorable ride likely occurred when he and Anquetil rode side by side for the final (10 kilometer (6¼-mile stretch of the Puy de Dome, the final ascent of the 1964 Tour. Poulider was the stronger climber, but Anquetil held a 56-second lead when he pulled next to Poulidor. The two riders stayed even for much of the final climb and occasionally bumped each other, a common occurrence in road race sprint finishes, but rare on mountaintops. Poulidor pulled away from Anquetil, the defending race titlist. But Anquetil knew what he was doing. He still had a 14-second margin for the final stage, a time trial — his specialty. Anquetil won the time trial easily and claimed his fifth Tour de France by 55 seconds over tough-luck Poulidor.

Merckx Attacked in the Mountains (1975)

As a five-time winner, Eddy Merckx of Belgium began the 1975 race as a surprisingly unknown factor. He was sick during the spring, missed the Tour of Italy, and didn't claim the other early season races he usually dominated.

When the Tour began, Merckx wasn't at his best, but he didn't give up easy. He won two stages of the '75 race — the last Tour stage wins of his career. But Merckx suffered often on climbs, crashed several times, and then faced the end of his Tour dominance because of a fan's outburst.

On Stage 14 — the longest of the race — Merckx was chasing eventual third-place overall finisher and compatriot Lucien Van Impe. A spectator suddenly jumped from the crowd and punched Merckx. Merckx lost time and stumbled across the line, vomiting. Despite his physical problems, Merckx rode down the hill after the race and identified his attacker to police. Merckx still had the race lead following the ordeal. But he lost more time in subsequent stages and ended up second overall. Two years later, Merckx returned to the Tour for the last time and finished sixth in the overall standings.

Hampsten Conquers L'Alpe d'Huez (1992)

Andy Hampsten twice won the Tour of Switzerland (1986 and 1987) and also won the Tour of Italy (1988). But his triumphant ascent and victory in the L'Alpe d'Huez stage of the 1992 Tour was likely his most well-known accomplishment.

While riding for the U.S.-based Motorola team, Hampsten became the first American to win the stage to the Tour's most recognized peak and ski resort. The climb to L'Alpe d'Huez is not the race's most difficult, but its 21 switchbacks provide great drama for on-site spectators and television viewers. Hampsten's triumph occurred two years after Greg LeMond's third and final Tour title. It was also televised on CBS, which meant that Hampsten gave American cycling a jolt of increased interest.

Hampsten finished as high as fourth overall in the Tour, and his L'Alpe d'Huez title added his name to the list of now six U.S. riders who have claimed Tour stage wins. Hampsten, founder of Cinghiale Cycling Tours and co-owner of Hampsten Bikes with his brother Steve, gave one of his road bikes the name Alpe d'Huez.

LeMond Rides into History (1989)

Greg LeMond had a singular focus during the final stage of the 1989 Tour. He didn't wear a watch and told his handlers not to tell him his time during his ride; he then went on to ride the race of his Tour career. Riding in a tuck position provided by aerodynamically configured handlebars (like the tuck of an alpine skier), LeMond overcame a 50-second deficit to Frenchman Laurent Fignon and claimed his second Tour title by 8 seconds, the closest margin of victory in race history.

LeMond knew he had ridden spectacularly, and it was quickly confirmed when his finishing time showed an average speed of 54.5 kph (33.8 mph), the fastest stage in Tour history. But LeMond still had to wait for Fignon, the last rider on course, to finish. But Fignon couldn't make up the deficit. When he knew he had won, LeMond leaped into the air, mouth agape, and then hugged his wife. Fignon, the 1983 and '84 Tour winner, collapsed near the finish, defeated in his quest for a third title by just 8 seconds.

Armstrong Salutes Fallen Fabio (1995)

Lance Armstrong and Fabio Casartelli of Italy were young team-mates and good friends, and they both were part of the U.S.-based Motorola squad competing in the 1995 Tour. Casartelli won the 1992 Olympic Road Race; Armstrong claimed the 1993 World Championship Road Race.

But something went terribly wrong in Stage 15 of the 1995 Tour. Frenchman climbing specialist Richard Virenque of France was at the front of the group pedaling toward a stage win. Well behind the stage leader, a helmetless Casartelli crashed with several other riders on the descent of the Portet d'Aspet.

While racing at approximately 50 mph, Casartelli hit his head hard against a cement railing and died en route to the hospital. The next day's stage was nullified out of respect to the deceased rider. Near the stage finish, the entire remaining Motorola team was allowed to come to the front of the *peloton* and cross the line together to honor its fallen teammate. Two days later at Stage 18, which finished in Limoges, Armstrong got into a small breakaway group and then powered to a solo win. As he approached the finish line, Armstrong raised both index fingers toward the sky, acknowledging Casartelli. He later dedicated the win to his deceased teammate and friend.

Sitting Down on the Job (1998)

Willy Voet was a *soigneur* for the French team Festina. When he was stopped in his car en route to a cross-channel ferry headed for the start of the 1998 Tour in Dublin, it marked the beginning of the end of the most tumultuous Tour in history.

Part of Voet's cargo was vials of EPO, the human growth hormone. Voet was arrested and subsequently revealed his team's doping practices to law enforcement officials. As the Tour progressed, other teams' hotel rooms were raided and other riders were arrested, including the entire Festina team. The race was in jeopardy.

Riders felt their rights were infringed upon, and during Stage 9, they began a series of protests by dismounting their bikes and sitting down on the road for two hours. The *peloton* eventually resumed racing, and there was much discussion with race officials.

Protests continued throughout the race, and tempers flared. By the time Italian Marco Pantani claimed the title in Paris, less than half the field remained, and the Tour was in the midst of a huge identity crisis and massive drug controversy.

Hamilton Shows His Mettle in the Mountains (2003)

For two weeks, Tyler Hamilton rode with the pain of a fractured *clavicle* (collarbone). But Hamilton wanted something more as his legacy. After riding for more than 70 miles with the *peloton,* Hamilton pedaled to the front of the main pack while climbing the Col de Bargargui in the 16th stage of the 2003 Tour from Pau to Bayonne. He steadily built a 5-minute lead and rode more than 50 miles alone at the front of the race.

Still heavily wrapped in bandages from the injury suffered in the opening stage, Hamilton stayed in front, despite a strong effort from the *peloton,* and he became only the sixth American to win a Tour stage, joining Greg LeMond, Andy Hampsten, Davis Phinney, Lance Armstrong, and Jeff Pierce.

Hamilton's impressive solo win also endeared him to Tour fans, who respected his ability to remain in the race despite an injury that usually forces riders to abandon. Hamilton's stage win and his strong effort throughout the race prompted his finish in fourth place, the highest of his Tour career.

Riding through Hay Fields (2003)

Lance Armstrong's tenure at the Tour has included many exhilarating moments. Perhaps the most dramatic occurred in 2003 in Stage 9 from Bourg d'Osians to Gap.

French roads are often resurfaced for Tour stages. But in the nearly omnipresent heat of the 100th anniversary Tour edition, a slight downhill section melted while Spain's Joseba Beloki and Armstrong began to furiously chase stage leader Alexandre Vinokourov of Kazakhstan.

With Beloki slightly ahead of Armstrong, the duo accelerated to an estimated 40 mph (65 kph). Beloki's rear wheel suddenly spun out in the melting tar. He swung back and forth for a few seconds, then hit the pavement hard.

Armstrong reacted instantly and swerved to the left. He exited the pavement and rode across a recently plowed field of hay and back toward the race course. Armstrong dismounted his bike, jumped with it across an irrigation ditch and joined a group of riders, just arriving in another chasing pack. Beloki was escorted to a local hospital with several broken bones, lacerations, and other injuries. Armstrong finished second in the stage and went on to claim his record-tying fifth consecutive Tour de France.

Chapter 16

Ten Great Tour Climbs and Mountaintops

*G*reat climbers tend to win the Tour de France, and races are won and lost on the mountains. Dozens of famous and infamous peaks have been used during stages and as finishing summits. Although some climbs remain nearly the same every time they're contested, Tour organizers also look for mountain innovation, like the introduction of the climb to L'Alpe d'Huez as an individual time trial during the 2004 Tour. Just like the diverse styles of race riders, Tour mountains have their own personalities.

Selecting the Tour's ten most noteworthy ascents and mountaintop finishes is next to impossible. But here are our choices of ten (well, thirteen, but who's counting?) unique, famous, infamous, unheralded, and wondrous Tour de France mountains, presented alphabetically.

Aspin

One of several Pyrenees peaks added to the Tour in 1910, Aspin (as-pan) been visited 64 times. The peak is 1,489 meters (4,888 feet) after a 12.5-kilometer (7¾-mile) climb at an average 6.3 percent gradient. Roads are narrow, rough, and hazardous.

French race winner Octave Lapize was the first rider over the summit in its 1910 debut. Since then, many legendary Tour performers and its current riders have crested Aspin first en route to stage wins, overall Tour wins, and infamous days in the Pyrenees. Claudio Chiappucci of Italy was twice the first rider to the top (in 1990 and 1992). But Chiappucci rode during Miguel Indurain's Tour career, so he never won the race. Chiappucci's strong climbing, however, catapulted him to two second-place and one third-place overall finishes during his Tour heyday (1990–1992).

American Bobby Julich, third overall in the 1998 Tour, is also among riders who've reached the top of Aspin first, en route to 18th in the General Classification (the overall finish) in the 2001 Tour. Three years later, Julich was Olympic time trial bronze medalist in Athens, Greece.

Aubisque

The Aubisque (oh-beesk), a legendary Tour peak added in 1910, has been conquered by great climbers, but it has also humbled countless cyclists.

The Aubisque culminates at 1,709 meters (5,605 feet), and riders as varied as Firmin Lambot of France (1920), Gino Bartali (1938) and Fausto Coppi of Italy (1949 and 1952), Charly Gaul of Luxembourg (1955), Eddy Merckx of Belgium (1969), Miguel Indurain of Spain (1989), and Laurent Jalabert of France (2002) all mastered the mountain.

Now part of the Tour more than 60 times, the Aubisque progresses for 16.5 kilometers (10¼ miles) with an average grade of 7.1 percent (see Figure 16-1).

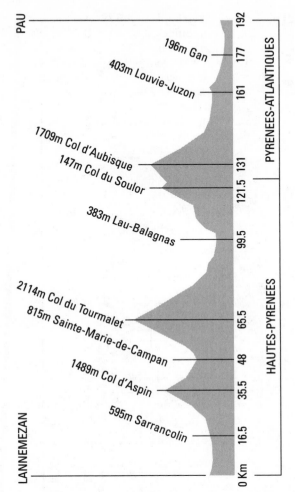

Figure 16-1: Lannemezann-Pau, Stage 16 of the 1999 Tour that included Col d'Aubisque.

Courchevel

Courchevel (core-sha-vell), a ski resort in the Alps, is a newcomer to the Tour and has only twice hosted a stage finish. Richard Virenque, the seven-time winner of the best-climber jersey, was victorious in 1997. Marco Pantani, 1998 race winner, tamed the 21.8-kilometer (13.5-mile) and 6.3 percent average gradient ascent (see Figure 16-2) en route to his stage win to Courchevel in 2000.

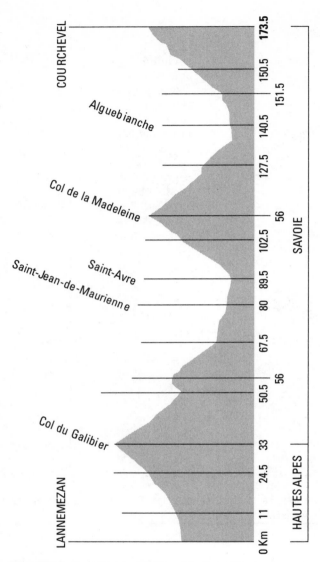

Figure 16-2: Course map of Briancon to Courchevel.

Opened in 1946, Courchevel stands at 2004 meters (6,573 feet) and is among the highest mountaintops used in the Tour. Often considered among the world's most prestigious ski resorts, the ski events at the 1992 Winter Olympics were held there.

Galibier

Among the Tour's longest climbs, the Galibier (gahl-eeb-bee-yay) is often presented in the same stage as the Col du Telegraphe and is among the race's oldest ascents. It was first added in 1911 when, like other notable Tour climbs, it was still a dirt road; riders often got off their bikes and walked sections of the 29.5-kilometer (18.3-mile) trek. Today, like all race mountains, the Galibier is a place for great climbers to showcase their talents.

The climb has an average gradient of 6.8 percent, and that suited Jacques Anquetil just fine. He dominated the 1,566-meter (5,136-foot) climb in 1957, and many others have also contributed to their legends with leading ascents of the climb and its 6.8 percent gradient — Charley Gaul (1959), Eddy Merckx (1969), Joop Zoetemelk (1972), Tony Rominger (1993), and Marco Pantani (1998).

Glandon

Introduced in 1947, Glandon peaks at 1,924 meters (6,240 feet) and is often incorporated into a series of climbs during the Tour's most difficult days. Many of the Tour's finest riders — three-time race winner Louison Bobet of France (1948), Fausto Coppi of Italy (1952), Stephen Rooks of the Netherlands (1988), Thierry Claveyrolet of France (1990), and Frenchman Richard Virenque (1994 and 1997) — all ruled the climb to Glandon.

Now part of the Tour on 13 occasions, the climb to Glandon is 27 kilometers (16.7 miles) with an average 4.5 percent gradient.

Izoard

Many of the Tour's legendary riders have mastered Izoard (aye-zore), the steep ascent into the Alps; the best known include Fausto Coppi (1949 and 1951) and Louison Bobet (1950, 1953, and 1954). This mountain debuted in 1922 and quickly built its reputation as among the race's most difficult climbs that peaks at 2,361 meters (7,744 feet).

The climb continues for 19.3 kilometers (12 miles) and at an average gradient of 5.9 percent while advancing along dusty, winding roads and through other varying landscape. Greg LeMond and Laurent Fignon dueled on this mountain in 1989 (see Chapter 15).

L'Alpe d'Huez

It's not the hardest ascent, but since its debut in 1952, L'Alpe d'Huez (lalp-dwhez) has defined the mystique of Tour de France mountains. Fausto Coppi won the inaugural ascent, a 9.5-mile climb that included 21 switchbacks and an average gradient of 7.9 percent. This mountain isn't included every year, but in each of its more than 20 editions, it's the most highly anticipated race stage, particularly for race fans.

Hundreds of thousands of spectators line the course, many arriving days in advance. It's a party from start to finish, often to excess, for spectators; it's a dangerous grind for cyclists who often have to negotiate their way through tight and rowdy crowds. The finishing climb ends at 6,102 feet.

American Andy Hampsten, who twice finished fourth overall in the Tour, won the stage in 1992 — a first for an American. Lance Armstrong claimed the stage in 2004 when, for the first time, the 21 switchbacks comprised an uphill individual time trial.

La Mongie

A ski resort near the top of the Tourmalet (tor-ma-lay), La Mongie (lah moan-jee) has been a Tour stage finish area only three times. The climb is 16.9 kilometers (10.5 miles) and the average gradient of the Pyrenees climb is 8 percent (see Figure 16-3). Bernard Thevenet of France (1970) was the inaugural winner at La Mongie. Lance Armstrong has one victory (2002) and one second place (2004) in the resort's two other arrival years.

La Mongie stands at 1,715 meters (5,625 feet) and its nearby summit, the top of the Tourmalet, is one of cycling's grand monoliths at 2,114 meters (6,934 feet), the highest peak in the Pyrenees. The Tourmalet was first included in 1910 and was nicknamed *Circle of Death*, and this Pyrenees climb is where the legendary rider Octave Lapize called race officials "assassins" as he negotiated the mountain in its Tour debut (see Chapter 15). Eddy Merckx, Claudio Chiappucci, and Richard Virenque have also been victorious on the Tourmalet. At the peak of the Tourmalet, a monument honors race founder Henri Desgrange.

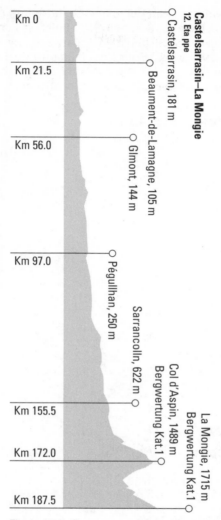

Figure 16-3: Course map of Castelsarrasin to La Mongie.

Luz-Ardiden

One of the most popular ascents in recent Tours, Luz-Ardiden (luze-ar-dee-dan) was first part of the Tour in 1985 when Spain's Pedro Delgado won the Pyrenees stage.

The *peloton* has returned ten more times to this ski station that concludes with 13.4 kilometers (8.3 miles) at an average 7.6 percent gradient (see Figure 16-4). Dag Otto Lauritzen of Norway

(1987), Miguel Indurain of Spain (1990), and Richard Virenque of France (2001) have claimed Luz-Ardiden stage finishes. Lance Armstrong and Jan Ullrich contested a great battle on the climb during the 15th stage of the 2003 Tour from Bagneres de Bigorre to Luz Ardiden. Armstrong won and Ullrich was third in one of the more memorable Tour mountain ascents in recent years.

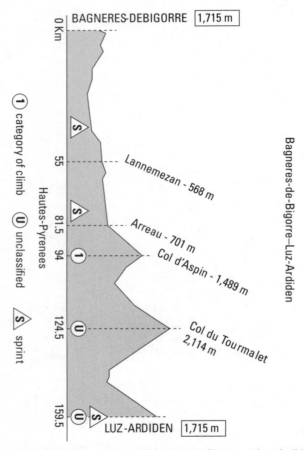

Figure 16-4: Course map of Bagners-de-Bigorre to Luz-Ardiden.

Madeleine

Introduced to the Tour in 1969, Col de la Madeleine (coal-duh-luh-mad-ah-lahn) is often presented as a three-part mountain package in the Alps, with Telegraphe and Galibier. Lucien Van Impe of Belgium (1983), Pedro Delgado of Spain (1984), Richard Virenque of

France (1995–1997), Jan Ullrich of Germany (1998), Michael Boogerd of the Netherlands (2002), and Gilberto Simoni of Italy (2004) all claimed the Madeleine climb.

The climb to Madeleine is 25.4 kilometers (15.8 miles) and has an average gradient of 6.1 percent. During the 2004 Tour, Madeleine was the highest point of the Tour.

Mont Ventoux

First included in the Tour in 1951, this climb to the barren peak above the French countryside is as infamous as it is famous. It plateaus at 1,909 meters (6,261 feet); one kilometer from the top is where British cyclist Tom Simpson collapsed and subsequently died in 1967.

Like all great Tour mountains, Mont Ventoux (mon-von-too) is steep and long. But it's the legendary *Mistral winds* — the cold, strong gusts that can surpass 100 mph (160 kph) — that most affect the race. The brutal winds have swept away most vegetation on the mountain, leaving it barren and brutally difficult for riders. Mont Ventoux is called the *Windy Mountain* and sometimes, the *Tour of the Moon.*

Mont Ventoux has been part of the Tour only 13 times, but it has produced epic battles, including the 2000 challenge between Lance Armstrong and Marco Pantani. Armstrong's strategically eased up at the finish line, allowing Pantani to claim the stage win. Pantani was upset, stating he didn't need Armstrong's sympathy, and duo began a nasty battle of words for the remainder of the Tour.

Puy de Dome

Like several other Tour ascents, Fausto Coppi of Italy first conquered Puy de Dome (pwee-dah-dome) in its debut in the 1952 Tour. Spain's Luis Ocana (1971) and Joop Zoetemelk of Holland (1976 and 1978) also mastered the climb to the peak at 1,415 meters (4,461 feet). The peak has been utilized a mid-race climb, and as a stage finish.

Puy de Dome is also the location of two of the Tour's most storied moments. Frenchmen Raymond Poulider and Jacques Anquetil staged one the most respected and intense final climbs on the mountains in 1964. It's also where a fan punched Eddy Merckx of Belgium as he rode past in 1975. Merckx never fully recovered from the attack, and the punch was likely responsible for ending his career.

Sestrieres

A respected ski resort, Sestrieres (ses-tree-air) is just across the French border in the Italian Alps. It has been used as both a mid-stage climb and as a finish point at 2,003 meters (6,668 feet) — see Figure 16-5. Sestrieres made its debut in 1952; Italian Fausto Coppi was victorious that year, and the mountain has been mastered by Claudio Chiappucci (1992) and Bjarne Riis of Denmark, the 1996 Tour winner on a solo breakaway win. Charly Gaul of Luxembourg (1956) and Jose Jimenez of Spain (1966) are also Sestrieres climb winners.

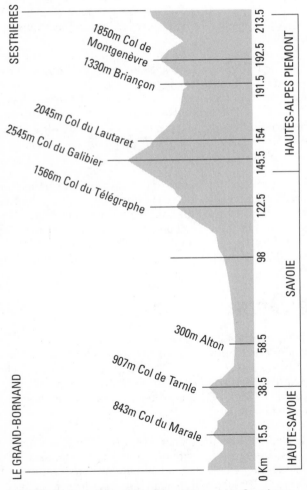

Figure 16-5: Course map of Le Grand Bornand to Sestrieres.

Lance Armstrong had plenty of nonbelievers when he returned to the Tour de France in 1999. But he had many fewer detractors after claiming the 9th stage from Le Grand Bornand to Sestrieres over Alex Zulle of Switzerland and Fernando Escartin of Spain. Armstrong had assumed the race lead the day before with a time trial win in Metz, but his mountain stage win in Italy proved he could climb with the sport's best. After winning in Sestrieres, he maintained the race lead en route to his first Tour title.

Chapter 17

Ten Other Important Races

There's no doubt that the Tour de France is cycling's prestige event. But cycling is increasingly competitive with a yearly calendar that begins in January and continues through December. Beyond the Tour, the *Giro d'Italia* (Tour of Italy) and *Vuelta a Espana* (Tour of Spain) are cycling's other Grand Tours. The three-week races have the highest rating of difficulty, according to *Union Cycliste Internationale* (International Cycling Union), the sport's global governing body.

Winning the Tour of Italy is considered cycling's second most important stage race title, followed by the Tour of Spain.

Stage routes of Grand Tours change yearly, although some cities are represented nearly every year. Routes for *classics* (longstanding races that are hotly contested) generally remain the same, with the exceptions of road construction changes or safety deviations. In addition, cycling has yearly world championships for track and road cycling, mountain biking, and *cyclo cross,* a road and mountain biking hybrid. Winners of world championships earn white jerseys featuring five horizontal rainbow stripes. Winning the World Championship Road Race is the most impressive single-day accomplishment in cycling.

Shorter stage races and myriad one-day races fill the calendar. For riders preparing for the Tour, spring races are ideal for training, testing fitness, and preparing the team. Cyclists, who excel as single-day or shorter stage race riders, look for their moments of opportunity, depending on the events' terrain and race-day circumstances.

With nearly a full year of races on the calendar, it's difficult to highlight only a select few non-Tour events. But here are ten important pro cycling events on the international calendar, listed alphabetically.

Amstel Gold Race

Still in its infancy compared with the historic classics, the Amstel Gold Race has steadily built its reputation since its 1966 debut. The event suits riders possessing strong, quick power, and savvy bike-handling skills.

Sponsored by Netherlands' most well-known brewery, the Amstel Gold Race is the country's only classic. The course meanders through southern Holland (see Figure 17-1), and features more than 30 climbs, some with 23 percent grades. Narrow, winding roads prevail for the classic held on the third week of April.

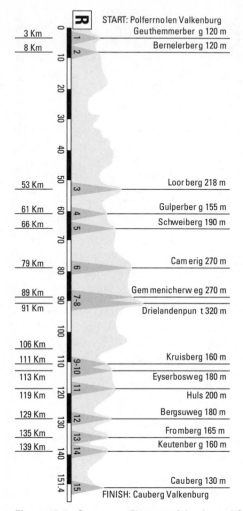

START: Polferrno len Valkenburg

3 Km		Geuthemmerber g 120 m
8 Km		Bernelerberg 120 m
53 Km		Loor berg 218 m
61 Km		Gulperber g 155 m
66 Km		Schweiberg 190 m
79 Km		Cam erig 270 m
89 Km		Gem menicherw eg 270 m
91 Km		Drielandenpun t 320 m
106 Km		
111 Km		Kruisberg 160 m
113 Km		Eyserbosw eg 180 m
119 Km		Huls 200 m
129 Km		Bergsuweg 180 m
135 Km		Fro mberg 165 m
139 Km		Keutenber g 160 m
151.4		Cau berg 130 m

FINISH: Cauberg Valkenburg

Figure 17-1: Course profile map of the Amstel Gold Race.

Clasica San Sebastian (San Sebastian Classic)

As Spain's only major classic, the San Sebastian Classic began in 1981 and is held on the second Saturday in August in the coastal city of the Basque region of northern Spain (see Figure 17-2). The 225-plus (140-mile) course features a half-dozen climbs, including Jaizkibel, the race's most difficult and often race-determining ascent. It begins with about 20 miles left in the race.

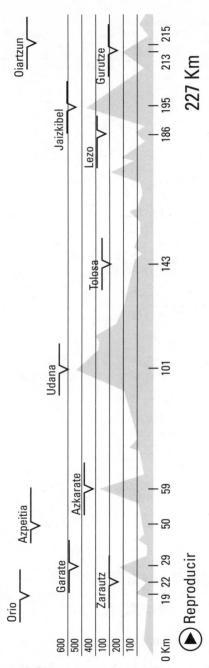

Figure 17-2: Course profile map of the San Sebastian Classic.

Spain is hot in August, and attrition is often a factor at the San Sebastian Classic, the newest of the European classics.

Lance Armstrong began his professional career at the event in 1992. He struggled, finished 111th (last place), and considered leaving cycling with only a one-race career. One year later, however, Armstrong won the world race title in Oslo, Norway.

Giro d'Italia (Tour of Italy)

Introduced in 1909 by its still-current sponsor, the Italian sports newspaper *Gazzetta dello Sport,* the Tour of Italy is conducted in very similar fashion to the Tour de France. It has flat road stages, time trials, and mountain ascents. The world's best teams participate, just like in the Tour de France and Tour of Spain.

The leader of the overall Giro competition since 1931 has worn the *Maglia Rosa* or pink jersey, the same color as the newsprint of *Gazetta dello Sport.* The Giro also has the *maglia verde* (green jersey) for best climber, *maglia ciclamino* (mauve jersey) for best sprinter, and the *intergiro* (blue jersey) for best intermediate stage competitor.

Since its early days, the Giro has attracted many of the sport's sports greats who achieved success before rabid fans. Italians Alfredo Binda (1925, '27, '28, '29, and '33) and Fausto Coppi ('40, '47, '49, '52, and '53), and Belgian's Eddy Merckx ('68, '70, '72, '73, and '74) are the only five-time winners. Italian riders claimed the race every year until 1950, but Giro winners now include cyclists from numerous countries.

Held in May and June, the Giro usually ends slightly more than one month before the start of the Tour. Numerous riders double by riding in the Tour of Italy, and then the Tour de France. Marco Pantani, the deceased Italian champion, was victorious in the 1998 Tour of Italy and Tour de France, the last rider to claim double Grand Tours in the same year.

It's only fitting another Italian, Mario Cipollini, has a record 42 career Giro stage wins. Andy Hampsten (1988) is the only American winner of the Giro, although Greg LeMond was third in 1985 and Tyler Hamilton placed second in 2002. Lance Armstrong has never competed.

Liege-Bastogne-Liege

Cycling's oldest classic began in 1892 and will be held for the 91st time in 2005. The course is out-and-back from the city of Liege to Bastogne in Belgium and is around 160 miles. It progresses through tall pine trees; along tricky, cobblestoned roads; along vast green fields; and into the Adrennes Mountains.

Considered among cycling's most grueling one-day events, the strenuous outbound segment to Bastogne is outdone by the more hilly and difficult return trip. The route (see Figure 17-3) includes ten climbs, many of them long, steep, and technical.

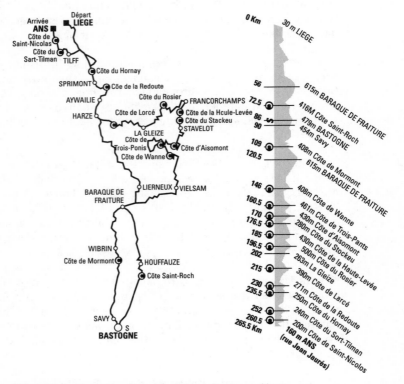

Figure 17-3: Course profile map of Liege-Bastogne-Liege.

Unpredictable weather is the norm in Belgium, particularly in April when the Liege-Bastogne-Liege is held on the fourth Sunday of the month. Eddy Merckx, the nation's hero, won the race five times, and he's honored with a monument along the course.

Milan–San Remo

The first World Cup race of the season is called La Primavera, and is named after a flower that blooms in early spring. Milan/San Remo began in 1907 and is held on the third Saturday of March. The route extends from Milan to San Remo, a city on the Italian Riviera.

While long (290 kilometers; 180 miles), Milan-San Remo is not as difficult as its ancient course brethren, and the course includes one major climb, the Turchino, and several less strenuous ascents (see Figure 17-4). The race is largely flat and fast and it often finishes with a group sprint. American Fred Rodriguez was second in 2002.

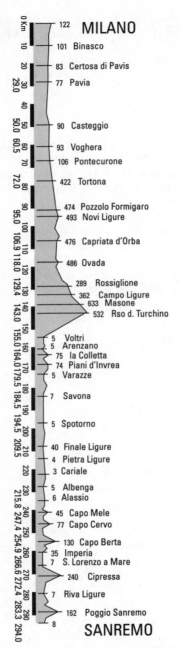

Km		
0 Km	122	MILANO
10	101	Binasco
20	83	Certosa di Pavis
30 29.0	77	Pavia
40		
50 50.0	90	Casteggio
60 60.5	93	Voghera
70	106	Pontecurone
80 72.0	422	Tortona
90	474	Pozzolo Formigaro
95.0	493	Novi Ligure
100		
110 106.9 118.0	476	Capriata d'Orba
120	486	Ovada
130 129.4	289	Rossiglione
	362	Campo Ligure
140	633	Masone
143.0	532	Rso d. Turchino
150		
155.0	5	Voltri
160	5	Arenzano
164.0	75	la Colletta
170 179.5	74	Piani d'Invrea
	5	Varazze
180 184.5	7	Savona
190		
200 194.5	5	Spotorno
210 209.5	40	Finale Ligure
	4	Pietra Ligure
220	3	Cariale
230 215.8	5	Albenga
	6	Alassio
240 247.4	45	Capo Mele
250	77	Capo Cervo
254.9	130	Capo Berta
260	35	Imperia
266.6	7	S. Lorenzo a Mare
270	240	Cipressa
280 272.4	7	Riva Ligure
290 283.3	162	Poggio Sanremo
294.0	8	SANREMO

Figure 17-4: Course profile map of Milan–San Remo

Olympic Road Race

Part of the Summer Olympics since 1896, the Olympic Road Race is prestigious, but it presents a riders' dilemma. Like the World Championships, the Olympic Road Race is contested by five-rider teams competing for their respective countries, not for their international trade teams.

Open to professionals since 1996, riders participate in the Olympic Road Race after already riding for the bulk of the season. If selected by their respective countries to participate, cyclists may ride with countrymen whom they ride *against* for most of the year. Likewise, riders from other countries may form alliances with trade team teammates competing for other countries. It's not officially allowed, but it happens.

Because the Olympics are held in varying countries, the Olympic Road Race course is never the same. Pascal Richard of Switzerland (1996), Jan Ullrich of Germany (2000), and Paolo Bettini of Italy (2004) have won the Olympic Road Race since its pro-rider debut.

The Olympic Road Race for women was added to the Summer Olympics in Los Angeles in 1984; Americans Connie-Carpenter-Phinney and Rebecca Twigg won the gold and silver, respectively.

Paris Roubaix

This race is simultaneously famous and infamous, and it's often called *The Queen of the Classics* or *The Hell of the North*. Like cycling in the Summer Olympics, Paris Roubaix began in 1896 and is considered cycling's most grueling one-day race.

Although sections have changed, the estimated 250-kilometer (155-mile) course now includes 26 segments of often gnarly, muddy, and treacherous cobblestones that have ruined many riders' days for the last century or so. If weather is perfect, the race (held the second Sunday in April) is brutally difficult for even the strongest cyclists. During inclement weather years, even riders' greatest skills can be nullified instantaneously by bad luck. Great riders do well at Paris Roubaix, but lucky great riders often emerge victorious.

George Hincapie's second-place finish to Tom Boonen of Belguim in 2005 was the only podium finish by an American in Paris Roubaix.

Tour of Flanders

The most prestigious classic in Belgium, the Tour of Flanders is held on the first weekend of April. Its 260-kilometer (160-mile) course meanders through small villages, past windmills, and through the Belgian countryside. Along with Paris-Roubaix, the Amstel Gold Race, and Liege-Bastgone-Liege, the Tour of Flanders commences cycling's finest month of classics.

Introduced in 1913, the Tour of Flanders is flat and fast. The race's second half features several cobblestone climbs that can quickly divide the field into contenders and riders seeking only to finish and escape severe suffering. This race has a total of 18 climbs, including the famed Koppenburg climb.

Vuelta a Espana (Tour of Spain)

Last of the Grand Tours, the Tour of Spain has gained prestige in recent years, particularly since it was moved from the spring to fall. It's the least heralded of the Grand Tours and dates to 1935.

Like the Tour de France and Tour of Italy, the Tour of Spain has an overall competition and race leader's jersey, the *jersey oro* or golden jersey. Various sub-competitions for best climber and sprinter are contested, too. Held in September, the course profile showcases the golden, rolling hills of Spain. Its steep climbs are legendary.

While not as popular as the Tour de France or Tour of Italy, the Tour of Spain is the country's cycling showcase and is often dominated by Spanish riders. While competing in one or two Grand Tours per season is a fine accomplishment for any pro cyclist, a small, hearty fraternity of riders through the years has completed all three Grand Tours in one season. In 2001, Levi Lephiemer was third overall, the first American to stand afoot the podium in Spain while riding for the U.S. Postal Service Cycling Team (now called the Discovery Channel Pro Cycling Team).

World Championship (Road Race)

Cycling's most prestigious one-day race, the World Championship Road Race is the final event of the world competition, and is held in a different country every year. Besides the Olympic Road Race, it's the only event in which riders compete for their countries, not their trade teams.

The route is all-important in the World Championship Road Race. Courses are usually repeated circuits of a lengthy loop around the hosting city. Hilly courses are conducive to skilled stage racers, while flat world courses favor a pack finish, with superior sprinters likely at the front. Most World Championship Road Races are held at high speeds, and they often become races of attrition, with less than 50 percent of starters finishing.

The winner of the World Championship Road Race is awarded the rainbow jersey. It's a white jersey with five horizontal stripes (blue, red, black, yellow, and green) around the chest and arms of the jersey. The World Champion wears the rainbow jersey for one year at all road races, and his jersey is the second most coveted in cycling, after the Tour's yellow jersey.

Glossary

● ●

Cycling has its own colorful and unique language. Keep this quick reference at hand when you're following the Tour de France.

abandon: Riders drop out, or "abandon" a stage, and official race rules don't allow them to continue in the event. Race results may indicate DNF (did not finish) or DNS (did not start).

arrivée: Finish line

attack: Quick acceleration to pull ahead of another rider or the *peloton*

attacker: A rider who attacks

autobus: Riders at the back of the *peloton*

bidon: Water bottle

blown: A rider is depleted physically or is mentally spent and unable to continue to race well

bonking: A rider's body is depleted of glycogen and, thus, has no energy left and may even lose his form

Boss: The most respected rider in the *peloton,* often the race leader or defending titlist

breakaway: Escaping from *peloton* to take the lead

broom wagon: With the exception of police cars, it's the last vehicle in the race caravan. The broom wagon began in 1903 and was used "to sweep" riders off the course when they couldn't continue. Today, the broom wagon is part tradition, but it's still a transportation option for an abandoning rider. Known as *voiture balai* in French.

caravan: Team cars, official cars, media cars, police vehicles, and emergency vehicles that precede or follow riders

caravane publicitaire: Tour sponsors' publicity vehicles driven along each stage route, often 90 minutes prior to riders; literally translates to "publicity caravan"

contre la montre: A time trial or a race in which riders race individually, against only the clock; literally translates to "race against the clock"

counter attacks: Attacking the attackers

directeur sportif: Team manager and coach

domestiques: Support riders for a race leader who sacrifice their chances of their own individual goals to ensure the leader is protected and that he has every opportunity to win. *Domestiques* are sometimes allowed to win stages or other races as payback for their dedication to the leader.

doping: Use of banned substances or procedures by racers

drafting: Riding closely behind another rider to decrease wind resistance

drop: To leave a rider behind

échelon: Riders forming a single line or double line, which is usually diagonal to the wind direction

entourage: The group following and/or attending to some important racer or team; the group may be staff, the press, or fans

étape: A term used for any stage of the Tour; translates literally to "stage"

Federation Francoise de Cyclisme: French Cycling Federation

gap: The amount of time or distance between one rider or group of riders and other riders or the pack.

Gardes Republicaines: Elite French motorcycle police

gendarme: French police

General Classification: Each rider's overall standing in the Tour, determined by calculating the accumulated individual time of each rider, adding time for bonuses and deducting time for penalties; also known as the GC

Grand Tours: Professional cycling's three major three-week races: the Giro d'Italia, the Vuelta a Espana, and the Tour de France

gruppetto: Stragglers who barely make the time limit; see also **time limit**

hors catégorie: A mountain so steep it's beyond categorizing

hot spots: Designated sprint locations during stages

kilometer: Metric unit equal to 0.62 mile

King of the Mountains: Rider awarded the polka-dot jersey as winner of the Tour's climbing competition, designated by points, after each stage and cumulatively at the end of the race

kit: Cycling jersey and shorts

lanterne rouge: Cyclist last in General Classification who has the "honor" of the red lantern, which by tradition hangs from the caboose to signify the end of a train; see also *General Classification*

leadout: A race strategy in which one rider rapidly accelerates, with a second rider (usually a top sprinter) following just inches behind, drafting at high speed; the first rider pulls aside, and the sprinter then speeds on past to the finish line; see also *drafting*

Le Grand Boucle: The Tour de France; literally translates to "the big loop"

ligne de arrivée: The finish line

maillot aux pois rouges: The polka-dot jersey, awarded to the best climber

maillot blanc: The white jersey, awarded to the best young rider age 25 and under

maillot jaune: The yellow jersey, awarded to the overall leader

maillot vert: The green jersey, awarded to the best sprinter

musette: A pouch or purse containing food that is given to riders along the course

Patron, The: A term of respect earned by a race leader

peloton: The main pack or group of riders

pileup: Several riders crashing

Prologue: A short, preliminary race; usually a time trial; see also *time trial*

pulling: Taking a turn at the front of the *peloton*

Race of Truth: An individual time trial, in which each rider competes alone, without teammates, against the clock

riding tempo: A rider's long, steady pace near the limit of his aerobic capacity; often used by riders to control the pace at the front of the *peloton*

rouleur: A specialist on long, flat stages whose job is to stay in front of the *peloton*, expending most of his energy by trying to control the stage pace. *Rouleurs* rarely have remaining strength to compete for stage wins; literally translates to "wheeler"

sitting on/in: A rider or riders getting protection from the wind from a rider or riders in front

soigneur: Masseurs and multifunction support staff hired by a cycling team

spinning: Pedaling at a fast cadence

stage: One day's competition in a multiday race

tarmac: Pavement

throw: Thrusting your bike forward in a sprint to gain a slight advantage

tifosi: Italian word meaning "fans"

time limit: Percentage of time allowed for a rider to finish behind the winner and still continue racing in the next day's stage

time trial: A race in which individual riders or the riders on one team ride together against the clock

Union Cycliste Internationale: International Cycling Union; cycling's international governing body that establishes and enforces rules and regulations, issues racing licenses, and manages world rankings

USADA: United States Anti Doping Association; responsible for in-competition and out-of-competition doping control testing for competing USA athletes

vélo: French word meaning "bicycle"

village départ: Sponsors' hosting area at the start line

WADA: World Anti Doping Association; responsible for in-competition and out-of-competition doping control testing for athletes belonging to organizations who have accepted the World Anti-Doping Code, including the Union Cycliste Internationale

wrench: Bike mechanic hired by a cycling team

zone de ravitaillement: Designated area of the race route where team staff hand out water bottles and musettes to riders; literally translates to "feed zone"; see also ***musette***

Index

• *H* •

• *N* •

• *O* •

• *P* •

Notes

Notes

Notes

Notes

Notes

BUSINESS, CAREERS & PERSONAL FINANCE

0-7645-5307-0

0-7645-5331-3 *†

Also available:

- Accounting For Dummies †
  0-7645-5314-3
- Business Plans Kit For Dummies †
  0-7645-5365-8
- Cover Letters For Dummies
  0-7645-5224-4
- Frugal Living For Dummies
  0-7645-5403-4
- Leadership For Dummies
  0-7645-5176-0
- Managing For Dummies
  0-7645-1771-6

- Marketing For Dummies
  0-7645-5600-2
- Personal Finance For Dummies *
  0-7645-2590-5
- Project Management
  For Dummies
  0-7645-5283-X
- Resumes For Dummies †
  0-7645-5471-9
- Selling For Dummies
  0-7645-5363-1
- Small Business Kit For Dummies *†
  0-7645-5093-4

HOME & BUSINESS COMPUTER BASICS

0-7645-4074-2

0-7645-3758-X

Also available:

- ACT! 6 For Dummies
  0-7645-2645-6
- iLife '04 All-in-One Desk Reference
  For Dummies
  0-7645-7347-0
- iPAQ For Dummies
  0-7645-6769-1
- Mac OS X Panther Timesaving
  Techniques For Dummies
  0-7645-5812-9
- Macs For Dummies
  0-7645-5656-8
- Microsoft Money 2004 For Dummies
  0-7645-4195-1

- Office 2003 All-in-One Desk
  Reference For Dummies
  0-7645-3883-7
- Outlook 2003 For Dummies
  0-7645-3759-8
- PCs For Dummies
  0-7645-4074-2
- TiVo For Dummies
  0-7645-6923-6
- Upgrading and Fixing PCs
  For Dummies
  0-7645-1665-5
- Windows XP Timesaving
  Techniques For Dummies
  0-7645-3748-2

FOOD, HOME, GARDEN, HOBBIES, MUSIC & PETS

0-7645-5295-3

0-7645-5232-5

Also available:

- Bass Guitar For Dummies
  0-7645-2487-9
- Diabetes Cookbook For Dummies
  0-7645-5230-9
- Gardening For Dummies *
  0-7645-5130-2
- Guitar For Dummies
  0-7645-5106-X
- Holiday Decorating For Dummies
  0-7645-2570-0
- Home Improvement All-in-One
  For Dummies
  0-7645-5680-0

- Knitting For Dummies
  0-7645-5395-X
- Piano For Dummies
  0-7645-5105-1
- Puppies For Dummies
  0-7645-5255-4
- Scrapbooking For Dummies
  0-7645-7208-3
- Senior Dogs For Dummies
  0-7645-5818-8
- Singing For Dummies
  0-7645-2475-5
- 30-Minute Meals For Dummies
  0-7645-2589-1

INTERNET & DIGITAL MEDIA

0-7645-1664-7

0-7645-6924-4

Also available:

- 2005 Online Shopping Directory
  For Dummies
  0-7645-7495-7
- CD & DVD Recording For Dummies
  0-7645-5956-7
- eBay For Dummies
  0-7645-5654-1
- Fighting Spam For Dummies
  0-7645-5965-6
- Genealogy Online For Dummies
  0-7645-5964-8
- Google For Dummies
  0-7645-4420-9

- Home Recording For Musicians
  For Dummies
  0-7645-1634-5
- The Internet For Dummies
  0-7645-4173-0
- iPod & iTunes For Dummies
  0-7645-7772-7
- Preventing Identity Theft
  For Dummies
  0-7645-7336-5
- Pro Tools All-in-One Desk
  Reference For Dummies
  0-7645-5714-9
- Roxio Easy Media Creator
  For Dummies
  0-7645-7131-1

* Separate Canadian edition also available
† Separate U.K. edition also available

Available wherever books are sold. For more information or to order direct: U.S. customers
visit www.dummies.com or call 1-877-762-2974.
U.K. customers visit www.wileyeurope.com or call 0800 243407. Canadian customers visit
www.wiley.ca or call 1-800-567-4797.

SPORTS, FITNESS, PARENTING, RELIGION & SPIRITUALITY

0-7645-5146-9

0-7645-5418-2

Also available:
- Adoption For Dummies
  0-7645-5488-3
- Basketball For Dummies
  0-7645-5248-1
- The Bible For Dummies
  0-7645-5296-1
- Buddhism For Dummies
  0-7645-5359-3
- Catholicism For Dummies
  0-7645-5391-7
- Hockey For Dummies
  0-7645-5228-7

- Judaism For Dummies
  0-7645-5299-6
- Martial Arts For Dummies
  0-7645-5358-5
- Pilates For Dummies
  0-7645-5397-6
- Religion For Dummies
  0-7645-5264-3
- Teaching Kids to Read
  For Dummies
  0-7645-4043-2
- Weight Training For Dummies
  0-7645-5168-X
- Yoga For Dummies
  0-7645-5117-5

TRAVEL

0-7645-5438-7

0-7645-5453-0

Also available:
- Alaska For Dummies
  0-7645-1761-9
- Arizona For Dummies
  0-7645-6938-4
- Cancún and the Yucatán
  For Dummies
  0-7645-2437-2
- Cruise Vacations For Dummies
  0-7645-6941-4
- Europe For Dummies
  0-7645-5456-5
- Ireland For Dummies
  0-7645-5455-7

- Las Vegas For Dummies
  0-7645-5448-4
- London For Dummies
  0-7645-4277-X
- New York City For Dummies
  0-7645-6945-7
- Paris For Dummies
  0-7645-5494-8
- RV Vacations For Dummies
  0-7645-5443-3
- Walt Disney World & Orlando
  For Dummies
  0-7645-6943-0

GRAPHICS, DESIGN & WEB DEVELOPMENT

0-7645-4345-8

0-7645-5589-8

Also available:
- Adobe Acrobat 6 PDF
  For Dummies
  0-7645-3760-1
- Building a Web Site For Dummies
  0-7645-7144-3
- Dreamweaver MX 2004
  For Dummies
  0-7645-4342-3
- FrontPage 2003 For Dummies
  0-7645-3882-9
- HTML 4 For Dummies
  0-7645-1995-6
- Illustrator CS For Dummies
  0-7645-4084-X

- Macromedia Flash MX 2004
  For Dummies
  0-7645-4358-X
- Photoshop 7 All-in-One Desk
  Reference For Dummies
  0-7645-1667-1
- Photoshop CS Timesaving
  Techniques For Dummies
  0-7645-6782-9
- PHP 5 For Dummies
  0-7645-4166-8
- PowerPoint 2003 For Dummies
  0-7645-3908-6
- QuarkXPress 6 For Dummies
  0-7645-2593-X

NETWORKING, SECURITY, PROGRAMMING & DATABASES

0-7645-6852-3

0-7645-5784-X

Also available:
- A+ Certification For Dummies
  0-7645-4187-0
- Access 2003 All-in-One Desk
  Reference For Dummies
  0-7645-3988-4
- Beginning Programming
  For Dummies
  0-7645-4997-9
- C For Dummies
  0-7645-7068-4
- Firewalls For Dummies
  0-7645-4048-3
- Home Networking For Dummies
  0-7645-42796

- Network Security For Dummies
  0-7645-1679-5
- Networking For Dummies
  0-7645-1677-9
- TCP/IP For Dummies
  0-7645-1760-0
- VBA For Dummies
  0-7645-3989-2
- Wireless All In-One Desk Reference
  For Dummies
  0-7645-7496-5
- Wireless Home Networking
  For Dummies
  0-7645-3910-8

HEALTH & SELF-HELP

Diabetes FOR DUMMIES

A Reference for the Rest of Us!

0-7645-6820-5 *†

Low-Carb Dieting FOR DUMMIES

A Reference for the Rest of Us!

0-7645-2566-2

Also available:
- Alzheimer's For Dummies
  0-7645-3899-3
- Asthma For Dummies
  0-7645-4233-8
- Controlling Cholesterol For Dummies
  0-7645-5440-9
- Depression For Dummies
  0-7645-3900-0
- Dieting For Dummies
  0-7645-4149-8
- Fertility For Dummies
  0-7645-2549-2

- Fibromyalgia For Dummies
  0-7645-5441-7
- Improving Your Memory For Dummies
  0-7645-5435-2
- Pregnancy For Dummies †
  0-7645-4483-7
- Quitting Smoking For Dummies
  0-7645-2629-4
- Relationships For Dummies
  0-7645-5384-4
- Thyroid For Dummies
  0-7645-5385-2

EDUCATION, HISTORY, REFERENCE & TEST PREPARATION

Spanish FOR DUMMIES

A Reference for the Rest of Us!

0-7645-5194-9

The Origins of Tolkien's Middle-earth FOR DUMMIES

A Reference for the Rest of Us!

0-7645-4186-2

Also available:
- Algebra For Dummies
  0-7645-5325-9
- British History For Dummies
  0-7645-7021-8
- Calculus For Dummies
  0-7645-2498-4
- English Grammar For Dummies
  0-7645-5322-4
- Forensics For Dummies
  0-7645-5580-4
- The GMAT For Dummies
  0-7645-5251-1
- Inglés Para Dummies
  0-7645-5427-1

- Italian For Dummies
  0-7645-5196-5
- Latin For Dummies
  0-7645-5431-X
- Lewis & Clark For Dummies
  0-7645-2545-X
- Research Papers For Dummies
  0-7645-5426-3
- The SAT I For Dummies
  0-7645-7193-1
- Science Fair Projects For Dummies
  0-7645-5460-3
- U.S. History For Dummies
  0-7645-5249-X

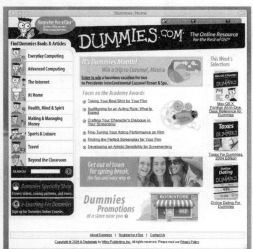

Get smart @ dummies.com®

- **Find a full list of Dummies titles**
- **Look into loads of FREE on-site articles**
- **Sign up for FREE eTips e-mailed to you weekly**
- **See what other products carry the Dummies name**
- **Shop directly from the Dummies bookstore**
- **Enter to win new prizes every month!**

---

* **Separate Canadian edition also available**
† **Separate U.K. edition also available**

Available wherever books are sold. For more information or to order direct: U.S. customers visit www.dummies.com or call 1-877-762-2974.
U.K. customers visit www.wileyeurope.com or call 0800 243407. Canadian customers visit www.wiley.ca or call 1-800-567-4797.